Catherine Happer • ⌐
William Me
Editors

Trump's Media War

palgrave
macmillan

Editors
Catherine Happer
University of Glasgow
Glasgow, UK

Andrew Hoskins
University of Glasgow
Glasgow, UK

William Merrin
Swansea University
Swansea, UK

ISBN 978-3-319-94068-7   ISBN 978-3-319-94069-4   (eBook)
https://doi.org/10.1007/978-3-319-94069-4

Library of Congress Control Number: 2018950072

Cover illustration: RetroSupply Co.
Cover design by Ian Wilson and Oscar Spigolon

This Palgrave Macmillan imprint is published by the registered company Springer Nature Switzerland AG
The registered company address is: Gewerbestrasse 11, 6330 Cham, Switzerland

PREFACE

Bewildered, exasperated, and exhausted, the liberal left mainstream news media appeared defeated a year into President Trump's openly declared war against them.

Katy Waldman (2018) in an essay in *Slate* entitled 'There's Nothing More to Learn About Trump' concedes, 'The more we cover him, the more we excite the desire to explain away, account for, and tame his outrageous behavior. But we can't. All we can do is stoke the fever with fresh data points, new revelations'.

Kyle Pope (2018), editor-in-chief of *Columbia Journalism Review*, writes, 'We continue to spend our days, and our audience's time, reacting to the president's bumbling with a level of disbelief and outrage that has boiled over into a stinking froth'.

And several months earlier, Mark Danner (2017) in *The New York Review of Books* wrote,

'It is our outrage, our disgust, our knee-jerk shock and condemnation that animate the play and give verisimilitude to the battle being fought. We are the enemy and our screams of dismay are vital to the drama'.

And yet this 'we', this 'media', that Trump is at war with, is merely a ghost of what was the liberal left mainstream media. The media's disbelief at Trump is increasingly a cover for their own anger at having been pushed out of that place from where they once painted the world in their own colours. The catastrophic fall of the mainstream is not a matter of the digital tsunami upending the business of news but is rather the widespread 'post-trust' (Happer and Hoskins forthcoming) contempt from the left and the right it is now held in. As Angela Nagle (2017, 2–3) describes, 'It is a career disaster now to signal your left-behind cluelessness as a basic bitch, a normie or a member of the corrupt media mainstream in any way'.

Trump's war on media continues to be fundamentally armed by a uniquely potent mix of a new critical mass of anti-establishment fervour and the mainstream's deep resentment of precisely this, or at least its acting in the vain hope that the multitude will stop hating it and that it will shake off its Trump dependency. The latter seems more likely to arrive—resulting from Trump leaving office—than the former (hatred of the establishment) but only because Trump's period in office has term limits.

To tell the story of Trump's war on media then requires a holistic vehicle that can at least illuminate the right and left's collusion in outrage alongside a vision of the imploding mainstream.

Through a series of short interventions from academics and journalists, this volume interrogates the emergent media war fought by Donald Trump in a fluid digital media ecology. Rather than a standard edited volume of extended essays, we use a series of interconnected clustered themes to set an agenda for exploration of Trump as the principal beneficiary as well as a sign of the shattering of mainstream consensual reality.

This work began through a symposium hosted by the College of Social Sciences at the University of Glasgow in June 2017. We are very grateful to all our participants and our contributors here for their innovative work on this project. Finally, thanks to Lina Aboujieb, Heloise Harding, Connie Li, Martina O'Sullivan, Lucy Batrouney, and the proposal reviewers in helping guide us through to these final pages.

Glasgow, UK   Catherine Happer
                                                        Andrew Hoskins
Swansea, UK   William Merrin

REFERENCES

Danner, Mark. 2017. What He Could Do. *The New York Review of Books.* 23 March. http://www.nybooks.com/articles/2017/03/23/what-trump-could-do/

Happer, Catherine, and Hoskins, Andrew. Forthcoming. *Broken Media: The Post-Trust Crisis of the Mainstream.*

Nagle, Angela. 2017. *Kill All Normies: Online Culture Wars from 4chan and Tumblr to Trump and the Alt-right.* Alresford: Zero Books.

Pope, Kyle. 2018. It's time to rethink how we cover Trump. *Columbia Journalism Review*. 22 January. https://www.cjr.org/covering_trump/trump-coverage-inauguration-press-media.php

Waldman, Katy. 2018. There's Nothing More to Learn About Trump. Please enjoy this essay about him. *Slate*. 22 January. https://slate.com/news-and-politics/2018/01/theres-nothing-more-to-learn-about-trump-please-enjoy-this-essay-about-him.html

Contents

Notes on Contributors

Abdullah K. Al-Saud is the Director of Research, and Head of the Security Studies Research Unit at King Faisal Center for Research and Islamic Studies (KFCRIS). He is also an assistant professor at the College of Strategic Sciences at Naif Arab University for Security Sciences (NAUSS) in Riyadh. Between September 2016 and March 2018, he was a visiting research fellow at the International Centre for the Study of Radicalisation (ICSR), King's College London. His research interests include security studies in general, with a special focus on radicalisation, terrorism, armed non-state actors, political violence, and the ideology of political Islamism.

Stuart Allan is a professor and Head of the School of Journalism, Media and Cultural Studies at Cardiff University, UK. He is the author of several books, including *Citizen Witnessing: Revisioning Journalism in Times of Crisis* (2013), and editor of numerous edited collections, including *Photojournalism and Citizen Journalism: Co-operation, Collaboration and Connectivity* (2017).

Tom Allbeson is Lecturer in Modern History at Swansea University. His research addresses post-conflict societies, photographic history, and cultural memory. His articles have been published in the *Journal of Modern History, Modern Intellectual History* and the *Journal of War & Culture Studies*. He and Stuart Allan are co-authoring a book on the history of war photography.

Peter Geoghegan is an investigative journalist and writer living in Glasgow and a lecturer at the University of the West of Scotland. His latest book, *The People's Referendum: Why Scotland Will Never Be the Same Again,* was published in January 2015, and was nominated for the Saltire Society First Book Prize. He is a co-founder and director of The Ferret, an investigative platform launched in 2015 and nominated for a British Journalism Prize for its work. He has written and reported from numerous countries for a wide range of publications including the *Guardian,* the *Times Literary Supplement,* the *Scotsman,* and the *Irish Times.*

Catherine Happer is Lecturer in Sociology and a member of the Glasgow University Media Group. She is co-author of *Communicating Climate Change and Energy Security: New Methods for Understanding Audiences* (2013) and her work has been published in international journals including the *European Journal of Communications and New Political Economy.* She has collaborated with Chatham House on a major international study, has given evidence at the House of Commons Select Committee on Climate, Policy and Public Understanding, and appeared on the BBC and Al Jazeera. She was previously a Factual programme-maker with the BBC. *Broken Media: The Post-Trust Crisis of the Mainstream,* with Andrew Hoskins, is her forthcoming work (https://brokenmedia.net).

Michael Higgins is senior lecturer in the School of Humanities at the University of Strathclyde. His writings on media and politics have been widely published, and his books include *Media and Their Publics* (2008), *The Cambridge Companion to Modern British Culture* (2010), and most recently *Belligerent Broadcasting* (2017).

Andrew Hoskins is Interdisciplinary Research Professor in Social Sciences at the University of Glasgow. His research connects multiple aspects of emergent digital society: media, memory, war, risk, security, and privacy. His latest books are (with John Tulloch) *Risk and Hyperconnectivity: Media and Memories of Neoliberalism* (2016) and (edited) *Digital Memory Studies: Media Pasts in Transition* (2018). *Broken Media: The Post-Trust Crisis of the Mainstream,* with Catherine Happer, is his forthcoming work (https://brokenmedia.net).

Jeff Jarvis is the Leonard Tow Professor of Journalistic Innovation and Director of the Tow-Knight Center for Entrepreneurial Journalism at the City University of New York's Graduate School of Journalism. He is author of numerous books including *Geeks Bearing Gifts: Imagining New Futures for News* (2014), *What Would Google Do?* (2009), and *Public Parts* (2011). He blogs about media and news at Buzzmachine.com and co-hosts the podcast *This Week in Google*. Jarvis was creator and founding editor of *Entertainment Weekly*; Sunday editor and associate publisher of the *New York Daily News*; TV critic for *TV Guide and People*; a columnist on the *San Francisco Examiner*; and assistant city editor and reporter for the *Chicago Tribune*.

Douglas Kellner is George Kneller Chair in the Philosophy of Education at UCLA, and is author of many books on social theory, politics, history, and culture, including *Camera Politica: The Politics and Ideology of Contemporary Hollywood Film*, co-authored with Michael Ryan; *Critical Theory, Marxism, and Modernity*; and *Jean Baudrillard: From Marxism to Postmodernism and Beyond*; works in cultural studies such as *Media Culture and Media Spectacle*; a trilogy of books on postmodern theory with Steve Best; and a trilogy of books on the media and the Bush administration, encompassing *Grand Theft 2000, From 9/11 to Terror War*, and *Media Spectacle and the Crisis of Democracy*.

Lisa W. Kelly is Lecturer in Television Studies at the University of Glasgow. She is the co-author of *The Television Entrepreneurs: Social Change and Public Understanding of Business* (2012) and *The Rise and Fall of the UK Film Council* (2015). Her research interests are around talent and diversity in film and TV, both onscreen and behind the scenes.

Paul Levinson is Professor of Communication and Media Studies at Fordham University. He has appeared on CNN, MSNBC, Fox News, the BBC, NPR, and numerous radio and television news shows. His non-fiction books, including *The Soft Edge, Digital McLuhan, Realspace, Cellphone, New New Media, McLuhan in an Age of Social Media*, and *Fake News in Real Context*, have been translated into 12 languages. His novels include *The Silk Code* (winner of Locus Award for Best First Science Fiction Novel of 1999), *Borrowed Tides, The Consciousness Plague, The Pixel Eye, The Plot To Save Socrates, Unburning Alexandria*, and *Chronica*. His stories and novels have been nominated for Hugo, Nebula, Sturgeon, Edgar, Prometheus, and Audie Awards.

Ben O'Loughlin is Professor of International Relations and Co-Director of the New Political Communication Unit at Royal Holloway, University of London. He is co-editor of the Sage journal *Media, War & Conflict*.

His latest book is *Forging the World: Strategic Narratives and International Relations* (2017). He was Specialist Advisor to the UK Parliament's Select Committee on Soft Power, producing the report *Power and Persuasion in the Modern World*. He is about to complete a book on narrative diplomacy and the 2015 Iran peace deal.

Dounia Mahlouly is a research associate at the International Centre for the Study of Radicalisation (ICSR), King's College London, as part of the VOX-Pol Network of Excellence. She holds a PhD from the University of Glasgow. Her thesis investigates the role of social media campaigning in the constitutional and presidential debates in post-revolutionary Tunisia and Egypt. It discusses the process through which different political groups incorporated participative media as part of their campaigning strategy and assesses to what extent such tools might contribute to consolidate a sustainable ideological message.

William Merrin is Associate Professor of Media Studies at Swansea University. His research and teaching focus on media and cultural theory, contemporary developments in digital media, and the history and philosophy of technology. Merrin developed the concept of 'Media Studies 2.0', starting the blog of the same name in November 2006 to follow developments in digital media and critically reflect upon the state and future of media studies. His books include *Media Studies 2.0* (2015) and *Digital War: A Critical Introduction* (2018).

Jennifer Pybus is Lecturer in Digital Culture and Society in the Department of Digital Humanities, King's College London. Her research looks at the politics of datafication and everyday life, specifically in relation to those critical points of tension that lie at the intersections between digital culture, Big Data and emerging advertising and marketing practices. This includes research around youth and privacy which relates to how third party ecosystems found on social media platforms are transforming the advertising industry via the rise of data analytics and algorithmic processes.

Alex Symons is Assistant Professor of Communication and Media Studies at LIM College, New York. His publications include *Mel Brooks in the Cultural Industries* (2012), as well as articles in *Celebrity Studies*, the *Journal of Popular Film and Television*, and the *Journal of Adaptation in Film and Performance*. His most recent work examines social media and podcasting in the careers of Doug Stanhope, Louis CK, and Marc Maron.

David Torrance is a freelance writer, journalist, and broadcaster with the specialist topic of Scottish independence and the constitutional debate more generally at *The Herald*. He holds a PhD from the University of the West of Scotland. He is also the author of a number of books on Scottish politics including *We in Scotland – Thatcherism in a Cold Climate* (2009), *Salmond: Against the Odds* (2010 & 2011), and, his most recent, *The Battle for Britain – Scotland and the Independence Referendum* (2013). His contribution to this volume was written in late 2017.

John Tulloch taught and researched between 1973 and 2015 at four universities in Australia (UNSW, Macquarie, Charles Stuart, and Newcastle) and three universities in Britain (Cardiff, Brunel, and Glasgow) after his undergraduate degree in History at Cambridge University, England, and his Masters in the Sociology of Art and Literature (and Media) at Sussex University, England, followed by his Sussex PhD in the History, Sociology and Aesthetics of Anton Chekhov. Tulloch has researched and published for fifty years across (and between) the disciplinary fields of film studies, media and cultural studies, photojournalism theory, literary theory, theatre and performance studies, political science, social psychology, and sociology (with a particular emphasis on 'risk society' theory and debate). In other fields, his most recent books are *Risk and Hyperconnectivity* (with Andrew Hoskins) and *Real Sex Cinema* (with Belinda Middleweek).

Killing the Media

CHAPTER 1

Weaponizing Reality: An Introduction to Trump's War on the Media

Catherine Happer, Andrew Hoskins, and William Merrin

When the world woke on 9 November 2016 to find Donald Trump had won the US presidential election, it was like a break in mainstream, consensual reality. This topped even *Back to the Future*'s joke, when Doc Brown asked Marty, 'Then tell me future-boy, who's president of the United States in 1985?' and his incredulity at being told it was Ronald Reagan, the actor—'Then who's Vice-President? Jerry Lewis?' Reagan, at least, had a political career. Trump was a celebrity-businessman, cameo film-actor, member of the WWE Hall of Fame and reality-TV host who had never held any public office.

Sweeping aside the conventions of professional political polish and presentation, Trump blustered, bluffed, fluffed, and incoherently shouted, threatened and tweeted his way to the presidency, surviving—and even gaining in strength from—character flaws and failures that would have torpedoed a normal campaign. Now he'd defeated probably the best-qualified presidential candidate in living memory. In the aftermath of his election,

C. Happer • A. Hoskins (✉)
University of Glasgow, Glasgow, UK

W. Merrin
Swansea University, Swansea, UK

© The Author(s) 2019
C. Happer et al. (eds.), *Trump's Media War*,
https://doi.org/10.1007/978-3-319-94069-4_1

reality itself seemed broken. The fourth wall of the television screen had been smashed and the public had 'hired' the boss of *The Apprentice*.

But Trump wasn't just a sign of a broken reality; he was the beneficiary of it. Mainstream consensual reality had shattered a long time ago; it was just that shattering *hadn't gone mainstream*. Trump was the moment when that alt-reality seized the political stage. His success was the result of a violent abreaction, an outpouring and release of dispossessed discontent that had one credo: continually articulating itself against the establishment, the elite, the mainstream, the political order, the neo-liberal economic order, the global order, the established way of doing things—against, that is, the entirety of the hitherto existing mainstream reality. Much of this discontent was justified, such as the pain of the economically marginalized Rust Belt workers, and there were many good reasons to vote for an outsider against Hilary Clinton's more-of-the-same neo-liberal centrism. But much of the discontent had a more dubious origin and cause, such as the 'Whitelash' of left-behind, angry white males, lamenting the multicultural PC-world where they thought only black lives now mattered and taking revenge on eight years of a black presidency.

There was, if you looked into it, a world of these claims, entire worldviews disconnected from what appeared in the mainstream media, in an inter-linked, pick-and-mix online ecology of information, opinions, facts, narratives, and claims. Trying to decipher the world-view of these Trump voters, the press soon found their scapegoat. It was precisely this unreality that was responsible: it was 'fake news' that had won Trump the election. It was a convenient explanation too, allowing the mainstream media to direct blame at the internet—that upstart threat to their eyeballs and advertising revenue—and especially at the apparent cause of all this fake news, social media.

Within days, Facebook was getting the blame. Most people today get their news from Facebook, the argument went, hence their susceptibility to any and every story appearing in their feed. Fake stories, pushed into its ecology for political reasons, gathered attention and garnered shares and 'likes', projecting them virally through the network, spreading lies through social media and, therefore, through the heart of the social itself. By 11 November, Zuckerberg was on the defensive, telling a Californian technology conference, 'The idea that fake news on Facebook, which is a very small amount of the content, influenced the election in any way I think is a pretty crazy idea...Voters make decisions based on their lived experience'.[1] Zuckerberg criticized the media's interpretation of the result, saying, 'I do think there is a certain profound lack of empathy in asserting that the only reason someone could have voted the way they did is because they saw some fake news. If you believe that, then I don't think you have internalized the message that Trump supporters are trying to send in this election'.[2]

Others disagreed. On the 17th, ex-president Obama aimed some very-pointed remarks in Facebook's direction at a press conference, saying, 'If we are not serious about facts and what's true and what's not, if we can't discriminate between serious arguments and propaganda, then we have problems...If everything seems to be the same and no distinctions are made, then we won't know what to protect'.[3] The problem was fundamental to democracy: 'We won't know what to fight for. And we can lose so much of what we've gained in terms of the kind of democratic freedoms and market-based economies and prosperity that we've come to take for granted'.[4]

Coming under increasing criticism, Facebook was forced to respond. On 19 November, Zuckerberg reversed his scepticism, acknowledging the issue and announcing new steps to counter fake news. 'We take misinformation seriously', he wrote in a post, 'We know people want accurate information. We've been working on this problem for a long time and we take this responsibility seriously.[5]' He said the company has 'relied on our community to help us understand what is fake and what is not', and claimed Facebook penalizes misinformation in the News Feed, just as it does clickbait, spams, and scams, 'so it's much less likely to spread'.[6] By 6 December, Facebook was reported to be testing a tool designed to identify and hide fake news, and on 15 December, Facebook announced it would now be flagging fake news stories with the help of users and outside fact-checkers. Reader alerts would now lead to stories being sent to five independent fact-checking agencies, including ABC News, AP, Factcheck. org, Politifact, and Snopes. Stories that failed the test would be flagged with the warning 'disputed by 3rd-party fact-checkers'.[7]

This was a significant reversal. Facebook had long denied being a media or news company and claimed not to be responsible for what its users post on it. Indeed, this was the default position of all Internet Service Providers (ISPs) and web platforms, based on Section 230(1) of the 1996 US Communications Decency Act which established the principle of immunity from liability for providers of an 'interactive computer service' who publish information produced by others. The problem was, Facebook's denial was disingenuous. They had a long history of removing material that offended against their 'Community Standards' and Terms of Service. Only a few months before, in September 2016, they had made headlines worldwide for their decision to delete a post by Norwegian writer Tom Egeland that featured 'The Terror of War', a Pulitzer Prize-winning photograph by Nick Ut showing children, including the naked nine-year-old Kim Phúc, running away from a napalm attack during the Vietnam War.[8] Facebook may not have wanted to be a media company, but they published information and exerted editorial control over it.

Importantly, Facebook also drew from liberal US traditions of freedom of speech and had declared on 12 November, 'I believe we must be extremely cautious about becoming arbiters of truth ourselves'.[9] Their own censorship and control compromised that lofty aim, though not fatally, but the new flagging and fact-checking system put them squarely in the position they had recently disavowed. The fake news scandal finally forced Zuckerberg to accept a different definition of his company. In a post on his own Facebook page announcing the changes, he admitted the business had a 'greater responsibility' to the public than just being a technology company:

> While we don't write the news stories you read and share, we also recognize we're more than just a distributor of news. We're a new kind of platform for public discourse – and that means we have a new kind of responsibility to enable people to have the most meaningful conversations, and to build a space where people can be informed.[10]

Facebook was 'a new kind of platform for public discourse', with 'a new kind of responsibility'.[11] It made for a bad end-of-year for the previously unassailable and reverentially treated social media giant.

Of course, the outrage at Facebook and the technology companies was most vociferously expressed in the traditional news organizations, especially in newspapers. The mainstream press hadn't simply lost the fight with the internet—accepting declining print sales and developing online sites where they mostly gave their work away for free—more importantly, they had lost control of people's attention and interest to social media. There was a deep resentment within journalism that their profession didn't matter as much now. Their entire livelihood was built on a technological system and in an age in which only a select few could broadcast their opinions to the masses. Now, anyone could, and we were more interested in our friends' opinions—or, if we were honest, *our own opinions*—than those of a professional elite. Journalists had spotted the change. In a column in January 2007 entitled 'Dear reader, please don't email me', *LA Times* journalist Joel Stein honestly expressed his disdain for the public's opinions:

> That address on the bottom of this column? That is the pathetic, confused death knell of the once-proud newspaper industry, and I want nothing to do with it. Sending an email to that address is about as useful as sending your study group report about Iraq to the president.
>
> Here's what my internet-fearing editors have failed to understand: I don't want to talk to you; I want to talk at you. A column is not my attempt to engage in a conversation with you. I have more than enough people to converse with. And I don't listen to them either.[12]

'I get that you have opinions you want to share', he says. 'I just don't have any interest in them'.[13] The Web 2.0 world, therefore, had turned everyone into a writer and publisher. It was true that few said much worth reading, but it was important to them and their friends and it didn't need an audience anyway as it wasn't trying to gather advertising revenue or justify public funding. This is a cultural shift whose import we are still barely beginning to understand.

But social media were also part of the economic threat to journalists' livelihoods. As far as they were concerned, social media was a parasitic organism which allowed its users to post their journalism for free whilst benefiting from the resulting advertising revenue that had shifted from the newspapers themselves. Hence their hostility to social media, their schadenfreude at its difficulties now and the sometimes-self-righteous tone of their fake-news-scandal reportage: whilst social media posted lies that threatened democracy, *they* were the repositories of truth, of quality, of fact-checked information, of verified, objective and impartial reporting. Suddenly, it seemed, journalists had rediscovered their values. They wrote about truth and objectivity as if they were employed by *The Washington Post* or *The New York Times*, standing in a smoke-filled, 1970s newsroom, all wide-lapels and sideburns, pulling all-nighters on the typewriter whilst publishing the Watergate stories or Pentagon Papers. Facebook, it turned out, wasn't the only one being disingenuous about its activities.

Because the problem of 'fake news' isn't confined to social media. What began as a highly-specific problem of deliberately written false stories designed to gain traction online in order to hurt a specific political cause or candidate soon mushroomed into a broader crisis of truth and trust, a questioning of validity and invalidity, and a recognition of the difficulty of dividing truth from opinion. Informational production and distribution suddenly underwent a very public crisis of legitimacy, with doubts raised over who had the right to lay claim to an audience or to truth. The mainstream media, however, didn't see this coming. Instead, they watched from the moral high ground, certain that the fake news scandal increased their importance and demonstrated their superiority to social media, even if they'd lost their position to them. And then one day, the claim was reversed back onto them.

It was, perhaps, Pope Francis, who kick-started the attack on the mainstream media over fake news. It had been a mantra of the alt-right for a long time, but it didn't really gain traction as an idea until after the election. On 7 December 2016, the Pope weighed into the fake news controversy, telling the Belgian Catholic weekly, *Tertio*, 'I think the media have to be very clear, very transparent, and not fall into – no offence intended – the sickness of coprophilia, that is, always wanting to cover scandals, covering nasty things, even if they are true',[14] he said. 'And since people have a tendency towards the sickness of coprophagia, a lot of damage can be done'.[15] Importantly, he didn't seem to be talking about social media, this was a critique of 'the media'—albeit it a highly-unusual critique, essentially accusing the media and the public of eating shit.

The media were confused. Suddenly 'fake news' was what the alt-right, Trump supporters and Trump himself was accusing *them* of. In his first White House press conference, on 16 February 2017, President Trump immediately demonstrated his departure not only from the preceding administration, but from almost the entire history of presidential appearances, launching into a free-form, 77-minute, near-monologue in which he took aim at anything he suddenly remembered he disliked, including the media:

> The press has become so dishonest that if we don't talk about it, we are doing a tremendous disservice to the American people. Tremendous disservice. We have to talk about it. We have to find out what's going on because the press, honestly, is out of control. The level of dishonesty is out of control. I ran for president to represent the citizens of our country. I am here to change the broken system so it serves their families and their communities well. I am talking, and really talking, on this very entrenched power structure and what we're doing is we're talking about the power structure.

We're talking about its entrenchment. As a result, the media's going through what they have to go through to oftentimes distort — not all the time — and some of the media's fantastic, I have to say, honest and fantastic — but much of it is not. The distortion, and we'll talk about it, you'll be able to ask me questions about it. We're not going to let it happen because I'm here, again, to take my message straight to the people.[16]

Though the argument lost its way towards the start, this was perfect, Trump-honed 'dog-whistle politics'. Forget the rambling and lack of evidence or cohesion, the key words were all here for his supporters to hear and react to: the press as liars, as out of control, journalism as a broken system, and the media as an entrenched power structure. If, in the final months of 2016 'fake news' had meant false social media stories, from now it increasingly meant the idea that the mainstream media were liars.

This accusation stung because, essentially, it is true. Journalism likes to believe its own mythology. This is the liberal theory of the press as 'the fourth estate': as a mediatory force standing between the people and authority, playing a key role in democracy in informing the public and in holding authority to account through its investigations and publications. The journalist as an indomitable, unwavering, dogged crusader-for-truth and heroic public servant is, however, a relatively recent invention. Journalists had actually begun as one of the lowest classes of people, let alone classes of employment, with one seventeenth-century English pamphleteer referring to them as 'This filthy Aviary, this moth-eaten crew of News-mongers, Every Jack-sprat that hath but a pen in his ink-horn is ready to gather up the Excrements of the Kingdom'.[17] The term 'hack' originated with Hackney carriages, a horse-driven cab that could be hired, before being applied to prostitutes who were similarly hired, and then was finally applied to journalists as hired writers. Though, for many, journalism has never quite left that low-level of company, the late nineteenth-century industrialization and capitalization of the press brought with it a more established role, a mass audience, increased legitimacy, a key role in the political public sphere, and a gradual professionalization of the trade. With that came professional organizations and a professional code of ethics, and with it too came an impressive record of public-interest investigative journalism.

There is no denying this record, but it isn't the full truth of journalism, because newspapers have, from the first, been commercial businesses: they are created not simply to inform or hold authority to account, but also—arguably primarily—to make money. The impact of the market on newspapers has been fundamental. There is a history of sensationalism and public-interest stories traceable from the broadside ballads sold at public executions, through the illustrated press of the 1830s, the Sunday papers from the mid-nineteenth century, to the mass-market dailies and tabloids of the late nineteenth century–early twentieth century. In the twentieth century, the 'Northcliffe Revolution', which transferred the profits of newspapers from cover-price to advertisements, would redefine the entire future of the newspaper: from then on, pleasing your demographic to accumulate readers was all that mattered.

Clearly, therefore, the press are not simply the repositories of truth they claimed to be in the wake of the fake news scandal, being distorted by market forces to please their readers. But their relationship to truth is also more complex than this and requires a deeper analysis. That analysis would be provided by a new academic field that rose in the late nineteenth century–early twentieth century, accompanying the rise of the modern media: journalism and mass communications research. This wasn't initially a critical discipline. Journalism was taught as a skill, and early communications research was concerned with *serving* the industry and government, being funded by them to study reception in order to increase the effectiveness of messages. Few looked inward at the industry itself, with the Frankfurt School being among the first to question what the communications industry itself was and how it operated. That kind of research only took-off in the post-war period.

The analysis of the operation of media industries has been a central element of post-war media studies. In a sense, the discipline has devoted itself to the exposure of the media and to understanding, if not their fakery, then certainly their *construction* of news and truth. David Manning White's 1950 article on 'the gatekeeper', for example, considered how an individual decided what was going to make the newspaper based on his personal decisions of worthiness; Warren Breed's 1955 article on 'social control in the newsroom' explored how individual journalists learnt how to fit into the editorial line and policy and produce what was required; Galtung and Ruge's 1973 work on 'news values' looked at the criteria employed for the selection of 'news'; Chomsky and Herman's 1988 'propaganda model' defined the 'five filters' information has to pass through to get printed, whilst Bourdieu's 1996 work on 'the journalistic field' traced the invisible background of the profession that is reproduced by each new member.

What these traditions showed is that all media involve fakery: news is not simply a truth in the world that is transparently mediated: it is always a *production* in which a range of biases, values and meanings are incarnated. Very often, as a result of these biases—especially political biases and market-needs—stories are published which serve particular agendas, which are intended to manipulate and cajole, which have an at-best ambiguous relationship to reality or which—if we are honest—are completely made-up. This is because journalism has always been as much about bullshit as about truth.

There were more radical traditions too, querying the 'reality' of media production. One of the most remarkable analyses was Daniel Boorstin's *The Image* (1962), whose subject matter was 'the world of our making, how we have used our wealth, our literacy, our technology and our progress, to create the thicket of unreality which stands between us and the facts of life'. In a world where news is expected and demanded, we have passed from 'news-gathering' to 'news-making', Boorstin writes, leading to the media creation of 'pseudo-events'—of events that are not spontaneous but are planned and produced to be reported, with an 'ambiguous' relationship to reality. Such media events, he says, now comprise more and more of our experience, flooding our consciousness. In giving rise to other events, the pseudo-event makes the 'original' of any phenomenon impossible to discover, ultimately 'reshaping...our very concept of truth'[18] in producing 'new categories of experience...no longer simply classifiable by the old common-sense tests of true and false'.[19] Aided by a 'graphic revolution', the world's complexity is reduced to intelligible and simplified images, 'more vivid, more attractive and more persuasive than reality itself'.[20] This is a world where the image replaces the original, until 'we make, we seek and finally we enjoy, the contrivance of all experience. We fill our lives not with experience, but with the images of experience'.[21]

It was a critique that would inspire Guy Debord's *Society of the Spectacle* (1967) with its description of a 'spectaclist' society—a world where 'all of life presents itself as an immense accumulation of spectacles[22]', with the images fusing in a common stream, forming 'a pseudo-world apart, an object of mere contemplation[23]'. And it would inspire too, Debord's heir, Jean Baudrillard, and his critique of the media 'simulacra' that were produced as our real experience, eclipsing the real (in a phrase taken directly from Boorstin) by being 'more real than the reality'.[24] This critical tradition is important here because it goes much further than simply identifying news as a construction. It suggests instead that the media create an epistemological environment: they produce entire *realities* that we live in and through.

Much has been written in recent years about the 'filter bubble', of social media and online lives—how much each of us lives in a filtered ecology of information tailored to what we already know and like. And some critics argue that 'echo chambers' are mere myth.[25] Moreover, so many have forgotten life lived in the powerful bubble of an earlier media ecology. For a long time the mainstream, broadcast media functioned as a 'mainstream bubble': a mass, consensual reality which we experienced almost as the horizon of our thought and expectations. Mass media worked on a mass principle, broadcasting to the widest audiences possible, with tastes playing to the mainstream and the broadest demographics. With a small number of channels of information and a dominance of the public's attention, the mainstream media ensured we all, broadly speaking, watched and experienced the same things the same way. Mass media were tightly controlled and couldn't afford to offend either their legal regulators or their advertisers and audiences; hence, they brought us news, information, and entertainment in certain, established and *acceptable* ways. Anything too far from this acceptability wouldn't be broadcast: sexual content could only go so far; certain political opinions wouldn't be covered; and although the views of the public might be solicited, they couldn't just be allowed to say anything they liked.

This began to change before the internet took off, with changes in media regulation and provision. In 1987 the US Federal Communications Commission stopped enforcing the Fairness Doctrine which defined the boundaries for political talk. In August 1988 Rush Limbaugh began appearing on 56 radio stations across the country, leading to a new wave of radio 'shock-jocks' whose success was built on saying things that their listeners thought and in giving a voice to those who didn't think the mainstream represented their opinions. The regulators tried to hit shock-jocks with fines—Howard Stern's employers were fined nearly $2 million—but the market was too great for them to stop. Most of the shock-jocks gave voice to right wing and even extreme right-wing ideas, with their rise linked to their fury at political correctness and at a Democratic incumbent in the White House (causes that today sound familiar). The Clintons, especially, infuriated the right in the 1990s and the shock-jocks gave vent to this hatred. In 1993 the *National Review* described Limbaugh as 'the leader of the opposition'. The other major change was the ongoing expansion of cable and satellite television through the 1990s. In providing more and more channels it fractured the mainstream media, allowing niche interests and programming to flourish and also allowing niche news. The Fox News Channel was established in 1996, for example, to deliver highly partisan and selective conservative news to an audience who wouldn't get this from the more mainstream CBS, NBC, and ABC.

But, yes, it was the internet that would eventually burst the bubble of mainstream media and its reality. On the internet, anything went. It became a haven for extreme material that would never—could never—appear in the mainstream media. The hardest of hard-core pornography wasn't available in the afternoon on the television; 'Two Girls, One Cup' would never show at a cinema near you; and you'd never open up a newspaper and see a Goatse. People with interests and opinions outside the mainstream found a home online, a means to promote their causes and an opportunity to communicate with others that was otherwise unavailable. As Chris Anderson would note, the internet liberated 'the long tail' of lifestyles, ideas, and hobbies that mainstream media and entertainment wouldn't or couldn't cater for.[26] This wasn't necessarily bad. It meant anything from people's more obscure sexual identities and interests to their love of the most niche music or popular culture could find an outlet and others to share it with. Inevitably, however, it included extreme political opinions that had no alternative media space to express themselves in.

The far right embraced the internet early on: the US' leading neo-Nazi website 'Stormfront' was created in 1995, the white nationalist website 'VDare' in 1998 and 'Vanguard News Network' (VNN) in 2000. The Patriot movement, white supremacists, white nationalists, racists, and neo-Nazis all found a home online, building a network of sites and an online presence that would later prove important. There were others too, whose views would coalesce with the far right online into the broad movement that became known as the 'alt-right'. Paleoconservatives, Neoreactionaries, and Accelerationists all had an online audience. 4Chan, founded in 2003, and the centre of online memes and trolling, was part of the anything-goes, libertarian culture of the internet, but its desire to shock and drift to the right would eventually make it and Reddit key sites for the alt-right. The 'manosphere'—the sites and personalities around the 'men's movement' and 'pick-up-artists'—was another online culture, one with a natural affinity with the alt-right due to its misogyny and anti-feminism. Right-wing news sites, such as Breitbart News Network, founded in 2007, all fed upon and into the same online audiences.

One of the best examples of an anti-mainstream, online culture was conspiracy theorism. This had a long, off-line history, but the internet liberated it in new ways. When, in April 2000, Deborah Lipstadt and Penguin Books won the libel case brought by David Irving over claims in her 1993 book *Denying the Holocaust* that he was a 'Holocaust denier', it was widely seen at the time as a major victory over denialists, with the trial involving the detailed destruction of Irving's historical claims and proof of his distortions. Denialism, however, was not only not defeated, the internet dumbed it down and made it available to anyone. You no longer needed to be a historian with a publishing contract: Web 2.0 would allow anyone with a camera and no historical research, knowledge, or qualifications to post their own denunciations of historical reality on YouTube.

Conspiracy theorism online proved to be a gateway drug to the alt-right: there was a truth about the world that *they*—the New World Order, the Illuminati, the Deep State, the establishment, the mass media, the liberal elite, and quite possibly democratic alien lizards—didn't want the people to know. The emerging alt-right spent much of the 2000s developing their theories—about September 11 as a 'false flag' operation carried out by Jews; about the 'Birther' conspiracy that alleged Obama wasn't American; about Obama being a Muslim; about illegal immigrants being part of a plan by democrats to rig future elections; about multiculturalism as a planned takeover of white culture and immigration as a demographic 'white genocide'; about climate change as a hoax; about FEMA concentration camps being readied for the American people; and about mainstream politicians as secret pawns of a New World Order.

These weren't just online. Fox News, in the person especially of Glenn Beck, would push many conspiracy theories, but the most famous outlet for them was Alex Jones' 'Infowars' website. Reportedly receiving over 10 million monthly visits, this 'news site' has proven extremely influential. Donald Trump has long expressed an interest in conspiracy theories and was one of the main figures in the 'Birther' conspiracy; hence it wasn't entirely surprising that, on 2 December 2015, he appeared for an interview on Jones' Infowars show. Trump's campaign was even built around conspiracy theories, especially about how the election was already rigged.

Conspiracy theorism is easy to dismiss, but it's important because it can be understood as part of a broader phenomenon: it resonates today especially as its part of an epochal shift in how we gather and share information, in a movement to a 'me-dia' world where individuals create their own, personal ecology of technologies, platforms, media, content, information, opinions, experiences, and knowledge. In such a world, they no longer have to listen to traditional informational sources: today, you really can think whatever you want and make your own reality. As McLuhan noted, 'All the world's a sage'.[27]

The shattering of reality that Trump exposed, therefore, was actually the shattering of the media's 'mainstream bubble'—of a consensual, acceptable, one-size-fits-all reality—into the infinite shards of individualized me-dia realities. Personalized 'filter bubbles' only became possible once the 'mainstream bubble' was burst. Hence the debate over 'fake news' shifted quickly from being about fabricated, nonsensical news shared on social media to being an attack on the entirety of the mainstream mass media and their reality. Let us be clear, this was a politically motivated attack by the right wing, including Trump and his supporters, against the liberal press and their ideals of holding authority to account at precisely a time when authoritarians were seizing power. But it was an attack that was so easy to make and so powerful because it had a basis in reality—the mass media did produce news and had a long history of bias.

In a way, journalists had long ago squandered the public goodwill and their rediscovery of their values was too late. The public knew the media cynically printed whatever would sell or titillate, whatever fitted their policies, biases, and politics, and whatever served the interests, personal connections, and aspirations of their owners or of the powers they supported. By 2016, their stock had never been so low. But there was also, perhaps, another, deeper shift here. The entire structure of the mass media was unilateral: *they* talked at *us* and had done for decades, if not centuries. Now, in a world where everyone's opinions had been liberated and everyone was talking to everyone, the mainstream media appeared too self-important, haranguing, too self-referential and concerned with themselves and their opinions, and even, as the UK phone-hacking scandal showed, out of control: in short, exactly like that biased, informational elite the Trump supporters accused them of being. As Jeff Jarvis argues (in this volume), the mass media are dead and journalism needs reinvention for this age.[28]

But the media alone weren't responsible for the 'mainstream bubble'. Politicians too had maintained a set of ideas about how the world worked, how the economy should work, what democracy was, and what was acceptable and unacceptable and had excluded from the debate all those who thought differently. Trust in politicians had already been eroded by the 2003 Iraq War and Bush and Blair's blatant manufacture of evidence about Saddam's Weapons of Mass Destruction (WMDs) and links to terrorists that had led to hundreds of thousands killed in a chaotic conflict that has continued to the present. Following the 2008 global economic crisis, politicians retrenched. The Conservative government in the UK erroneously blamed Labour public spending and embarked on an extension of neo-liberal economic policies that had caused the crisis, whilst in the US Obama similarly refused to steer away from neo-liberal free-trade policies. By 2013 there were signs of trouble. In the UK, the celebrity Russell Brand's call for the young not to vote on behalf of a 'disenfranchised, disillusioned underclass' that the system fails to serve was widely criticized, but he presciently identified a sentiment that would grow in the following years: 'It is not that I am not voting out of apathy. I am not voting out of absolute indifference and weariness and exhaustion from the lies, treachery and deceit of the political class that has been going on for generations[29]', he said.

By June 2016, UKIP and immigration, hatred for the political and media 'elite', anger at 'austerity' politics and the pro-market neo-liberal orthodoxy, alienation from the political system, MPs, Westminster, London and the cosmopolitan centre, and the feeling of being left behind in favour of the rich, all combined to create a Brexit vote. Brexit was certainly the product of 'Fake News'—from decades of stories from the UK's right-wing press about what the Brussel's bureaucracy wanted to do now, to numerous 'Leave' claims and the famous Brexit battle-bus slogan 'We send the EU £350 million a week. Let's fund our NHS instead' which turned out not to actually be a promise to do so—but it was equally a response to the manufactured, 'mainstream bubble' of reality created in the political system that had excluded so many other voices and experiences and fears. Similar sentiments spread across Europe, aiding the rise of far-right parties, and in the US, being mobilized by the far right to push the Trump candidature.

The political element of fake news is important here because what we've seen in the US isn't an entirely home-grown phenomenon. The fracturing of reality may have had technological, cultural, and economic causes, but it was a process that was politically exploited by the alt-right and Trump supporters and this exploitation wasn't entirely their own idea. In fact, it came straight out of the Kremlin playbook. Russia had long embraced the idea of 'information war'. In 1998, Sergei P. Rastorguev, a Russian military analyst, published *Philosophy of*

Information Warfare, in which he argued that one of the most important weapons was disinformation, in allowing nations to be weakened from within. It was an idea applied within Russia itself by Putin's aid, Vladislav Surkov, a 'political technologist' who from 1999 to 2011, as Pomerantsev says, directed Russian society like a 'great reality show'. Surkov was inspired in part by the science-fiction of the Strugatsky brothers, especially their 1972 novel, *Roadside Picnic* (the basis for Tarkovsky's 1979 film, *Stalker*). In the novel, aliens have passed over the earth, leaving behind 'zones' where reality itself is unstable, fluid, changing minute by minute and affecting people differently at different times. As Adam Curtis argues in his 2016 film *Hypernormalisation*, for Surkov, this became the basis for a new political strategy: where previously Soviet authorities retained power by controlling the state's narrative and vision of reality, allowing only their version to appear, now, promoting multiple realities and an instability of the real, where anything could mean something else and where nothing was certain, allowed Putin to retain his position. Critique became impossible when everyone believed anything and no common position could be agreed.

It was Surkov's tactics that were employed against Crimea and Ukraine in 2014, where Russian media immersed every political event in a maelstrom of competing claims and lies in order to confuse all discourse, with the mass dissemination of fake news allowing the control and redefinition of reality itself. Surkov's 2014 novel *Without Sky* had explained some of this, describing a 'non-linear warfare'—a state of war where instead of two sides, there were multiple sides, all with shifting allegiances, in a war of 'all against all'. The year before, in February 2013, in an influential article in the Russian journal *Military-Industrial Courier* entitled 'The Value of Science is in the Foresight', Valery Gerasimov, the chief of the general staff of the Russian military, had set out a vision of precisely this 'hybrid' or 'non-linear' warfare where 'the lines between war and peace are blurred'.[30] As he argued there, 'The very "rules of war" have changed.[31] The role of non-military means of achieving political and strategic goals has grown, and, in many cases, they have exceeded the power of force of weapons in their effectiveness'. Ultimately, 'Long distance contactless actions against the enemy are becoming the main means of achieving combat and operational goals'.[32] 'The Gerasimov doctrine', as it's become known, has been applied to the west in an ongoing Russian informational war, active since at least March 2016.

The Russian informational war has three main elements: political hacking in order to undermine particular campaigns and candidates; direct support for favoured parties, candidates, and causes; and an online informational psy-ops and propaganda campaign that penetrates deep into the heart of the target state. All three were seen in the US elections in 2016. Hacking groups such as 'Fancy Bear' (named APT28 by the west) and 'Cozy Bear' (APT29) with probable links to GRU, the Russian Main Intelligence Directorate, hacked the Clinton campaign and Democratic National Committee, passing their emails onto WikiLeaks to publish, to publicly embarrass the Democratic campaign. Links between the Trump campaign and Russian figures and Russian offers of help against Clinton have been admitted and are currently being investigated in the US. And there is evidence that Russia has employed its informational resources during the US election.

Online, Russia targets social media such as Twitter, Facebook, YouTube, and Instagram. 'Troll Farms' such as the pro-Kremlin, Internet Research Agency (IRA) in St. Petersburg hired hundreds of workers to produce online stories, videos, photos, memes, comments, and contributions promoting Russian interests. These farms and other operatives created and disseminated explicit 'fake news', but they also created fake profiles ('sock puppets'), in order to post about controversial and divisive issues such as race, immigration, and Islam. In the US, for example, Russians targeted the Black Lives Matter (BLM) movement, setting up accounts such as the Facebook 'Blacktivist' page honouring Freddie Gray who had died in police custody. The page gathered 360,000 'likes' and regularly posted comments intending to inflame anger.

In October 2017, it was also reported that Russian trolls posing as Americans made payments to genuine activists in the US, to fund protest movements on socially divisive issues, spending about $80,000 in two years on campaigns on race relations, Texan independence, and gun rights. Meanwhile Twitter-bots automatically produced and retweeted stories and comments, and ads were bought on Facebook to promote particular political positions. The IRA, for example, was revealed in September 2017 to have spent $100,000 on 3000 Facebook ads in the two years before May 2017. Russian news-outlets, such as RT (Russia Today) and Sputnik, then picked up on these manufactured stories and reported on the claimed controversies, to push them further into the news. The initial stories about 'fake news' on Facebook, therefore, were correct, but they only spotted a tiny part of the problem.

Russia's aim here is simple. It is a mode of cyberwar: an attack on the *social and cultural* critical infrastructure of the west, being designed to manipulate political discourse, to exacerbate and weaken existing divisions, to polarize political beliefs, to sow disorder and create real internal conflict, to spread fake stories and create contradictory realities to undermine cohesion or reasoned debate, and, ultimately, to undermine faith in the democratic process and the concept of democracy itself. Because what Russia wants most in the west are weakened democracies too caught up in their own internal conflicts; a divided west moving away from the unity offered by NATO and the EU; authoritarian nations accepting of Russia's own politics; the discrediting of democracy itself and a relativistic international order that would jettison discussion of human rights in favour of great powers and their sphere of influence. Military weapons will never achieve this, but informational weapons might.

But Russia couldn't achieve all this alone. To be effective these social media productions needed to be taken up *within the target country*. And this is what happened. As Jonathan Albright's post-election analysis showed, the right was highly organized online, having spent years building a propaganda machine consisting of over 300 fake news sites and consisting of 1.3 million hyperlink connections.[33] They not only created their own fake news and opinion pieces to push through the online ecology, they also—knowingly or not—picked up on and promoted Russian-produced material too. As did anyone online who agreed with what the Russian operatives were posting, including, as we've seen BLM democrats. In October 2017, Facebook identified about 80,000 Russian posts published from June 2015 to August 2017, reaching 29 million Americans directly and being amplified and spread through reposts, comments, and 'likes' to around 126 million Americans. The scale of the Russian campaign, its ability to reach deep inside the everyday media platforms and informational experiences of the public, and the ability, effectively, to crowd-source its informational warfare through the target country by getting the population themselves to repost and contribute towards it, all gave this campaign a diffuse, online, real-time efficacy, one dissolved through the everyday life of the polity.

The fracturing of the mainstream consensus reality was exploited, therefore, by a range of actors, including the Russian state, the alt-right, Trump supporters, and Trump himself as part of his push for power. As Surkov showed, a world with multiple, unstable, debatable, personal realities dissolves all dissent and critique into just another opinion. In a world where everyone's views are liberated and all extremes can be expressed, the traditional, ideal, communicative and democratic space of the Habermasian 'public sphere' is exposed as the privileged and controlled simulation it always was and shattered. Hence, unfortunately, the mainstream media and journalism's attempt to defend themselves by rediscovering their values, by laying claim to an elevated position of truth-telling and by promoting their fact-checking services is bound to fail. In a fractal informational environment, that consensus of the real is irrecoverable. Instead, as the right understood, when reality becomes a free-for-all, then reality becomes available for the taking. It becomes *a weaponizable force* for anyone with the power to seize and lay claim to it. This is what Trump achieved. Reality itself was seized, and the valid claims of 'fake news' were reversed back against the mainstream media themselves, sucking the reality out of their journalism and out of their profession to leave the accusation and appearance of hollow 'fakery'.

America didn't need to look to Russian science-fiction to explain this. It had its own native prophet of the unstable and weaponized real: Philip K. Dick. His work simultaneously articulates both Trump-supporter, conspiracy-theory paranoia at the machinations of the media, the elites and politicians and an eerily prescient, critical vision of Trump's America. In his novels, fake-news proliferates, manufactured, simulacral presidents and their celebrity wives govern through the media, America becomes a Nazi state, false memories and fake experiences dominate, truth and falsity and human and non-human merge, reality fractures and splinters, alternative and virtual realities are manufactured, and people become trapped in their own personal realities. Something similar has now happened. With the rise of Trump, we entered into an alternative Dickian timeline. 'If you think this universe is bad', Dick once said, 'You should see some of the others'. That is indeed what we are doing.

NOTES

1. Techonomy 2016. https://techonomy.com/2016/11/live-techonomy-2016/
2. Ibid.
3. President Barack Obama Says Fake News Is a Problem for 'Democratic Freedoms', *Time*, 18 November 2016. http://time.com/4575981/barack-obama-fake-news-democracy-facebook/
4. Ibid.

5. https://www.facebook.com/zuck/posts/10103269806149061
6. Ibid.
7. Facebook to begin flagging fake news in response to mounting criticism, *The Guardian*, 15 December 2016. https://www.theguardian.com/technology/2016/dec/15/facebook-flag-fake-news-fact-check
8. Facebook deletes Norwegian PM's post as 'napalm girl' row escalates. *The Guardian*: 9 September 2016. https://www.theguardian.com/technology/2016/sep/09/facebook-deletes-norway-pms-post-napalm-girl-post-row
9. https://www.facebook.com/zuck/posts/10103253901916271
10. https://www.facebook.com/zuck/posts/10103338789106661
11. Ibid.
12. Dear reader, please don't email me. *The Guardian*. 8 January 2007. https://www.theguardian.com/media/2007/jan/08/mondaymediasection13
13. Ibid.
14. Pope warns media over 'sin' of spreading fake news, smearing politicians. Reuters. 7 December 2016. https://www.reuters.com/article/us-pope-media/pope-warns-media-over-sin-of-spreading-fake-news-smearing-politicians-idUSKBN13W1TU
15. Ibid.
16. Full transcript and video: Trump news conference. *The New York Times*. 16 February 2017. https://www.nytimes.com/2017/02/16/us/politics/donald-trump-press-conference-transcript.html
17. Bob Clarke. Lecture: From Grub Street to Fleet Street: The Development of the Early English Newspaper. 3 June 2013. https://www.gresham.ac.uk/lectures-and-events/from-grub-street-to-fleet-street-the-development-of-the-early-english-newspaper
18. Daniel J. Boorstin. 1962. The Image: A Guide to Pseudo-Events in America. New York: Harper Colophon, p. 205.
19. Boorstin p. 211.
20. Boorstin p. 36.
21. Boorstin p. 252.
22. Guy Debord (1967/1994). Society of the spectacle (translated by D. Nicholson-Smith) New York: Zone Books.-
23. Ibid.
24. Boorstin p. 249.
25. Elizabeth Dubois and Grant Blank. 2018. The myth of the echo chamber. The Conversation. 8 March 2018. https://theconversation.com/the-myth-of-the-echo-chamber-92544
26. Chris Anderson. The Long Tail. Wired. 1 October 2004. https://www.wired.com/2004/10/tail/
27. Marshall McLuhan and Quentin Fiore. 1996. The Medium is the Massage. San Francisco: Hardwired.

28. Jeff Jarvis, Trump and the Press: A Murder-Suicide Pact. In Happer, Catherine, Andrew Hoskins and William Merrin (Eds.) Trump's War on the Media. Basingstoke: Palgrave Macmillan.
29. Russell Brand. BBC News. 23 October 2013. http://www.bbc.co.uk/news/av/uk-24648651/russell-brand-i-ve-never-voted-never-will
30. Gerasimov, Valery (2013) 'The Value of Science is in the Foresight', *Military Review*, Jan–Feb, pp. 23–29, http://usacac.army.mil/CAC2/MilitaryReview/Archives/English/MilitaryReview_20160228_art008.pdf
31. Ibid.
32. Ibid.
33. Jonathan Albright. The #Election2016 Micro-Propaganda Machine. Medium. 18 November 2016. https://medium.com/@d1gi/the-election2016-micro-propaganda-machine-383449cc1fba

CHAPTER 2

Trump and the Press: A Murder-Suicide Pact

Jeff Jarvis

The Press will Destroy Trump and Trump will Destroy the Press.

Consider that trust in media began falling in the 1970s,[1] coincident with what we believe was our zenith: Watergate. We brought down a President. A Republican President.

Now the press is the nation's last, best hope to bring down a compromised, corrupt, bigoted, narcissistic, likely insane, incompetent, and possibly dangerous President. A Republican President. Donald Trump.

If the press does what Congress is so far unwilling to do—investigate him—then these two Republican presidencies will bookend the beginning of the end and the end of the end of American mass media. Any last, small hope that anyone on the right would ever again trust, listen to, and be informed by the press will disappear. It doesn't matter if we are correct or righteous. We won't be heard. Mass media dies, as does the notion of the mass.

This essay was originally published on Medium: https://medium.com/whither-news/trump-the-press-a-murder-suicide-pact-460ce4480c2d. We are grateful for the kind permission of Jeff Jarvis to reproduce it here.

J. Jarvis (✉)
Tow-Knight Center for Entrepreneurial Journalism, The City University of New York' Graduate School of Journalism, New York, NY, USA

© The Author(s) 2019
C. Happer et al. (eds.), *Trump's Media War*,
https://doi.org/10.1007/978-3-319-94069-4_2

23

Therein lies the final Trump paradox: In failing, he would succeed in killing the press. And his final projection: The enemy of the people convinces the people that we are the enemy.[2]

The press that survives, the liberal press, will end up with more prizes and subscriptions,[3] oh joy, but with little hope of guiding or informing the nation's conversation. Say *The New York Times* reaches its audacious dream of 10 million paying subscribers.[4] So what? That's 3% of the US population (and some number of those subscribers will be from elsewhere). And they said that blogs were echo chambers. We in liberal media will be speaking to ourselves—or, being liberal, more likely arguing with ourselves.

No number of empathetic articles[5] that try to understand and reflect the worldview of the angry core of America will do a damned bit of good getting them to read, trust, and learn from *The New York Times*. My own dear parents will not read The New York Times. They are left to be <cough> informed by Fox News, Breitbart, Drudge, RT,[6] and worse.

In February 2017, Jim Rutenberg[7] and David Leonhardt[8] of *The Times* wrote tough columns about turmoil in Rupert Murdoch's *Wall Street Journal* over journalists' fears that they find themselves working for an agent of Trump. They missed the longer story: What we are living through right now was the brainchild of Rupert Murdoch. It started in 1976 (note the timeline of trust above) when he bought the *New York Post* to be, in his words, his bully pulpit—and he added new meaning to that phrase. Yes, Rush Limbaugh and his like came along in the next decade to turn American radio into a vehicle for spreading fear, hate, and conspiracy. But it was in the following decade, in 1996, when Murdoch started Fox News, adding new, ironic meaning to another phrase: "fair and balanced." He and his henchman, Roger Ailes, used every technique, conceit, and cliché of American television news to co-opt the form and forward his worldview, agenda, and war.

Murdoch could have resurrected the ideological diversity that was lost in the American press when broadcast TV culled newspapers in competitive markets and the survivors took on the impossible veil of objectivity. Instead, he made the rest of the press into the enemy: not us "and" them but us "or" them; not "let us give you another perspective" but "their perspective is bad."

What's a liberal journo to do? We are stuck in endless paradoxical loops. If we do our job and catch the President in a lie, we are labeled liars. When we counteract fake news with real news, everything becomes fake news. If I get angry about being attacked by angry white men I end up becoming an angry white man. Liberals tell us to be nice to conservatives to win them over but then they only mock us for being weak.[9] Snowflakes. Cucks. Liberal tears.

I commend to your reading this essay by Dale Beran[10] explaining the ultimate political irony of our day: The alt-right is made up of losers and when we call them losers they win. So we can't win. "Trump is Pepe. Trump is loserdom embraced," Beran explains. "Trump supporters voted for the con-man, the labyrinth with no center, because the labyrinth with no center is how they feel, how they feel the world works around them. A labyrinth with no center is a perfect description of their mother's basement with a terminal to an endless array of escapist fantasy worlds."

How do you argue with that worldview? How do you inform it? How do you win somebody over when all they want is enemies? (Watch this[11] at your own peril.) You probably can't. There are some chunks of America that likely need to be written off because they have fenced themselves off from reasonable, fact-based, intellectually honest, civil debate and now wallow in hate. Is that condescending of me to say? No, it's pragmatic. *Realjournalismus.*

So then am I giving up on journalism and democracy? No, dammit, not yet. I am giving up on mass media. The internet wounded it; Rupert Murdoch and Donald Trump finally killed it.

So now what? Now we reinvent journalism. Now we learn how to serve communities, listening to them to reflect their worldviews and gain their trust so we can inform them. Now we give up on the belief that we are entitled to act as gatekeeper and to set the agenda as well as the prices of information and advertising. Now we must learn to work well with others. Now we must bring diversity not just to our surviving newsrooms—which we must—but to the larger news ecosystem, building new, sustainable news services and businesses to listen to, understand, empathize with, and meet the needs of many communities.

Our goal is not to herd all the lost sheep back into our fence. I will disagree with those[12] who[13] say that we must grinfuck Trump voters to woo them to our side of the ballot. No, we must stay angry and incredulous that they—the fanatical core of them—brought us Trump, and we prove our worth by fixing that. I say there is no hope of convincing frogs and eggs in our Twitter feeds; let's not waste our time. Instead, our goal is to bring out the people who regretted their vote; there must be some. Far more important, our goal is to bring out the people who did not vote, who were not sufficiently informed of the risk of their inaction and thus not motivated to act. We can do that. Journalism can. That is why journalism exists, for civic engagement. (This is why starting Social Journalism at CUNY[14] was a revolutionary act.)

Start, for example, with the many communities who are lumped together as Latino Americans. Meet them not as a demographic bucket imagined by Anglo Americans and marketers but as distinct groups of people who have distinct needs and interests. (This is why I am proud that CUNY started a bilingual journalism program.[15]) Do the same with so many other underserved and these days abused communities: immigrants, Muslims, LGBT communities, people who will lose health insurance—communities organized not just around identity but also around need.

To be clear, this does not mean that the last mass-media companies can abandon these communities to media ghettos. *The New York Times*, *The Washington Post*, *The Guardian*, CNN, every newspaper company, and every broadcast company must work much harder to bring diversity into their newsrooms and executive ranks to do their jobs better. (One last plug for CUNY: This is why we work so hard to recruit a diverse student body.) We can improve mass media. But I don't think we can fix it as it is—that is, return it to its lost scale. And I don't think that mass media can fix the mess we are in.

So I would advise media companies old and new to invent and invest in new services to serve new communities. If I wanted to save a struggling mass-media company—think, Time Inc.—I would start scores of new services, building new and valued relationships with new communities.

And, yes, I would start a new service for conservative America. I would hire the best conservative journalists I could find not just to write commentary but to report from a different worldview (if anyone can define conservatism these days). I would underwrite scholarships at journalism schools (I promised to stop plugging mine) to recruit students from towns wracked by unemployment, from evangelical colleges, from the military. I would take advantage of a tremendous business opportunity to fight back against Murdoch's and Trump's destruction of the American press in the full belief that there are enough people in this nation on the right who want facts, who want to be informed, who will listen to their own uncomfortable truths. I would welcome that diversity, too.

Finally, I would stop listening to the entitled whining of journalists about the state of their business.[16] Yes, Murdoch fired a first bullet and Trump hammered a last nail but we bear the most responsibility for abandoning large swaths of America and for refusing to change. I disagree with Adrienne LaFrance that Mark Zuckerberg is out to "destroy journalism." His manifesto about the future of communities and an informed society shows we have much to learn from him.[17] "Online communities are a bright spot," he writes, ever the optimist. "Research suggests the best solutions for improving discourse may come from getting to know each other as whole people instead of just opinions—something Facebook may be uniquely suited to do."

OK, but I will also push him, too. Facebook, Twitter, and all the platforms should invest their considerable intelligence, imagination, and resources in helping reinvent journalism for this age. New tools bring new opportunities and new responsibilities. I would like to see Facebook help news companies understand how to serve communities and how to reimagine how we inform citizens' conversations where they occur. I wish that Facebook would find more ways to introduce us to new people who can tell their stories in safe spaces where we can come to learn about each other. I would like Facebook and media to collaborate convening communities in conflict to informed and productive discourse. I would like to see Twitter finally address its and perhaps society's key problem: Can we be open and also civil? I hope Google will be more transparent about those who would manipulate it and thus us. I hope they all help us invent new business models that no longer reward just clickbait and fame, cats and Kardashians, sensationalism and polarization (Zuckerberg's words). The platforms should spend less effort trying to help journalism as it is— except insofar as it buys us time for innovation—but instead support journalism as it can be.

Let Donald Trump kill the mass media that made him President. Let his ego and his hate suck all his attention and hostility from its last dying embers. Let his election be the last gasp, the nadir of this dying institution. Then let the rest of us—God willing a comfortable majority in this already-great nation—find a path to resume a civil and informed conversation about our shared future.

NOTES

1. GALLUP, Confidence in Institutions: http://news.gallup.com/poll/1597/confidence-institutions.aspx
2. Reena Flores, 'White House chief of staff says take Trump seriously when he calls press "the enemy"', CBS News, 18 February 2017: https://www.cbsnews.com/news/white-house-chief-of-staff-says-take-trump-seriously-press-is-the-enemy/
3. Joseph Lichterman, 'After Trump's win, news organizations see a bump in subscriptions and donations', NiemanLab, 14 November 2016: http://www.niemanlab.org/2016/11/after-trumps-election-news-organizations-see-a-bump-in-subscriptions-and-donations/
4. Ken Doctor, 'Newsonomics: The New York Times is setting its sights on 10 million digital subscribers', NiemanLab, 5 December 2016: http://www.niemanlab.org/2016/12/newsonomics-the-new-york-times-is-setting-its-sights-on-10-million-digital-subscribers/
5. Laurie Goodstein, 'Torn Over Donald Trump and Cut Off by Culture Wars, Evangelicals Despair', *The New York Times*, 29 September 2016: https://www.nytimes.com/2016/09/30/us/donald-trump-christians-gay-marriage.html?rref=collection%2Fbyline%2Flaurie-goodstein&action=click&contentCollection=undefined&region=stream&module=stream_unit&version=latest&contentPlacement=1&pgtype=collection
6. https://twitter.com/TomNamako/status/833113928238526465
7. Jim Rutenberg, 'When a Pillar of the Fourth Estate Rests on a Trump-Murdoch Axis', *The New York Times*, 12 February 2017:https://www.nytimes.com/2017/02/12/business/media/rupert-murdoch-donald-trump-news-corporation.html
8. David Leonhardt, 'The Struggle Inside The Wall Street Journal', *The New York Times*, 14 February 2017: https://www.nytimes.com/2017/02/14/opinion/the-struggle-inside-the-wall-street-journal.html
9. Sabrina Tavernise, 'Are Liberals Helping Trump?' *The New York Times*, 18 February 2017: https://www.nytimes.com/2017/02/18/opinion/sunday/are-liberals-helping-trump.html?action=click&pgtype=Homepage&clickSource=story-heading&module=opinion-c-col-right-region&region=opinion-c-col-right-region&WT.nav=opinion-c-col-right-region&_r=0
10. Dale Beran, '4chan: The Skeleton Key to the Rise of Trump', Medium, 14 February 2017: https://medium.com/@DaleBeran/4chan-the-skeleton-key-to-the-rise-of-trump-624e7cb798cb
11. 'MILO Confronts the Panel', Overtime with Bill Maher, HBO, 17 February 2017: https://www.youtube.com/watch?v=3cDLflyQ8TA&feature=youtu.be

12. https://twitter.com/NickKristof/status/833317718422016000
13. https://twitter.com/CitiSam/status/833328363049725952
14. https://www.journalism.cuny.edu/future-students/m-a-social-journalism/
15. https://www.journalism.cuny.edu/future-students/m-a-in-journalism/subject-concentrations/spanish-language-journalism/
16. Adrienne LaFrance, 'The Mark Zuckerberg Manifesto Is a Blueprint for Destroying Journalism', *The Atlantic*, 17 February 2017: https://www.theatlantic.com/technology/archive/2017/02/the-mark-zuckerberg-manifesto-is-a-blueprint-for-destroying-journalism/517113/
17. Mark Zuckerberg, 'Building Global Community', Facebook, 16 February 2017: https://www.facebook.com/notes/mark-zuckerberg/building-global-community/10154544292806634

PART II

Fake News

Turning the Tables: How Trump Turned Fake News from a Weapon of Deception to a Weapon of Mass Destruction of Legitimate News

Paul Levinson

Turning the tables and accusing your adversary of what has been claimed about you is a time-honored technique of sincere debate and deceptive propaganda. This essay examines Donald Trump's adept use of this strategy, beginning with his calling Hillary Clinton a "puppet" in a presidential debate after she said the same about him regarding Putin, and continuing after he was elected and from the White House with an ongoing campaign to disable his critics in the news media as purveyors of fake news after they began systematically demonstrating how Trump had long been wielding that same approach himself. The result of such a campaign is an increasing portion of the public that doesn't know what to believe—a situation singularly caustic to democracy, which depends upon a citizenry not only informed, but confident that the information they receive is accurate and true, to the best of the journalist or commentator's human ability.

P. Levinson (✉)
Communication and Media Studies, Fordham University, Bronx, NY, USA

© The Author(s) 2019
C. Happer et al. (eds.), *Trump's Media War*,
https://doi.org/10.1007/978-3-319-94069-4_3

33

The Roll-Out: Fake News Rears Its Ugly Head

Although there have been errors in reporting, publication, and broadcasting of news since the inception of these media—most unintentional but occasionally (as in the case of Jayson Blair and *The New York Times*, see Barry et al. 2003) deliberate—fake news first appeared as a major public concern in the immediate aftermath of the US presidential election of 2016, and the scramble to understand why Hillary Clinton lost the electoral college vote and thereby the election to Donald Trump. In her postmortem What *Happened*, published in September 2017, Clinton cites "fake news" along with James Comey's statements, Russian email hacks, and sexism as among the main causes of the election result (see Senior 2017, for a perceptive summary of the book).

Given the complex American electoral system, and the culturally and politically diverse population of voters, attributing an election result to any one factor, or even a group of factors, is a dicey proposition. In the case of fake news, evidence would be needed that, for some reason, the voters in the crucial Midwest states that went for Trump were for some reason more influenced by the fake news than voters in states as culturally diverse as New York, Nevada, New Hampshire, and California. There was indeed a report (see Stone and Gordon 2017) that US Senate, House of Representative, and Department of Justice investigators are attempting to determine if the Trump campaign pointed Russian-created fake news toward swing-state voters in the Midwest, but this is a long way from actual evidence. Suffice to say that, whatever its impact on the 2016 presidential election, fake news is not a good thing for an election process, or any aspect of a democratic society and its need for a trustworthy press.

Thus, it is the contention of this essay that the most damaging effect of fake news was the weapon it gave Donald Trump to undermine the press by turning the tables and accusing his perceived enemies in the legitimate media of conveying, if not the same fake news stories that dogged the Clinton campaign, the same general category of news deliberately designed to deceive.

Turning the Tables: The Claim that Legitimate Media Traffic in Fake News

Trump was quick to launch his attack on unwelcome news reports as fake news—or, as he no doubt sees it, his counter-attack—with a tweet, just ten days after the start of the new year of 2017, characterizing reports of the Russians seeking to blackmail him with recordings of sexual escapades when he was in Moscow as "FAKE NEWS - A TOTAL POLITICAL WITCH HUNT!" (all caps in Tweet from Trump, see Beech 2017). This prompted MSNBC commentator Eugene Robinson (2017) to remark later that day that fake news had become a label for "news we don't like." Trump's use of Twitter, his favorite medium, to unleash this assault is also significant and worthy of note. Just as Adolf Hitler preferred radio to the press (see Hitler 1924/1971), because it afforded him direct access to the German people, so Trump likes Twitter, because it enables him to communicate directly and without media interpretation to his supporters, or without his words being misreported by a "dishonest" press (Phippen 2017). (No similarity of political views need be inferred—this is, rather, a statement of the similarity of authoritarian leaders and their predilection for unmediated communication to the public.)

Trump followed up his attack the very next day, on another unmediated forum—or less mediated than most television—live coverage of a press conference, where he shouted from the podium at CNN's senior White House correspondent: "You're fake news!" (*Daily Beast* 2017). This apparently was because CNN in Trump's view had reported with insufficient criticism *BuzzFeed*'s unverified charges about the Russian blackmail which Trump had just lambasted on Twitter. He developed this a few weeks later into an all-purpose self-serving view that "any negative polls are fake news, just like the CNN, ABC, NBC polls in the election" (Batchelor 2017). By the end of February 2017 and his first month as President, Trump had progressed from ungrammatically trumpeting on Twitter that "FAKE NEWS media knowingly doesn't tell the truth" ("media" is a plural term, though I'll freely admit that holding the line on that Latin construction is a losing battle, and Trump has a legion of company, far more people than voted for him in the election, happily misusing that term) to actually locking out perceived offenders CNN and *The New York Times* from White House briefings (Davis and Grynbaum 2017). For this *Man in the High Castle* (Dick 1962), real news had become fake news and fake news had become real. Of course, all science fiction—for that matter, all fiction—is a form of fake news, except it doesn't pretend to be true, or pretends to be true only insofar as it tries to persuade us to willingly suspend our disbelief, as Coleridge (1817) prescribed, so that we may be entertained.

STORMING THE BARRICADES OF TRUTH

But there was and is nothing entertaining in Trump's assault on the all-too-real world of the open society and its enemies (as per Karl Popper 1945) in which we live, and the demonization of real news as fake news took an even uglier turn by the summer of 2017. Rachel Maddow reported on her MSNBC hour on July 6, 2017, that the show had been shopped a cleverly concocted and nearly convincing fake news story about the Russians working with the Trump campaign during the 2016 election. The motive clearly was to erode public trust in MSNBC's reporting—widely and corrected viewed as progressive—and Maddow hypothesized that Dan Rather had been victimized by a similar operation when he was obliged to resign as anchor of the *CBS Evening News* in 2005 after broadcasting a story in 2004 about George W. Bush's avoidance of the draft during the Vietnam War (MacVean 2004)—a story based on apparently forged documents provided by sources that to this day remain unclear.

In some ways an even more disturbing scenario surfaced in August 2017, when a lawsuit cited Fox News as a co-conspirator with the White House in a deliberate concoction of a fake news story that attempted to utilize the murder of Democratic National Committee (DNC) staff member Seth Rich to discredit the findings of US intelligent agencies that Russia was behind the hacking of DNC emails which were later published in WikiLeaks (Darcy 2017). If true, this would be the first time that a major news organization was accused not just of purveying fake news but actively working to create it with the knowledge and help of the highest level of government. Unlike Breitbart News, which is frank and blatant in its over-the-top, often absurd reporting on what it regards as the progressive left (see Clinton 2017, for some choice examples, such as "Birth Control Makes Women Unattractive and Crazy" and "Fact Check: Were Obama and Hillary Founders of ISIS? You Bet"), Fox at least gave lip-service to not only being factual but "Fair and Balanced" in its reporting, though it wisely abandoned that motto in June 2017. Fox claimed they did this because the slogan had "been mocked" (Sherman 2017), but my hope would be that they abandoned the tagline in the interest of accuracy.

Meanwhile, in effect complementing the dismissal of unwelcome news as fake news, Trump spokesperson Kellyanne Conway characterized as "alternative facts" the obvious falsehood from then Press Secretary Sean Spicer that the crowd gathered for the inauguration of Donald Trump in

Washington, DC, "was the largest audience to ever witness an inauguration, period" (Conway 2017). In reality, the 1.5 million people assembled for Trump's inauguration were about a third of the number who came to see Barack Obama inaugurated in 2009 (Fandos 2017). Thus, in this new kind of double-speak, unpleasant true news is fake news, and palpably untrue news reports are alternative facts—or two sides of the same lethal-to-democracy coin. (As Allbeson and Allan 2019, point out, photography, its verisimilitude, and its manipulability were central to the refutation of Spicer's claim and Conway's attempt to support it via her neologism. See also Levinson 2016, for some history of photographic deception and fake news.)

Subsequent suggestions that Spicer was referring to television viewership as well as in-person attendance of Trump's inauguration are also refuted by the easily discoverable history of US presidential inauguration broadcasts, which attracted 41 million viewers for Ronald Reagan's inauguration in 1981, 38 million viewers for Barack Obama in 2009, and 33 million for Richard Nixon in 1973, in comparison to 31 million for Trump in 2017 (see Gorman 2017, for more details).

What Can Be Done About These Assaults?

These toxic attacks on the press and therefore our democracy deserve not only our condemnation but careful deconstruction—in other words, a response to bogus fake news or fake-fake news, which is what allegations that the legitimate press is fake amount to, require as clear as possible an identification of real fake news. We can begin by recognizing that there is a significant difference between news that we know with 100% certainty is fake—because, as in the case of Jestin Coler, its creator tells us so, and takes us through the steps via which it was fabricated and disseminated, and why he did this, which was to make money by attracting people to a website (see Soboroff 2016)—and news alleged to be fake. We furthermore need to draw a distinction between news that is unverified or even false (as in the case of unintended errors in the legitimate press, and that includes Blair's deliberate concoctions in *The New York Times*, which were not intended by its editors and publisher, and also includes not just professional reporters and media but citizen journalists—see Levinson 2016, for more on how citizen journalists and the crucial work they do need to be assessed in any taxonomy of real vs. fake news, with citizen journalism on the "real" side), and news that is fake, since fake implies a deliberate intent to deceive, from writing through publication. And we may need to draw brighter lines between fake news itself, and the reporting and dissemination of fake news with varying degrees of identification or not of the news as fake. Purchase by a Russian "troll farm" of political ads from 2015 onward on Facebook would be a recently uncovered example of the latter. Although ads are not in and of themselves fake news, Facebook had a moral and legal obligation to know their source and not publish the ads, since ads from foreign sources attempting to influence American elections are prohibited (see Shane and Goel 2017, for more).

The *Columbia Journalism Review* (Gezari 2017) also makes a distinction between "unverified" and "unverifiable" news reports. This is important because "unverified" implies reporting that was premature, or done by a lazy journalist, in contrast to "unverifiable," which connotes deeper possible reasons for the lack of verification, which may be newsworthy in themselves. (See also *Order of the Coif* 2017, which suggests the opposite, that "unverifiable" could also mean worthy of no further investigation.)

WHAT SHOULD NOT BE DONE TO STOP FAKE NEWS?

Ironically, a clearer identification of what is fake news in contrast to real news carries with it a need to identify what ought not be done to counter fake news because, in the case of what Trump and his minions have sought to do against real news—plainly an effort to undermine real news by labeling it fake—any sanctions against or censorship of fake news could result in real news (deliberately mislabeled as fake) being suppressed as well.

The First Amendment to the US Constitution and its insistence that government "shall make no law…abridging the freedom of speech, or of the press" is of paramount importance here, in making sure that truthful news isn't interred along with the detritus of false news. That's likely what Trump ultimately wants, when the true news is critical of him—a result that would also give fake news produced by Russian propagandists or white supremacists a privileged or even sole place in the marketplace of ideas, with no truth to contend with. Such a totalitarian situation would indeed destroy Milton's dynamic (*Areopagitica* 1644) of truth and falsity unhindered to fight it out in the marketplace of ideas, with human rationality awarding the victory to truth. But even if that's not what Trump implicitly has in mind about real news by painting it with the scarlet letter of F for Fake (with apologies to Orson Welles 1974), the banning of fake news would still be a very bad idea.

There has never been a time in our history in which the insistence of First Amendment "absolutists" such as mid-twentieth-century Supreme Court Justices Hugo Black and William Douglas that "no law" in the First Amendment means "no law" need be more strictly respected and followed to the letter. (See my "The Flouting of the First Amendment" 2005, for more.) Whether "falsely shouting fire in a theater" (Justice Oliver Wendell Holmes Jr.'s example in the *Schenck v. United States* 1919 Supreme Court decision of what the First Amendment should not protect) or fake news or truthful news spitefully labeled as fake, the government has no proper business restricting, preventing, or punishing any of it.

A better way of dealing with falsely shouting fire in crowded theaters is constructing theaters with numerous, easy means of egress which defuse trampling crowds. (Note that Holmes' exemption from First Amendment protection is "falsely" shouting fire. Penalizing the shouting of fire without the "falsely" in front, which is the way Holmes' injunction is often wrongly rendered, would have the unfortunate effect of stopping someone from shouting fire when there really is a fire burning, when shouting might be a good idea.) The lunatic who showed up with a gun at the Comet Ping Pong pizzeria in Washington, DC, after reading a fake news story about Hillary Clinton participating in a child predation ring at the pizza place (see Gillin 2016, for further details) could be far more effectively disarmed by a law which kept guns out of the hands of the mentally ill than a law that banned fake news. And the possibility of a true news story being censored because Trump and his supporters deemed it unfair and thus fake news should be reason enough never to ban anything that is fake news, be it really fake or not.

In a significant twist to this continuing tale of falsely shouting fake news, and the acute need for both non-fake news and its false identification as fake news to be protected by the First Amendment—that is, not excised by the government—we have CNN, ABC, CBS, and NBC (not Fox) refusing in May 2017 to air an ad by Trump supporters attacking those networks as purveyors of fake news. Since that ad is itself a form of fake news, or what we might call "meta-fake news" or fake news about fake news—because those networks are in fact not disseminating fake news—any refusal to broadcast the ad seems a useful step in the battle to reduce fake news. Nonetheless, Trump's daughter-in-law Lara, commenting about that refusal, observed that "mainstream media are champions of the First Amendment only when it serves their own political views" (see Hayden 2017). That's probably true enough not only about the networks but most human beings—since we most want to protect communication we love, and least want to protect communication we hate—but since the networks are not the government, they're certainly not violating the First Amendment or any law by refusing to air a political ad that is point-blank false.

But if not a violation of law, is the refusal a violation of what I like to call "the spirit of the First Amendment" (Levinson 2010), something which occurs any time a non-governmental public agent, whether TV network or university, seeks to limit or squelch communication? Had the networks not aired the ad because it didn't "fit their biased narrative," as Lara Trump also alleged (Hayden 2017), then I think that action would indeed have constituted a violation of the spirit of the First Amendment. But since the ad is demonstrably false, that surely trumps (to use that handy term) any bias that the networks might have had. The raison d'etre, again, of all forms of non-fake news reporting is to present the truth. And since the elimination of fake news is surely integral to that mandate, Lara Trump's criticism of the networks is wrong both in the legal sense, since there was no violation of the First Amendment per se, and in any ethical sense, since there was no violation of any spirit of the First Amendment, either.

Where We Go from Here

We can establish a general principle that the elimination of fake news by non-governmental means is not only not inconsistent with a strong commitment to the First Amendment, but assists the First Amendment, and Milton's ideal, by making the marketplace of ideas less likely to have landmines designed to disrupt and destroy the marketplace itself, or the capacity of people to encounter and consider truth as well as lies. Since there would be no laws against fake news, including false claims that true news is fake news, there would be no eclipse of freedom for Trump and anyone who wants to disseminate deception and undermine media. They would be free to express their mischaracterizations somewhere, anywhere. But the major media would be under no obligation to aid in their dissemination. A good starting point would be reducing the coverage that Donald Trump as President understandably receives. But there is a fine line between denying a lie the oxygen of publicity and exposing it to the sunlight of clarifying publicity, and the media need to take care not to do the first at the expense of the second.

In general, identification of fake news that is really fake is the best way of combatting false allegations that a true news story is fake, because it gives the public ongoing examples of what fake news is really like. But how can we know if a story we read online, or see on television, is fake? A good initial tactic is what we do with optical illusions. If we see a shimmering body of water far ahead down the highway, we can determine if the water is really there by slowly approaching it. This would give us multiple vantage points, far and near, and the media equivalent would be looking at more than one source for confirmation of a story, the more sources the better. Of course, if we're driving down the road and we see the shimmering water the day after a hurricane, the first glimpse might be more than enough to get us to turn around. But this would just be another example of consulting more than one source in reaching a judgment about whether we're seeing truth or illusion down the road—in this case, the source of our knowledge that there had been a hurricane, in addition to what we currently see on the road.

Other than the general advisability of calling on more than one source, there are many things that media and consumers can do to combat fake news. Facebook's plan to restrict fake news by identifying phony stories in its algorithms and inserting true news stories in feeds that display fake news stories (see Hoover 2016) is certainly a good idea. Other kinds of gatekeeping include:

- Humanly curated stories on Snapchat's "Discovery" (see Tiku 2016), and Google's "fact-check tag," which reports to what degree a statement is confirmed as true on other sites (Woollacott 2017).
- Facebook's deletion of 30,000 "fake" accounts in France prior to its national election in April 2017 (Kottasová 2017). These included not only purveyors of fake news but spam, and accounts used to artificially inflate Likes and Shares. Unfortunately, the ease with which new accounts can be created means that, as with Twitter's ongoing battle with accounts used by ISIS and terrorists, the purging of accounts is far from a complete or even effective solution. And Facebook needs to shed its reflex habit of denying any foreign purchase of political ads on its site, and then taking months to investigate and discover that there indeed was foreign involvement, as occurred with the revelation about the Russian trolls (Shane and Goel 2017).

- Validation or verification of accounts of people who post—as Twitter has done for years and Facebook more recently with the iconic blue checkmark next to the user's name—is a time-honored way on the Internet of combating trolls, and presumably has reduced publishing of some fake news. In February 2017, Authenticated Reality rolled out "The New Internet," a browser overlay that allows users to verify their accounts by providing their driver's license or passport. The goal, as with the blue checkmark, is to limit or eliminate fake news, online terrorists, and swindlers (Shah 2017). But anonymity and pseudonyms (which I never favored, since I don't like talking to people with bags over their heads) has also been cited since the inception of the Internet as one of its great advantages, encouraging frank conversation (see "The Dark Side of New New Media" in Levinson, 2009/2013, for more on trolls and anonymity), and there's no guarantee that a validated account won't spread fake news.
- Development and dissemination of apps that can detect alterations in audio and video recordings (see Adler 2017).
- Since pursuit of advertising revenue fuels the creation and dissemination of some fake news, public denouncement of advertisements that appear on pages with fake news, and perhaps boycotts of such advertised products and services, has been suggested (see Perlman 2017). Identification and denunciation of fake news is also something the government can do, as distinct from censorship and punishment (which, again, would violate the First Amendment).
- Seminars such as "Calling Bullshit" (Bergstrom and West 2016), unofficially offered at the University of Washington. These should be a necessary component of every college curriculum.

THE UNINTENDED BOUNCE

Media evolution teems with unintended consequences. No one expected the printing press in Europe to result in the Age of Discovery, the Protestant Reformation, the Scientific Revolution, and the rise of national states (see Levinson 1997). No one expected the Internet to generate the epidemic of fake news that currently afflicts our world. And no one expected, likely least of all Trump, that in this age of fake news and Trump's attempt to pin that label on legitimate sources of news, that readers would be flocking to reliable sources such as *The New York Times*, which posted a record-breaking increase of "276,000 digital news subscribers in the last quarter" of 2016 (Toonkel 2017). The ubiquity of fake news apparently increases the hunger of many people for truthful reporting.

And one professor of journalism, in effect adopting a Popperian approach that people learn via acquaintance with error, has argued that "truth should never be suppressed, and neither should lies, untruths or alternative facts," because "exploring these non-facts can, in reality, help us discover the truth" (Burris 2017; see Popper 1962, for learning from error). That's a good reason—in addition to its contradiction of the First Amendment—that fining or criminalizing the publication of fake news on websites (as per a new law enacted in July 2017 in Germany, see Faiola and Kirchner 2017; JTA 2017) is not the best solution.

In the end, as a biological model suggests, the epidemic of fake news can best be combatted by a variety of methods, including washing of hands or removal of pathogens before they enter the body (curating posts and validating accounts), antibiotics (aggressive introduction of truth to combat the lies), and strengthening the immune system (education about how to recognize fake news). But just as we can never eradicate all disease-causing viruses and bacteria, we can expect to be in a never-ending battle with fake news. And just as with illness, battling fake news can sometimes make us stronger. Like illness, fake news is a part of life. And like life, the spread of fake news may even have unexpected beneficial consequences, such as strengthening the need for and increasing the reach of the very media of truth that Trump is seeking to destroy.

References

Adler, Simon (2017) "Breaking News," *Radiolab* podcasts, 27 July. http://www.radiolab.org/story/breaking-news/

Allbeson, Stuart, & Allan, Tom (2019) "The War of Images in the Age of Trump" in Catherine Happer, Andrew Hoskins, and William Merrin, eds. *Trump's War on the Media*. Basingstoke, UK: Palgrave Macmillan, pp. 69–84.

Barry, Dan; Barstow, David; Glater, Jonathan D.; Liptak, Adam; and Steinberg, Jacques (2003) "CORRECTING THE RECORD; *Times* Reporter Who Resigned Leaves Long Trail of Deception," *The New York Times*, 11 May. http://www.nytimes.com/2003/05/11/us/correcting-the-record-times-reporter-who-resigned-leaves-long-trail-of-deception.html

Batchelor, Tom (2017) "Donald Trump: 'Negative polls are fake news'," *Independent*, 6 February. http://www.independent.co.uk/news/world/americas/donald-trump-negative-polls-fake-news-twitter-cnn-abc-nbc-a7564951.html

Beech, Eric (2017) "Trump calls Russia reports 'fake news – a total political witch hunt'," *Reuters*, 10 January. http://www.reuters.com/article/us-usa-cyber-russia-tweet-idUSKBN14V05T

Bergstrom, Carl T., & West, Jevin (2016) "Calling Bullshit In the Age of Big Data," unofficial seminar offered at University of Washington. http://callingbullshit.org/syllabus.html

Burris, Larry (2017) quoted in Baar, Aaron, "What's Search's Role in Combating Fake News?" *Media Post*, 24 January. https://www.mediapost.com/publications/article/293605/whats-searchs-role-in-combating-fake-news.html

Clinton, Hillary (2017) *What Happened*. New York: Simon & Schuster.

Coleridge, Samuel Taylor (1817) *Biographia Literaria*, edited 1907 by J. Shawcross. London: Oxford University Press.

Conway, Kellyanne (2017) Interview by Chuck Todd, *Meet the Press*, NBC-TV, 22 January. http://www.nbcnews.com/meet-the-press/video/conway-press-secretary-gave-alternative-facts-860142147643

Daily Beast, The (2017) "Trump Refuses to Let CNN's Jim Acosta Ask Question: 'You're Fake News!'" 11 January. http://www.thedailybeast.com/cheats/2017/01/11/jim-acosta-trump-cnn-reporter-spar-in-press-conference.html

Darcy, Oliver (2017) "Lawsuit: Fox News concocted Seth Rich story with oversight from White House," *CNN Money*, 2 August. http://money.cnn.com/2017/08/01/media/rod-wheeler-seth-rich-fox-news-lawsuit

Davis, Julie and Grynbaum, Michael (2017) "Trump Intensifies His Attacks on Journalists and Condemns F.B.I. 'Leakers'," *The New York Times*, 25 February. https://www.nytimes.com/2017/02/24/us/politics/white-house-sean-spicer-briefing.html?_r=0

Dick, Philip K. (1962) *The Man in the High Castle*. New York: Putnam's. Television series: Frank Spotnitz, Amazon, 2015/2016.

Faiola, Anthony, & Kirchner, Stephanie (2017) "How do you stop fake news? In Germany, with a law," *Washington Post*, 5 April. https://www.washingtonpost.com/world/europe/how-do-you-stop-fake-news-in-germany-with-a-law/2017/04/05/e6834ad6-1a08-11e7-bcc2-7d1a0973e7b2_story.html

Fandos, Nicholas (2017) "White House Pushes 'Alternative Facts.' Here Are the Real Ones," *The New York Times*, 22 January. https://www.nytimes.com/2017/01/22/us/politics/president-trump-inauguration-crowd-white-house.html

Gezari, Vanessa M. (2017) "BuzzFeed was right to publish Trump-Russia files," *Columbia Journalism Review*, 11 January. http://www.cjr.org/criticism/buzzfeed_trump_russia_memos.php

Gillin, Joshua (2016) "How Pizzagate went from fake news to a real problem for a D.C. business," *POLITIFACT*, 5 December. http://www.politifact.com/truth-o-meter/article/2016/dec/05/how-pizzagate-went-fake-news-real-problem-dc-busin/

Gorman, Steve (2017) "Trump inauguration draws nearly 31 million U.S. television viewers," *Reuters*, 22 January. http://www.reuters.com/article/us-usa-trump-inauguration-ratings-idUSKBN15600S

Hayden, Eric (2017) "Trump's 'Fake News' Ad Refused by More Major TV Networks," *The Hollywood Reporter*, 5 May. http://www.hollywoodreporter.com/news/more-major-networks-refuse-trumps-fake-news-ad-1000615

Hitler, Adolf (1924/1971) *Mein Kampf*, trans. R. Manheim, Boston: Houghton-Mifflin.

Hoover, Amanda (2016) "How curated articles could help Facebook fight fake news," *Christian Science Monitor*, 4 December. http://www.csmonitor.com/Technology/2016/1204/How-curated-articles-could-help-Facebook-fight-fake-news

Kottasová, Ivana (2017) "Facebook targets 30,000 fake accounts in France," *CNN Media*, 21 April. http://money.cnn.com/2017/04/14/media/facebook-fake-news-france-election/

JTA (2017) "Germany curbs Holocaust denial and hate speech on social networks," 2 July. http://www.jta.org/2017/07/02/news-opinion/world/new-german-law-curbs-hate-speech-including-holocaust-denial-on-social-networks

Levinson, Paul (1997) *The Soft Edge: A Natural History and Future of the Information Revolution*. London: Routledge.

———. (2005) "The Flouting of the First Amendment," Keynote Address, Sixth Annual Convention of the Media Ecology Association, Fordham University, New York City, 23 June. transcript: http://paullevinson.blogspot.com/2007/07/flouting-of-first-amendment-transcript.html video: https://www.youtube.com/watch?v=qXwcC0MTME8

———. (2009/2013) *New New Media*. New York: Pearson.

———. (2010) "Blagojevich and Fair Trial 1, Fitzgerald 0," *Infinite Regress* blog, 10 April. http://paullevinson.blogspot.com/2010/08/blagojevich-and-fair-trial-1-fitzgerald.html

———. (2016) *Fake News in Real Context*. New York: Connected Editions.

MacVean, Mary (2004) "Dan Rather to Quit 'CBS Evening News'," *Los Angeles Times*, 23 November. http://www.latimes.com/la-112304rather_lat-story.html

Maddow, Rachel (2017) *The Rachel Maddow Show*, MSNBC, 6 July 2017.

Milton, John (1644) *Areopagitica*.

Order of the Coif (2017) "Buzzfeed and the Manchurian Candidate," 12 January. https://orderofthecoif.wordpress.com/2017/01/12/buzzfeed-and-the-manchurian-candidate/

Perlman, Elisabeth (2017) "Fool's gold: Remove the financial incentive of fake news," *Verdict*, 15 February. http://www.verdict.co.uk/fools-gold-remove-financial-incentive-fake-news

Phippen, Thomas (2017) "Trump Says His Twitter Account Will Continue To Get Around The 'Dishonest' Press," *The Daily Caller*, January 16. http://dailycaller.com/2017/01/16/trump-says-his-twitter-account-will-continue-to-get-around-the-dishonest-press/

Popper, Karl (1945) *The Open Society and Its Enemies*. London: Routledge.

———. (1962) *Conjectures and Refutations*. London: Routledge.

Robinson, Eugene (2017) Commentary made on *The 11th Hour with Brian Williams*, MSNBC TV, 10 January.

Senior, Jennifer (2017) "Hillary Clinton Opens Up About 'What Happened,' With Candor, Defiance and Dark Humor," *The New York Times*, 12 September. https://www.nytimes.com/2017/09/12/books/review-hillary-clinton-what-happened.html

Shah, Angela (2017) "Amid Fake News, Authenticated Reality Launches 'The New Internet'," *Xconomy*, 13 February. http://www.xconomy.com/texas/2017/02/13/amid-fake-news-authenticated-reality-launches-the-new-internet

Shane, Scott, & Goel, Vindu (2017) "Fake Russian Facebook Accounts Bought $100,000 in Political Ads," *The New York Times*, 6 September. https://www.nytimes.com/2017/09/06/technology/facebook-russian-political-ads.html

Sherman, Gabriel (2017) "Fox News Is Dropping Its 'Fair & Balanced' Slogan," *New York*, 14 June. http://nymag.com/daily/intelligencer/2017/06/fox-news-is-dropping-its-fair-and-balanced-slogan.html

Soboroff, Jacob (2016) Interview of Jestin Coler, *The 11th Hour with Brian Williams*, MSNBC, 5 December. http://www.msnbc.com/brian-williams/watch/exclusive-interview-with-man-behind-fake-campaign-news-825635395578

Stone, Peter, & Gordon, Greg (2017) "Trump-Russia investigators probe Jared Kushner-run digital operation," *McClatchy DC Bureau*, 11 July. http://www.mcclatchydc.com/news/nation-world/national/article160803619.html

Tiku, Nitasha (2016) "Why Snapchat And Apple Don't Have A Fake News Problem," *Buzzfeed News*, 1 December. https://www.buzzfeed.com/nitashatiku/snapchat-fake-news

Toonkel, Jessica (2017) "Newspapers aim to ride 'Trump Bump' to reach readers, advertisers," *Reuters, Data Dive*, 16 February. http://www.reuters.com/article/us-newspapers-trump-campaigns-analysis-idUSKBN15V0GI

Welles, Orson (1974) *F for Fake*, motion picture directed and co-written by Welles.

Woollacott, Emma (2017) "Google Brings 'Fact Check' Tag To Search Results," *Forbes*, 7 April. https://www.forbes.com/sites/emmawoollacott/2017/04/07/google-brings-fact-check-tag-to-searchresults/#1208b6a86109

CHAPTER 4

Trump's War Against the Media, Fake News, and (A)Social Media

Douglas Kellner

From early in his improbable presidential campaign and into his mind-boggling presidency, Donald Trump has waged a war against the media. Trump's media bashing and daily attacks on the media via his campaign rallies, Twitter feeds, and off-the-cuff remarks have been a defining feature of both Trump's presidential campaign and the first 200 days of his presidency. When the media criticizes his statements or actions, Trump goes on the attack. When he makes questionable or demonstrably false statements and is confronted with contrary evidence, Trump and his handlers dismiss any critical claims about Trump as "fake news" and "alternative facts." Echoing Chairman Mao and Comrade Stalin, Trump calls the media "the enemy of the people" and rarely does a day go by without a barrage of attacks and rants against the media on his Twitter account.

Ironically, one could argue that Trump won the Republican primary contest and then the 2016 US presidential election, in part, because he is the master of *media spectacle*, a concept that I've been developing and applying to US politics and media since the mid-1990s.[1] In this study, I will first discuss Trump's use of media spectacle in his business career, in his effort to become a celebrity and reality-TV superstar, and his political

D. Kellner (✉)
UCLA, Los Angeles, CA, USA

© The Author(s) 2019
C. Happer et al. (eds.), *Trump's Media War*,
https://doi.org/10.1007/978-3-319-94069-4_4

47

campaigns. Then, I examine how Trump uses both broadcasting and social media in his campaign and presidency and deploys a war against the media to delegitimize criticism or opposition to his presidency. Yet Trump's war against the media has generated a momentous battle in which segments of the media are fighting back against Trump in what has to be the most contested media spectacle in modern US political history.

DONALD TRUMP AND THE POLITICS OF THE SPECTACLE

I first came up with the concept of media spectacle to describe the key phenomenon of US media and politics in the mid-1990s. This was the era of the O.J. Simpson murder case and trial, the Clinton sex scandals, and the rise of cable news networks like Fox, CNN, and MSNBC and the 24/7 news cycle that has dominated US politics and media since then.[2] The 1990s was also the period when the Internet and new media took off so that anyone could be a political commentator, player, and participant in the spectacle, a phenomenon that accelerated as new media morphed into social media and teenagers, celebrities, politicians, and others wanting to become part of the networked virtual world joined in.

The scope of the spectacle has thus increased in the past decades with the proliferation of new media and social networking like Facebook, YouTube, Twitter, Instagram, Skype, and the like that increases the scope and participation of the spectacle. By "media spectacles" I am referring to media constructs that present events which disrupt ordinary and habitual flows of information, and which become popular stories which capture the attention of the media and the public, and circulate through broadcasting networks, the Internet, social networking, smartphones, and other new media and communication technologies. In a global networked society, media spectacles proliferate instantaneously, become virtual and viral, and in some cases become tools of socio-political transformation, while other media spectacles become mere moments of media hype and tabloidized sensationalism.

I've argued since 2008 that the key to Barack Obama's success in two presidential elections is because he became a master of media spectacle, blending politics and performance in carefully orchestrated media spectacles (Kellner 2009, 2012). Previously, the model of the mastery of presidential spectacle was Ronald Reagan who every day performed his presidency in a well-scripted and orchestrated daily spectacle. Reagan was trained as an actor and every night Ron and Nancy reportedly practiced his lines for the next day performance like they had done in their Hollywood days. Reagan breezed through the day scripted with a teleprompter and well-orchestrated media events, smiling frequently, and pausing to sound-bite the line of the day.

Trump's biographies reveal that he was driven by a need to compete and win,[3] and entering the highly competitive real estate business in New York in the 1980s, Trump saw the need to use the media and publicity to promote his celebrity and image. It was a time of tabloid culture and media-driven celebrity, and Trump even adopted a pseudonym "John Baron" to give the media gossip items that touted his successes in businesses, with women, and as a rising man about town (Fisher and Hobson 2016).

Now in the 2016 election and into his presidency, obviously Trump has emerged as a major form of media spectacle and has long been a celebrity and master of the spectacle with promotion of his buildings and casinos from the 1980s to the present, his reality-TV shows, self-promoting events, and then his presidential campaign and election. Hence, Trump was arguably empowered and enabled to run for the presidency in part because media spectacle has become a major force in US politics, helping to determine elections, government, and more broadly the ethos and nature of our culture and political sphere.

The Apprentice, Twitter, and the Summer of Trump

Since Trump's national celebrity derived in part from his role in the reality-TV series *The Apprentice*,[4] we need to interrogate this popular TV phenomenon to help explain the Trump phenomenon. The opening theme music *For the Love of Money*, a 1973 R&B song by The O'Jays, established the capitalist ethos of the competition for the winning contestant to get a job with the Trump organization, and obviously money is the key to Trump's business and celebrity success, although there is much controversy over how rich Trump is, and so far he has not released his tax returns to quell rumors that he isn't as rich as he claims, that he does not contribute as much to charity as he has stated, and that many years he had paid little or no taxes.

In the original format to *The Apprentice*, several contestants formed teams to carry out a task dictated by Trump, and each "contest" resulted with a winner and Trump barking "you're fired" to the loser. Curiously, some commentators believe in the 2012 presidential election that Barack

Obama beat Mitt Romney handily because he early on characterized Romney as a billionaire who liked to fire people, which is ironic since this is Trump's signature personality trait in his business, reality-TV, and now political career, which saw him fire two campaign managers and more advisors by August 2016, and made dramatic firings of key officials a defining feature of his chaotic administration.

The Apprentice's TV Producer Mark Burnett broke into national consciousness with his reality-TV show *The Survivor*, a neo-Darwinian epic of alliances, backstabbing, and nastiness, which provides an allegory of how one succeeds in the dog-eat-dog business world in which Trump has thrived, and spectacularly failed as many of the books about him document. Both Burnett and Trump share the neo-Darwinian (a)social ethos of the nineteenth-century ultracompetitive capitalism with some of Trump's famous witticisms proclaiming:

> When somebody challenges you unfairly, fight back—be brutal, be tough—don't take it. It is always important to WIN!
> I think everyone's a threat to me.
> Everyone that's hit me so far has gone down. They've gone down big league.
> I want my generals kicking ass.
> I would bomb the shit out of them.
> You bomb the hell out of the oil. Don't worry about the cities. The cities are terrible. (Trump in Pogash 2016, pp. 30, 152, 153)

In any case, *The Apprentice* made Trump a national celebrity who became well-known enough to plausibly run for president and throughout the campaign Trump has used his celebrity to gain media time. In addition to his campaign's ability to manipulate broadcast media, Trump is also a heavy user of Twitter and tweets out his messages throughout the day and night. Indeed, Trump may be the first major Twitter candidate, and certainly he is the one using it most aggressively and frequently into his presidency. Twitter was launched in 2006, but I don't recall it being used in a major way in the 2008 election, although Obama used Facebook and his campaign bragged that he had over a million "Friends" and used Facebook as part of his daily campaign apparatus. I don't recall, however, previous presidential candidates using Twitter in a big way like Trump, although many have accounts. In the next section, I accordingly interrogate Trump's use of Twitter and social media and will highlight its' asocial and problematic aspects.

TWITTER, (A)SOCIAL MEDIA, AND TRUMP

Twitter is a perfect vehicle for Trump as you can use its 140 character framework for attack, bragging, and getting out simple messages or posts that engage receivers who feel they are in the know and involved in TrumpWorld when they get pinged and receive his tweets. When asked at an August 26, 2015, Iowa event as to why he uses Twitter so much, he replied that it was easy, it only took a couple of seconds, and that he could attack his media critics when he "wasn't treated fairly." Trump has also used Instagram—an online mobile photo-sharing, video-sharing, and social networking service that enables its users to take pictures and videos, and share them on a variety of social networking platforms, such as Facebook, Twitter, Tumblr, and Flickr.

Twitter is perfect for General Trump who can blast out his opinions and order his followers what to think. It enables Businessman and Politician Trump to define his brand and mobilize those who wish to consume or support it. Trump Twitter gratifies the need of Narcissist Trump to be noticed and recognized as a Master of Communication who can bind his warriors into an online community. Twitter enables the Pundit-in-Chief to opine, rant, attack, and proclaim on all and sundry subjects, and to subject TrumpWorld to the indoctrination of their Fearless Leader.

Hence, Trump has mastered social media as well as dominating television and old media through his orchestration of media events as spectacles and his daily Twitter Feed. In Trump's presidential campaign kickoff speech on June 16, 2015, when he announced he was running for president, Trump and his wife Melania dramatically ascended down the stairway at Trump Towers, and the Donald strode up to a gaggle of microphones and dominated media attention for days with his drama. The opening speech of his campaign made a typically inflammatory remark that held in thrall news cycles for days when he stated that "The U.S. has become a dumping ground for everybody else's problems. [Applause] Thank you. It's true, and these are the best and the finest. When Mexico sends its people, they're not sending their best. They're not sending you. They're not sending you. They're sending people that have lots of problems, and they're bringing those problems with us. They're bringing drugs. They're bringing crime. They're rapists. And some, I assume, are good people."

This comment ignited a firestorm of controversy and a preview of Things to Come concerning vile racism, xenophobia, Islamophobia, and the other hallmarks of Trump's Cacophony of Hate. Debate over Trump's assault on undocumented immigrants would come to dominate daily news cycles of the Republican primaries and would continue to play out in the general election in fall 2016. In the lead up to the first Republican primary debate in fall 2015, Trump got the majority of media time, and his daily campaign appearances and the Republican primary debates became media spectacle dominated by him. Every day that Trump had a campaign event, the cable news networks would hype the event with crawlers on the bottom of the TV screen proclaiming "Waiting for Trump," with air-time on cable TV dominated by speculation on what he would talk about. Trump's speeches were usually broadcast live, often in their entirety, a boon of free TV time that no candidate of either party was awarded. After the Trump event, the rest of the day the pundits would dissect what he had said and his standing vis-à-vis the other Republican candidates. If Trump had no campaign event planned, he would fire off a round of tweets against his opponents on his highly active Twitter account—which then would be featured on network cable news discussions as well as social media.

Hence, Trump's orchestration of media spectacle and a compliant mainstream media was a crucial factor in thrusting Trump ever further into the front-runner status in the Republican primaries and winning for him the overwhelming amount of media attention and eventually the Republican nomination. The first major quantitative study released notes that from mid-June 2015 after Trump announced he was running through mid-July, Trump was in 46% of the news media coverage of the Republican field, based on Google news hits; he also got 60% of Google news searches, and I will bet that later academic studies will show how he dominated all media from newspapers to television to Twitter and new media to social networking during the Republican primaries and then during the general election (Somaiya 2015).

Trump bragged during the primary campaign about how one major media insider told him that it was the "Summer of Trump," and that it was amazing how he was completely dominating news coverage. Trump also explained, correctly I think, why he was getting all the media attention: "RATINGS," he explained, "it's ratings, the people love me, they want to see me, so they watch TV when I'm on." And I do think it is ratings that lead the profit-oriented television networks to almost exclusively follow Trump's events and give him live TV control of the audience.

From the beginning of his business career into his presidency, Trump has been particularly assiduous in branding the Trump name and selling himself as a businessman, a celebrity, and in Election 2016 as a presidential candidate. Indeed, Trump's presidential campaign represents an obscene branding of a hypercapitalist pig into a political candidate whose campaign was run on bombast, dominating on a daily basis the mediascape, and gaining the attention of voters/consumers. Obviously, Trump is orchestrating political theater, his theatrics are sometimes entertaining, and, as I noted earlier, his candidacy represents another step in the merger between entertainment, celebrity, and politics (here Ronald Reagan played a key role, our first actor President). Yet Trump is arguably the first major candidate to pursue politics as entertainment and thus to collapse the distinction between entertainment, news, and politics, so that the 2016 presidential election and then the Trump presidency can be seen as a form of infotainment.

THE TRUMP PRESIDENCY, FAKE NEWS, AND THE WAR AGAINST THE MEDIA

Just as Trump ran his presidential campaign like a reality-TV show, so too has he run his presidency as a theatrical performance, playing to his base and the media which he continues to dominate, perhaps more than any previous president in history. Yet the Trump presidency has been perhaps the most controversial in recent times, and from the beginning the Trump presidency has been a war against the media.

Trump began his presidency with a Big Lie concerning the numbers of people attending the Obama versus Trump inaugurations, claiming that his inauguration was the biggest ever. When TV pictures showed that there were many more people at the 2008 Obama inauguration, with comparative pictures of crowds on the mall and lining parade routes, Trump sent out his hapless press secretary Sean Spicer to read a carefully and nastily written attack on the media for misrepresenting the amount of people who had attended Trump's inauguration, and threatened that the media would be held responsible for their lies and distortions. Spicer correctly argued that the Federal Parks Service did not do crowd estimates, but falsely claimed that many more people took the Metro the day of Trump's inauguration than on Obama's inauguration and provided what turned out to be completely false numbers in his false claim that Trump's inauguration was the biggest in history.

The DC Metro quickly released inauguration day rider statistics for the Trump and Obama events, and reported that many more took the Metro the day of Obama's inauguration, thus leading CNN and other media to report that the Trump administration began its reign with bald-faced lies on its first day in office, and had launched an attack on the media for allegedly lying, while available statistics and facts indicated that the media had in fact basically told the truth about comparative crowd size, Metro usage, and comparative pictures of the Obama and Trump administration inaugurations which showed that many more attended the former.

On Sunday morning of inauguration weekend, more evidence emerged that the Trump administration had gone full out post-factual as President Donald tweeted: "Wow, television ratings just out: 31 million people watched the Inauguration, 11 million more than the very good ratings from 4 years ago!" The still functioning media quickly pointed out, however, that "Nielsen reported Saturday that 30.6 million viewers watched inaugural coverage between 10 a.m. and 6 p.m. on Friday. That figure is higher than Obama's second inauguration in 2013, which drew 20.6 million viewers. But it's lower than that of Obama's first inauguration in 2009, when 38 million viewers tuned in, according to Nielsen. The record is held by Ronald Reagan, when 42 million watched his inaugural festivities in 1981" (Battaglio 2017).

The same morning, on *Meet The Press,* the Trumpsters multiple and multiplying by the minute misrepresentations of inauguration numbers were cited by moderator Chuck Todd who asked Kellyanne Conway, counselor to the President: "Why put him [i.e. Press Secretary Sean Spicer] out there for the very first time, in front of that podium, to utter a provable falsehood? It's a small thing, but the first time he confronts the public, it's a falsehood?" Conway responded: "Don't be so overly dramatic about it, Chuck. You're saying it's a falsehood, and they're giving – our press secretary, Sean Spicer, gave alternative facts to that. But the point really is –" Todd jumped in and retorted: "Wait a minute. *Alternative facts!?* Alternative facts!? Four of the five facts he uttered…were just not true. Alternative facts are not facts; they're falsehoods."

The Trumpsters have obviously come to believe that they can define facts and reality, and that if the media doesn't validate their truths, Trump and his post-factual brigade of media flacks will take them on, presenting a challenge to the media to subject every word of Trumpspin to rigorous scrutiny and if necessary critique. It will be interesting to see how long Trump's minions will continue to tell bold and brazen lies that they and their media critics and informed audiences know to be untrue. In any case, Trump spinster Kellyanne Conway will evermore be remembered in the

Post-Truth Hall of Infamy as "alternative facts" Conway, and Sean Spicer earned the title of 4L4M Spicer (as in "four lies four minutes" Spicer), and everything they say should be subjected to the same rigorous scrutiny and criticism that should be applied to the ultimate source and King of Lies, Donald John Trump.

During the early days of the Trump presidency, 4L4M Spicer riled the media by his aggressive hectoring tone, threats that the media would be held responsible for its lying reporting, and then after loudly and aggressively repeating his litany of lies, he shouted: "And that's what you should be reporting!" The media does not like to be told what to report any more than politicians and their spinners like to be confronted with alternative facts that trump their facts. Democracy requires a separation of powers and the press serves classically as the "fourth estate" to provide part of a system of checks and balances against excessive, misused, or corrupt state power, including speaking truth to lying liars.

In the first full day of the Trump administration, Trump bragged of his "running war against the media" in front of CIA employees before the fabled CIA "Wall of Fame," and sent his flunkeys out to battle the press in the media for the next days, but the barrage of ridicule, criticism, and anger they stirred up suggest that Trump and Co. lost the battle of Day One. Of course, Trump's daily twitters, that he promised to continue despite contrary advice, and his "running" war against the media, could be a distraction in the real war to push through a rightwing and militarist agenda while the press is distracted chasing down the Daily Lies and shooting down "fake news" and alternative facts that are the epistemological novum of the newly minted Trump administration; that is, never had an administration run on a daily dosage of fake news and alternative facts as the Trumpsters. To this day Trump and his minions shoot down stories they don't like as "fake news" and for their rabid followers have labeled the mainstream and increasingly anti-Trump media as "false news" tout court, marking the first time that a president has so broadly attempted to delegitimize the mainstream media.

The State of the Union was not good as the Donald J. Trump White House Reality Show moved into its first weeks in office. The stock market had declined for five days straight before the inauguration and lost all of its gains for the year and continued to go down, although there would no doubt be roller coasters to come and indeed by summer 2017 Wall Street indexes were at an all-time high as finance capital speculated in an orgy of irrational exuberance, as if they were entering the Last Days. The Earth's temperature had risen to all-time highs for the third year in a row and a Trump administration full of climate deniers and contemptuous of science would no doubt continue to heat things up and indeed would shock the world some months later when Dumbass Donald announced that the US was leaving the Paris climate accord.

Inauguration weekend had seen extreme weather events from coast to coast as heavy rain continued to pound California after a severe drought and rational minds were undergoing shock and trauma at the unthinkable thought of a Trump presidency. Yet as in classic authoritarian movements, the followers accepted the pronouncements of the leader as gospel truth, and although Trump lied more outrageously than any candidate in recent US history, his followers turned out in droves throughout the country shouting hateful slogans and repeating Trump's lies and deception. Like classical authoritarian demagogues, Trump produced scapegoats and others who were seen as threats against whom Trump could mobilize his followers. The scapegoats Trump projected were not only Muslims and immigrants but "the establishment" and a shadowy cabal of global capital with which Trump identified Hillary Clinton, successfully making her part of the enemy against which Trump railed. Trump played the "forgotten men and women" card effectively, and presented himself as the people's savior, although it was not clear what he would actually deliver to his followers.

THE TRUMP ADMINISTRATION, RUSSIA, AND THE MEDIA WAR OVER THE TRUMP PRESIDENCY

In putting together his transition team, cabinet, and administration, Donald J. Trump went further than any previous US president in confirming Marx's view of capitalism and embodying Eisenhower's warning against the military-industrial complex, choosing an assortment of generals, billionaires, rightwing ideologues, and cronies for top positions in his government, often without qualifications in the area in which they were chosen to serve. They also included some of the worst racists, Islamophobes, sexists, homophobes, and creatures of the swamp imaginable, suggesting that rather than draining the swamp, Trump was constructing a morass of swamp creatures who were likely to create an era of unparalleled disruption, nastiness, conflict, crisis, precarity, and warfare that would put US democracy and global organizations to their more severe tests in its history (see Kellner 2017).

What was also totally bizarre was the number of strongly pro-Russian figures who Trump chose for the inner circle of his Government, and how Trump himself spoke so positively of Russian dictator Vladimir Putin and the Russians during his campaign and presidency going against Republican Cold War orthodoxy that villainized Russia, the Evil Empire, and The Enemy Red Menace during the Cold War. Many of us grew up in a Cold War culture which included many films and TV shows with evil Russians, and experienced broadcast and print media, schooling, and other institutions that presented the Cold War as a battle between Good and Evil with the US presenting Good, Democracy, and Freedom, while the Soviet Union represented Evil, with its authoritarian communism, dictators, and collectivism. In particular, Republicans vilified the Soviet Union with Ronald Reagan decrying the "evil empire" and every Republican presidential candidate in my lifetime taking a hard anti-communist and anti-Soviet line.

Enter Donald Trump with his famously friendly words toward Vladimir Putin during the election and a strikingly Russian-friendly inner circle of his campaign and administration. Trump initially chose as National Security Director, General Michael Flynn, who was one of a cadre of close Trump associates who had fond relations with Putin and the Russians, as pictures circulated throughout the media of Flynn next to Putin in Moscow as an event celebrating Russian Television (RT); Flynn was paid for this event but did not report Russian contacts on security forms and was fired, only belatedly admitting and signing documents which confirmed he was a foreign agent for Russia and a Russian-friendly group in Turkey. After Flynn was exited as these stories circulated in the press, Trump fired FBI Director James Comey who confirmed in Congressional hearings that Donald Trump, not known for friendship or loyalty, went out of his way to try to get Comey to lay off of the Flynn-Russian investigations, and told the FBI Director that he expected "loyalty" of himself, leading to charges of possible obstruction of justice and impeachment.

In addition, there hasn't been adequate discussion of how former ExxonMobil CEO Rex Tillerson, Trump's choice for Secretary of State, was one of several powerful positions within the Trump administration who had especially close relations with Vladimir Putin and the Russians. In over 30 years' service with ExxonMobil, Tillerson had particularly warm relations with Putin and the Russians, cutting big business deals, becoming a personal Friend of Vladimir, and even receiving Russia's Order of Friendship.[5] Typical anti-Russian Republicans were worried about the too-cozy relationship between Tillerson and the Russians: "'Let's put it this way: If you received an award from the Kremlin, order of friendship, then we're gonna have some talkin'. We'll have some questions,' Senator Lindsey Graham (Rep.-S.C.) said upon hearing Tillerson was going to be Trump's choice for the key Secretary of State office."[6]

As president of ExxonMobil, Tillerson was attempting to negotiate with Putin and the Russians a major oil deal to explore areas of the Arctic believed to contain vast mineral wealth, when President Obama imposed sanctions on Russia because of their intervention in Ukraine and Crimea.[7] If the Trump administration could eliminate these sanctions, Tillerson and his cronies could profit immensely, but such conflicts of interest did not bother Donald J. Trump, himself a walking and talking cauldron of conflicting interests, ranging from his hotel near the Capital in Washington, DC, to the outposts of his far-flung and largely mysterious business empire.

Trump's pro-Russian cabinet was unnerving to many because not only was Trump himself excessively well-disposed toward Putin and Russia, but Michael Flynn, Trump's national security advisor, was also close to Putin and the Russians, as was Tillerson. Tillerson's nomination was especially unsettling because the major story of the week of Tillerson's designation to lead the State Department was an uproar over the Russian's hacking the 2016 election, and a story in the *Washington Post*, that the Russians had intervened to help Donald Trump get elected (Entous et al. 2016). Trump himself denied that the Russians had hacked the Democrats, and had released selected information to help Trump and hurt Clinton, whereas major figures in both parties, the US intelligence services, and sectors of the media were all convinced that Russia had intervened in the US election. Moreover, President Obama had announced in the last weeks of his presidency a commission that would put out a report on the Russian intervention as soon as possible (Entous et al. 2016).

Of course, it would be wrong to claim that the US was an innocent who had never intervened in foreign elections in the light of an entire history of the US incursions in foreign elections, starting in a post-War Italy where the CIA did everything in its power to make sure the Christian Democrats beat the Italian Communist Party.[8] During the Reagan era, William Casey's CIA intervened in a number of Latin American countries, and after failing to oust the Nicaraguan Sandinistas through the electoral process funded an illegal Contra war that embarrassed the Reagan administration and destroyed the careers of some of its officials when it was uncovered that an illegal deal selling arms to Iran was funding the Contra war.[9]

Yet given that Republicans had been Cold War super-adversaries of Russian Communism, it was highly bizarre to see so many of Trump's inner circle and Trump himself so enamored of Putin and the Russians. These included Paul Manafort, his campaign manager for six months; Carter Page, who Trump described as a key foreign policy advisor and who US intelligence claimed was the target of a Russian intelligence operation; and Donald J. Trump who had made contact with a Russian lawyer who claimed she had "dirt" on Hillary Clinton and arranged a meeting in Trump Tower with the Russia, Manafort, and Trump's son-in-law Jarod Kushner, himself under investigation for Russian connections that he did not disclose on security forms necessary for White House government positions.

What can we make of the Trump-Russia connections, currently the focus of Special Counsel Robert Mueller and many Congressional committees that are investigating the linkages, as well as an intense focus of global investigative media? While more and more information comes out every day concerning the Trump-Russia connections, and much still remains to be revealed, we can reach some preliminary conclusions and advance some hypotheses concerning the role of Putin and the Russians, in the context of the 2016 US presidential election and the shocking and surprising victory of Donald Trump, and even more startling scandals of his administration.

CONCLUDING COMMENTS: TRUMP, RUSSIA, AND THE MEDIA

From a globalist perspective, the 2016 election and Trump presidency need to be interpreted in terms of Cold War and US-Russian relations. The Russian hack and intervention in the US election can be seen as revenge, blowback, for US interventions in Russian elections, as well as what the Russians saw as US interference in elections and political upheaval in Russian satellite countries, and other elections and countries around the world in which the Russians had interests. During the Cold War, both Russia and the US regularly intervened in elections throughout the world to support, in the case of the US, pro-US candidates while attacking leftist and progressive national candidates who would be conceived as supporting the Soviet Bloc or world socialism and communism. In turn, the former Soviet Union supported parties in its orbit while attacking governments seen as US allies.

While both the US and Russia have intervened in elections throughout the Cold War, yet, as far as we know, Election 2016 is the first time the Russians intervened massively and perhaps effectively in a US presidential election and may have influenced the outcome, although there is not yet enough evidence to make this claim. It is significant, however, that the revelations of Trump/Russian connections in the election make it clear that the Russians intervened on behalf of the Trump campaign, and that high-level members of the Trump team had many contacts with the Russians, although we do not know the nature of the collusion or extent of their coordination. There are, however, many questions to still be raised and some assertions that we can make as of the time of writing this text in mid-July 2017.

Why did the Russians intervene in favor of Donald Trump in the 2016 election? While there were reports that Trump had secret business connections with Russia and that the Russians had compromising material on Trump, it is clear that Putin and his crowd hated Hillary Clinton and preferred Donald Trump, although we still don't know why the Russians seemed to like Trump so much and why Trump gushed with enthusiasm over Putin during the election and then fawned over him at the G-20 conference in Hamburg when they allegedly first met in July 2017. US-Russia-Trump relations are now at the center of many House and Senate investigations, as well as Special Counsel Robert Muller's investigation of Trump and the election, so presumably we will eventually learn much more about this "special relationship." In addition, the Trump-Russia connection is the focus of US media doing its job investigating shady government actions and it appears that mainstream media like *The New York Times, The Washington Post, The Wall Street Journal* and some of the cable news networks are working feverishly to break new and startling daily revelations of the Trump-Russia saga, which is emerging as the most astonishing and jaw-dropping political spectacle of my lifetime.

There are also books published that help explain why Putin and Russia would take the risk of intervening in the 2016 election. Martha Gessen's *The Man Without a Face: The Unlikely Rise of Vladimir Putin*, initially published in 2012, argues that Putin was devastated by the collapse of the Soviet Union in 1989 when he was a KGB agent assigned to an embassy/ Russian government job in Dresden, probably spying for the KGB. Hence, Putin himself was close to seeing the Berlin Wall go down, the Soviet Empire collapse, and George H.W. Bush and others proclaiming that Russia lost the Cold War.[10]

From this optic, Putin was a super sore loser, who wanted revenge and made the choice to disrupt the 2016 election to delegitimize the US electoral system and attempt to help defeat Hillary Clinton, who he blamed for helping stir up anti-Russia revolts in Ukraine, Crimea, and other parts of Russia when she was Secretary of State under Obama. From this standpoint, the election of Donald J. Trump could be seen as Putin's revenge for the US role in helping take down the Soviet Union and undermining the USSR/Russia during the long Cold War period, and then interfering in Putin's affair during his reign.[11] I'm bracketing the issue explored in my book *The American Horror Show* whether Trump is Putin's Poodle, a Manchurian candidate, a Russian agent, or someone with deep financial Russian interests subject to blackmail, or something else, some of which we'll hopefully learn more about before it's too late.

The question then arises: how did Putin get his revenge and what are its nature and consequences? My thesis is that Russian hacking of 2016 election and helping to get Trump elected is rooted in longtime Russian Cold War policies and the psyche of its product Vladimir Putin. Note that I'm saying "helping to get Trump elected" and not causing, or directly influencing the outcome, as we obviously lack such evidence. In analyzing Election 2016 and most complex historical events, we need multicausal analysis that explicates the multiple causes and deep layers of economic, political, cultural, media, and other factors that help explain as of 2017 why Donald Trump won the 2016 presidential election—which I attempt to do in *The American Horror Show*, published after the election and first 30 days of the Trump administration (Kellner 2017).

We do know, however, that the Democratic National Committee email server and that of Clinton's campaign manager, John Podesta, among others, were hacked by the Russians, and that Putin and the Russians used WikiLeaks and various global Internet networks to circulate fake news, bots, and anti-Hillary stories.[12] From this perspective, key global-digital networks helped Trump win, which along with the anti-globalization discourse with which Trump conned his followers, makes Election 2016 the first US presidential election where global actors and networks, and global politics, played a significant and perhaps decisive role.

There are now ongoing investigations in Congress and by Special Prosecutor Robert Mueller into the extent to which the Russians deployed Facebook and Twitter to circulate fake news circulated by fake people generated by Russian bots and cyberwar tactics that attacked Hillary Clinton and advocated for Donald Trump.[13] *Facebook* is also under investigation for taking Russian money for ads against Clinton that were circulated throughout Facebook and other social media (Samuelsohn 2017; Emba 2017) in a cybercampaign perhaps unique in US history that will probably be investigated and analyzed for years to come.

Part of Trump's appeal for both the Russians and his devoted followers, who Trump claimed would vote for him if he shot someone on Fifth Avenue, was that at least in his campaign rhetoric Trump presented himself as anti-establishment and anti-globalist. On one hand, this is total BS as Trump is part of the global establishment with business connections throughout the world. Moreover, Trump's administration is full of the worst Swamp Creatures from the political and economic establishment and his policies have so far only helped the 1% while he has done nothing for his working class supporters angry about globalization and an establishment apparently hostile or blind to their interests. Yet, it appears that Trump was against the US political establishment and institutions of US democracy. The Donald loaded his cabinet and administration with establishment businessmen, generals, and Republican politicians, but he has acted from the beginning as a wrecking ball for the political institutions of liberal democracy and has arguably diminished severely the US role and standing in the world.

Highlights of the Trump administration's attack on the institutions of liberal democracy and the US political system during his first eight months in office, which arguably weakened the US polity and its position in the world include:

Trump's Travel Ban and attack on the judiciary during the opening days of his administration, a war still intensely being fought into his first year in office;

Trump's daily Twitter war, assaulting all and sundry aspects of the political, media, and global establishment which offend him in some way;

Trump's attack on Obamacare (aka the Affordable Care Act) and the US health system;

Trump's attacks on NATO and alienating of the US from NATO and other allies and efforts to weaken the US alliances and the US role as a global superpower, led to German Chancellor Angela Merkel stating that the US can no longer be counted on for leadership;

Trump's shocking pulling out of Paris climate accord and unleashing devastation on the environment, marked by attempts to defang the EPA, signing executive orders to cut regulations, build pipelines through sensitive environmental areas, intensify oil exploration, and even coal production, generating dangerous threats to climate change.

Yet perhaps the most distinctive feature so far of the Trump presidency is his daily attacks on the mainstream media, and on the truth itself. Mass media have been theorized in the modern era as the fourth estate, a necessary pillar of democracy where the people can speak truth to power and debate issues of the day. Yet Trump's Twitter war against the media presented them in one tirade as the media as "the enemy of the American people," a phrase that Comrade Stalin used to use against bourgeois media, a phrase resurrected by Comrade Trump that puts him in the Stalinist anti-media camp. Trump's equation of the media as a site of "fake news" is an attack on the truth itself, for it is the media that functions at its best to expose the lies, deceits, and corruption of those in power.

Other assaults on the political establishment include firing James Comey and carrying out attacks on the FBI, the CIA, and US intelligence services, astonishingly posing Trump against top institutions of US intelligence and crime detection and prevention. I might note that Trump's alt-right consigliere Steve Bannon has called the Trump project a "deconstruction of the administrative state," a use of the term by a barbarian who would appall the urbane Jacques Derrida. So from this perspective, the Trump presidency, so far, might be seen as the greatest victory for Russia in the Cold War, leaving the US divided and weakened.

Yet perhaps the most outrageous of Trump's use of media spectacle and (a)social media concern the uproar in August 2017 over Trump's failure to condemn Neo-Nazi, Klan, and white supremacist groups until more than two days after deadly alt-right demonstrations in Charlottesville, Virginia, over the weekend of August 11–13, 2017, which produced three deaths, many injuries, and tremendous outrage over the extremist demonstrations. In a news conference on August 15 that was strongly denounced by the media and political establishment, Trump symmetrized the white supremacist forces that had gathered in Charlottesville with protesters against neo-fascism and white supremacism, arguing they were equally responsible for violence, while defending Robert E. Lee and the Confederacy!

The next day Trump continued his war against the Union and for the Confederacy, mourning the loss of "beautiful statues and monuments" in the wake of demands for the removal of statues depicting Confederate military commander Robert E. Lee in the Charlottesville spectacle, followed by demands for removal of other monuments of the Confederacy throughout the country. As Trump hardened his support of far-right groups, executives from major corporations began resigning from advisory panels, leading Trump to cancel the panels, while major military leaders and some Republican congressmen and senators denounced white supremacism and the President's failure to more sharply criticize extremist groups.

The media responded with all-out war against an increasingly embattled Trump who was finding out that war against the media cut two ways. Bowing in to pressure, and perhaps wanting to change the media narrative, Trump fired Steve Bannon, the center of the alt-right in the White House on August 18, 2017, who promised that he would wage an all-out media war against the Republican establishment and his enemies in the Trump administration. Hence, while one cannot foresee the trajectory of the Trump presidency, one can be certain that it will involve continuing war with the media of huge intensity and consequence.

NOTES

1. On my concept of media spectacle, see (Kellner 2001, 2003a, b, 2005, 2008, 2012, 2016, 2017). This article draws upon and updates my two Trump books, Kellner (2016, 2017).
2. I provide accounts of the O.J. Simpson trial and the Clinton sex/impeachment scandal in the mid-1990s in Kellner (2003b); engage the stolen election of 2000 in the Bush/Gore presidential campaign in Kellner (2001); and describe the 9/11 terrorist attacks and their aftermath in *From 9/11 to Terror War* in Kellner (2003a).
3. See D'Antonio (2015), Blair (2000), and Kranish and Fisher (2016). Blair's chapter on "Born to Compete" (p. 223) documents Trump's competitiveness and drive for success at an early age.
4. Trump's book *The Art of the Deal*, co-written with Tony Schwartz (2005 [1987]), helped introduce him to a national audience and is a key source of the Trump mythology; see (Blair 2000, pp. 380ff).
5. On the Tillerson/Russian connections, see Coll (2013).
6. Coll, whose book *Private Empire: ExxonMobil and American Power*, (2013), is considered a major book on ExxonMobil, claimed: "reporting on Exxon was not only harder than reporting on the Bin Ladens, it was harder than reporting on the CIA by an order of magnitude," adding: "They have a culture of intimidation that they bring to bear in their external relations, and it is plenty understood inside the corporation too. They make people nervous, they make people afraid" Coll cited in Schwartz (2012).
7. On Russia's intervention into Ukraine and Crimea and ensuing global controversy, see Myers (2016).

8. On US and Russian intervention in previous elections, see Osnos et al. (2017), and Agrawal (2016).
9. On the Nicaraguan Sandinistas, the Contra war, and the Reagan administration, see Travis (2016).
10. This account is similar to that in the excellent overview of Putin's career in Myers (2016).
11. Putin has long believed that Hillary Clinton was the spearhead of US interference in Russian affairs during her role as Secretary of State under Obama; see Herszenhorn and Barry (2011).
12. The hacking is documented in Nance (2016), and many mainstream media sources, although it is denied in Kovalik (2017), and pro-Trump sources from the swamps and whacko-worlds of "alternative facts" which may be the enduring legacy of the Trump presidency. For a comprehensive analysis of how the Russian hacking interfered in the 2016 election and dangers for the future of US democracy, see Calabresi (2017, pp. 30–35).
13. See Nance (2016). For articles on the alleged Russian hacking, see Issie Lapowsky (2017), Williams (2017), and Calabresi (2017).

References

Agrawal, N. (2016) "U.S. disrupts elections too. Like Russia, America has a long history of meddling in foreign votes." *Los Angeles Times*, December 22: A2.

Battaglio, S. (2017) "Trump's inauguration is watched by 30.6 million viewers — 7 million fewer than Obama's first ceremony," *Los Angeles Times*, January 19, 2017, at http://www.latimes.com/business/hollywood/la-fi-ct-inauguration-ratings-20170119-story.html (accessed July 22, 2017).

Blair, G. (2000). *The Trumps*. New York: Simon and Schuster.

Calabresi, M. (2017) "Hacking Democracy. Inside Russia's Social Media War on America." *Time*, May 29, pp. 30–35.

Coll, S. (2013) *Private Empire: ExxonMobil and American Power.* Baltimore: Penguin Books.

D'Antonio, M. (2015) *Never Enough. Donald Trump and the Pursuit of Success.* New York: Thomas Dunne Books.

Emba, C. (2017) "When it comes to Facebook, Russia's $100,000 is worth more than you think," *Washington Post,* September 11, 2017, at https://www.washingtonpost.com/opinions/when-it-comes-to-facebook-russias-100000-is-worth-more-than-you-think/2017/09/11/b6f8dde6-94c7-11e7-aace-04b862b2b3f3_story.html?utm_term=.40de09712f6e (accessed September 11, 2017).

Entous, A., E. Nakashima and G. Miller, "Secret CIA assessment says Russia was trying to help Trump win White House *Washington Post*, December 9, 2016, at https://www.washingtonpost.com/world/national-security/obama-orders-review-of-russian-hacking-during-presidential-campaign/2016/12/09/31d6b300-be2a-11e6-94ac-3d324840106c_story.html?utm_term=.bb175270bfde (accessed December 9, 2016).

Fisher, Marc, and Will Hobson. 2016. "Donald Trump 'pretends to be his own spokesman to boast about himself.' Some reporters found the calls disturbing or even creepy; others thought they were just examples of Trump being playful." *The Independent,* May 13, 2016, at http://www.independent.co.uk/ news/world/americas/us-elections/donald-trump-pretends-to-be-his-own-spokesman-to-boast-about-himself-a7027991.html (accessed August 9, 2016).

Herszenhorn, D. M. and E. Barry (2011) "Putin Contends Clinton Incited Unrest Over Vote," *The New York Times,* December 8, 2011, at http://www.nytimes. com/2011/12/09/world/europe/putin-accuses-clinton-of-instigating-russian-protests.html (accessed July 17, 2017).

Kellner, D. (2009). "Barack Obama and Celebrity Spectacle." *International Journal of Communication,* Vol. 3: 1–20 at http://ijoc.org/ojs/index.php/ijoc/article/ view/559/350

Kellner, D. (2017) *The American Horror Show: Election 2016 and the Ascendency of Donald J. Trump.* Rotterdam, The Netherlands: Sense Publishers.

Kellner, D. (2016) *American Nightmare: Donald Trump, Media Spectacle, and Authoritarian Populism.* Rotterdam, The Netherlands: Sense Publishers.

Kellner, D. (2012) *Media Spectacle and Insurrection, 2011: From the Arab Uprisings to Occupy Everywhere.* London and New York: Continuum/Bloomsbury.

Kellner, D. (2005) *Media Spectacle and the Crisis of Democracy.* Boulder, Col.: Paradigm Press.

Kellner, D. (2003a) *From September 11 to Terror War: The Dangers of the Bush Legacy.* Lanham, Md.: Rowman and Littlefield.

Kellner, D. (2003b) *Media Spectacle.* London and New York: Routledge.

Kellner, D. (2001) *Grand Theft 2000. Media Spectacle and a Stolen Election.* Lanham, Md.: Rowman and Littlefield.

Kovalik, D. (2017) *The Plot to Scapegoat Russia. How the CIA and the Deep State Have Conspired to Vilify Russia.* New York: Skyhorse Publishing.

Kranish, M. and M. Fisher (2016) *Trump Revealed. An American Journey of Ambition, Ego, Money and Power.* New York: Scribner. Kirchgaessner, S. "Russia 'targeted Trump adviser in bid to infiltrate campaign.' CNN claims investigators have intelligence suggesting Russians may have used Carter Page to try to access Trump campaign," *The Guardian,* April 23, 2017, at https://www. theguardian.com/us-news/2017/apr/23/russia-tried-to-use-trump-advisers-to-influence-us-election-report (accessed July 10, 2017).

Lapowsky, I. (2017) "Russia Could Easily Spread Fake News Without Team Trump's Help," *Wired,* July 14, 2017, at https://www.wired.com/story/ russia-trump-targeting-fake-news/ (accessed September 9, 2017).

Myers, S.L. (2016) *The New Tsar: The Rise and Reign of Vladimir Putin.* New York: Vintage Books.

Nance, M. (2016) *The Plot to Hack America: How Putin's Cyberspies and WikiLeaks Tried to Steal the 2016 Election.* New York: Skyhorse Publishing.

Osnos, E., D. Remnick, and J. Yaffa, "Trump, Putin, and the New Cold War. What lay behind Russia's interference in the 2016 election—and what lies ahead?" *The New Yorker*, March 6, 2017 at http://www.newyorker.com/magazine/2017/03/06/trump-putin-and-the-new-cold-war5 (accessed July 22, 2017).

Pogash, C. Ed. (2016) *Quotations From Chairman Trump*. New York: Rosetta Books.

Samuelsohn, D. (2017) "Facebook: Russian-linked accounts bought $150,000 in ads during 2016 race," *Politico*, September 6, 2017, at http://www.politico.com/story/2017/09/06/facebook-ads-russia-linked-accounts-242401 (accessed July 22, 2017).

Schwartz, M. (2012) "An Extended Interview with Steve Coll," *Texas Monthly*. May 2012 at http://www.texasmonthly.com/articles/an-extended-interview-with-steve-coll/ (accessed December 9, 2016).

Somaiya, R. (2015) "Trump's Wealth and Early Poll Numbers Complicate News Media's Coverage Decisions." *The New York Times*, July 24, at http://www.nytimes.com/2015/07/25/business/media/donald-trumps-wealth-and-poll-numbers-complicate-news-medias-coverage.html (accessed July 22, 2016).

Travis, P.W. (2016) *Reagan's War on Terrorism in Nicaragua: The Outlaw State*. Lexington, Ky.: Lexington Books.

Trump, D. J., with T. Schwartz (2005 [1987]) *The Art of the Deal*. New York: Ballantine Books.

Williams, L.C. (2017) "Where are they now? The Russian bots that disrupted the 2016 election. Russia-linked social media bots played a big role in online conversation about the election. Here's what they've been up to since." *ThinkProgress*, May 5, 2017, at https://thinkprogress.org/russian-bots-where-are-they-now-e2674c19017b/ (accessed September 9, 2017).

CHAPTER 5

The War of Images in the Age of Trump

Tom Allbeson and Stuart Allan

This chapter aims to contribute to pressing debates surrounding the issue of 'fake news' by focusing on the politicisation of visual imagery. The Trump administration's use of 'fake news' as a term of critique directed at journalists and their news organisations represents a cynical strategy of deflection and deception, one that risks destabilising confidence in the free flow of information underpinning political deliberation in a democratic system. Gaming the journalist-source relationship in this manner—often orchestrating 'debate' regarding the truth-value of particular imagery—has proven to be both click-bait infotainment and effective image management. We aim to promote discussion by highlighting ways in which the public circulation of photographs prove consistent with purposeful, albeit inchoate strategies of distraction and diversion mobilised by the Trump administration and its supporters, as well as how publicly circulating photographic images can also occasionally disrupt or frustrate such strategies.

T. Allbeson (✉) • S. Allan
School of Journalism, Media and Culture, Cardiff University,
Cardiff, UK

© The Author(s) 2019
C. Happer et al. (eds.), *Trump's Media War*,
https://doi.org/10.1007/978-3-319-94069-4_5

To fully grasp the nature of contemporary media spectacles, we suggest the position of photography within the current newscape deserves careful scrutiny. From the illustrated magazines of the nineteenth century to the photo-magazines pioneered in the interwar period and the advent of television news in the post-war decades, the visual material has long been a formative facet of the news. Never incidental, news images have always been instrumental in making meaning; they are 'evidence of a practice whose history included the construction of the very objects and subjects they claimed to merely represent' (Hill and Schwartz 2015: 4). Moving from a period dominated by print or broadcast news to one dominated by digital platforms, however, has entailed a shift in the contours of media audiences. From Benedict Anderson's imagined national communities of the nineteenth century and Marshall McLuhan's purported global village of the late-twentieth century, the fear is now that—as a consequence of the algorithmic determination of online content—news audiences of the contemporary digital era are segmented in a series of dislocated echo chambers or filter bubbles (Krasodomski-Jones 2016). While the media infrastructure may have changed dramatically in recent decades, photographic images remain as significant in shaping the image of public figures and the perception of political events. Perhaps now more than ever, photographs are both basic building blocks of news content and vital vehicles of media spectacles. Certainly, they can journey much more readily between *The Guardian*, *New York Post*, or *Breitbart* websites and social media platforms such as Twitter, Facebook, or Instagram. The distinction, moreover, between user-generated content and that emanating from established news institutions or politically motivated organisations is often far from obvious.

Photography is central to fake news, both as a media phenomenon and a political discourse. From established media outlets to the social media platforms used to disseminate bogus stories, publicly circulating imagery is an integral component of the digital ecology of the twenty-first century. Indeed, it was public debate about a comparison between two photographs that prompted Kellyanne Conway, Counsellor to the President, to coin the phrase 'alternative facts.' Two photographic depictions of the Mall in Washington, taken on the inauguration days of Presidents Obama and Trump in 2009 and 2017 respectively, precipitated a controversy concerning the size of inauguration crowds. Seeking to explain away the discrepancy between the sizes of the crowds in each photograph, Sean Spicer, the then White House press secretary, claimed that plastic sheeting 'had the effect of highlighting areas people were not standing whereas in years past the grass eliminated this visual' (BBC News 2017a). It was this dissembling that Conway sought to categorise with the infamous coinage. Tellingly, from one perspective, discussion of the inauguration photographs was embarrassing for the new administration, while from another it was a fortuitous diversion from news coverage of the Women's March that took place in Washington and in cities around the world the day after the inauguration. This co-ordinated protest produced a multitude of eye-catching images disseminated by major news agencies. For instance, Reuters circulated various photographs by Steffi Loos and Gregor Fischer of a woman wearing a headscarf fashioned from the US flag at the rally in Berlin, while Getty Images made available a photograph of actor Scarlett Johansson in the crowd in Washington. Attention, however, was drawn away from the global protest concerning women's rights to the trivial issue of which President drew the largest crowd.

The inauguration photographs appear to come from a camera positioned on top of the Washington Monument. They are ostensibly ideologically neutral, having been mechanically captured as part of an objective visual relay. Familiar adages aptly characterise everyday attitudes to such imagery, such as 'The camera never lies' and 'Seeing is believing.' Even in a climate of considerable cynicism about media coverage, the sense of a technical, dispassionate point of view afforded by the camera continues to be central to journalistic authority. The resultant image's presumed status as unmediated visual evidence is typically taken for granted—at least until proven otherwise. Photographs such as this, and what they purport to show, are repeatedly the subject of fractious debate. In this context of the ambiguous epistemological status of the photographic image within a refashioned newscape, then, we address the role of particular images in pro- and anti-Trump discourse; anxieties about faked or staged images; and the need to critically engage more thoroughly with this partisan war of images to fully grasp the fluid, uneven dynamics of political communication.

We propose a typology of relatively distinct yet inter-related categories intended to facilitate efforts to attend to pertinent imagery with sufficient analytical specificity. This typology is based on insights drawn from consideration of news coverage and public debate across mainstream news organisations, as well as social media platforms. The coverage examined spans a roughly 12-month period from spring 2016 to summer 2017, encompassing the US presidential election campaign and the first months of the

Trump administration. These categories are neither exclusive nor exhaustive; one particular photograph may share characteristics with different types listed below and not all news imagery practices may be captured by the typology that follows. Rather, this is a formulation of illustrative examples, each of which helps to pinpoint pertinent tensions warranting closer inspection. Our proposed typology is intended to contribute to establishing the conceptual space necessary to investigate the relationship between photography and 'fake news.' Our hope is that this tentative typology may be a springboard to further critical engagement. Such analysis, we suggest, invites a reconceptualisation of the ways various modes of depicting Trump resonate with 'structures of feeling' (Williams 1961) consistent with cultural, and thereby rhetorical appeals characterised by the antagonistic political voice of an adversarial media profile aiming to advance the administration's ideological interests and priorities.

MISAPPROPRIATED PHOTOGRAPHS

On 7 August 2016, pictures by two photographers—Jonathan Ernst and Mark Makela—were published in a Breitbart story by Patrick Howley (2016), headlined 'Internet Melts Down over Photos of Hillary Clinton Getting Helped Up the Stairs.' The photos of the presidential candidate were actually taken months earlier in February. Nonetheless, the first line of the article, as well as painting a particular image of the Clinton campaign entourage, explicitly references the authenticating role the photographic illustration is supposed to fulfil: 'Hillary Clinton needed to be physically helped up a moderate flight of stairs by her team of staffers and handlers, according to campaign-trail photos that made the rounds on the Internet Sunday.' Complementing the minimal, but effective text are quotations from, videos about, and links to other stories insinuating 'Clinton's various health problems.' Makela, in a *Wired* interview, later recalled that the photographs captured a moment when, having slipped, Clinton was simply steadied by the aides standing next to her. He drew attention to what he characterised as a 'really bizarre and dispiriting' use of photojournalistic images in media discourse about politicians. 'We're always attuned to photographic manipulation,' Makela suggested, 'but what was more sinister in this situation was the misappropriation of a photo' (Mallonee 2016).

The familiar principle animating such misleading uses of photographic imagery—a commonplace from the work of pioneering Weimar-era photojournalists like Erich Salomon, through post-war paparazzi such as Tazio Secchiaroli—is that candid photographs can reveal truths that their subject is working hard to obscure. This imputed objectivity is central to the force of such images, as evident in the pointed highlighting by the Breitbart writer that the illustrations are 'Reuters and Getty photographs.' The presumed credibility of these two agencies underwrites the imagery's tacit promise to offer a view through a chink in the spectacle of modern politics. In this way, viewers are effectively invited to imaginatively join a virtual community of like-minded, interested individuals party to the same exposure. The sharing of such misappropriated photographs on social media platforms—presumably the prompt for the 'Internet Melts Down' assertion, as well as being promoted by it—amplifies this strategy of collective identification with its emotive undertones.

In the same vein, making acrimonious allegations about the 'liberal' media is a further aspect of the Trump media team's strategy, one where 'fake news' is used as a shorthand for supposedly deliberate distortions, even propaganda, advanced by the administration's 'enemies.' Such forms of finger pointing include making complaints about a lack of so-called appropriate, balanced, or fair coverage. On 10 August 2016, Breitbart again published Makela's photograph, this time under the headline, 'Physician: Mainstream Media "Strangely Silent" About Hillary Clinton's Health' (Berry 2016). The article, credited to Dr. Susan Berry, cites Dr. Jane Orient, 'executive director of the Association of American Physicians and Surgeons,' as raising questions about the spurious possibility that the photograph depicts the moment of a seizure or stroke. The operative element of the story, reliant on its recycling of photographic illustration as visible evidence, is the accusation that this proof is being denied by the 'mainstream media' for reasons of partisan bias, if not outright conspiracy.

While many such attacks directed at journalists by the Trump administration find their mark, some backfire. A key example is the 'Bowling Green Massacre.' In January 2017, Conway cited the event as evidence of the need for the travel ban or 'extreme vetting' to protect the country's interests.[1] As was quickly determined by journalists, however, while two Iraqi refugees had been arrested in Bowling Green, Kentucky, in 2011, no massacre occurred. Commentators—not least late-night television talk show hosts—were quick to ridicule Conway for proclaiming otherwise. Evidently, such criticisms did not make Trump think twice about making comparable claims about attacks in Sweden the following month.[2] Likewise in August 2017 at a now-notorious press conference addressing the violence in Charlottesville surrounding the 'Unite the Right' rally, the President attributed 'blame on both sides' and asserted that 'I saw the same pictures as you did' (Segarra 2017). The frequent suggestion that news stories, and often specifically photographic evidence, are being withheld is a common thread in the attacks on journalists and their news organisations by the Trump administration and its supporters. Misappropriated photographs and this sort of misdirection alluding to supposedly deficient photographic coverage are flip-sides of the same coin.

Manipulated Photographs

While misappropriation and misdirection seldom feature as talking points, the question of photographic manipulation—the faked photograph—provokes lively debate, particularly across social media platforms. The actual incidence of certified fake (as opposed to misappropriated) photographs is relatively rare, but this has not devalued the currency of this issue in contemporary political discourse. A salient example surfaced following the inauguration on 20 January 2017. President Trump, having been sworn in, shook hands with former-President Obama as he was about to board an air force helicopter. A photograph of this handshake was taken by a photographer attached to Getty Images and was reported by ABC News to have been framed and hung on a wall in the White House. Two versions of the same photograph subsequently surfaced, the difference between them being that Trump's left hand appears larger in one than in the other. The perceived discrepancy was highlighted in a tweet by Dana Schwartz, a writer for the New York *Observer*, suggesting the President-elect was manipulating his media image owing to insecurities about the size of his hands: 'Trump 100% photoshopped his hand bigger for this picture hanging in the white house, which is the most embarrassing thing I've ever seen.'[3] It soon became apparent, however, that while one version of the photo was doctored, it was not as Schwartz speculated. Someone had reduced the size of Trump's hand in the version she took to be the original, authentic photograph. As with most Twitter storms, Schwartz's error prompted intense anger from some respondents, including accusations about the dire state of twenty-first-century journalism. Schwartz—who writes on arts and entertainment—felt obliged to distance herself from political journalism, apologising for her error and writing it off as a bit of fun. Many failed to see the joke. Others weighing-in sought to clarify the precise nature of the confusion, reasserting the credentials of thorough, fact-checking journalistic practice (Bump 2017). In doing so, however, they implicitly set news journalism in opposition to photojournalism, suggesting that the former is the arbitrator of the latter.

The debate about (more than the instance of) photographic manipulation reveals the extent to which news photography, political journalism, and commentary on social media platforms are inextricably linked in the current digital ecology of news and social media. Moreover, this debate has Janus-faced ramifications. In drawing attention to contending discourses of facticity, it invites media audiences to be more sceptical about the truth-value of news imagery. Yet simultaneously, the revelation of falsification or forgery also works to underscore the general credibility of imagery: 'Fakes will be called out.' Back in 1990, at the dawn of digital news photography, art critic Andy Grundberg wrote in *The New York Times* about how photographic manipulation might change our attitudes to the medium:

> In the future, it seems almost certain, photographs will appear less like facts and more like factoids – as a kind of unsettled and unsettling hybrid imagery based not so much on observable reality and actual events as on the imagination. This shift [...] will fundamentally alter not only conventional ideas about the nature of photography but also many cherished conceptions about reality itself. [...] Those disciplines based on the veracity of photographic appearances, including photojournalism, will either change radically in appearance or wither. (Grundberg 1990)[4]

A quarter-century later, these seem a prescient set of insights. Twenty-first-century ideas of photographic representation are uneasily positioned between authenticity and unreliability. This equivocal conception of photography may not be novel, but photographs are more ubiquitous than ever, and integral to public debate at all levels. Arguably, the cognitive dissonance arising from this equivocal conception is such that while scepticism about photography may be widespread those images that confirm one's point of view can still carry the stamp of authenticity. Photographs that meet one's expectations may be experienced as 'real' or 'objective' images, while the photograph that jars with a pre-existing point of view can seem ideologically motivated, and as such less trustworthy.

The Photo-Opportunity

Far more ubiquitous than the faked photograph is the photograph of the staged or manufactured event—the event envisioned and dramatically performed, at least in part, with the purpose of producing a desirable image outcome. Such a 'photo-opportunity' is both a response to and a driver of image-saturated political cultures, where news values blur into those of advertising, public relations, and publicity. The highly contrived 'pseudo-event,' as Daniel J. Boorstin termed it in his classic study *The Image* published in 1961, 'comes about because someone has planned, planted or incited it,' more often than not 'for the immediate purpose of being reported or reproduced' (Boorstin 1961: 11–12). Today the stage-managed nature of the photo-opportunity is all but taken for granted; the absence of such effort likely to warrant greater news comment than its routine operationalisation in presidential media management from one day to the next.

In the plethora of photo-op images produced and circulated in the media, handshakes and signings are two of the most commonly featured subjects. Examples organised and set in motion by the Trump media team abound. On 11 January 2017, the President-elect held a press conference at Trump Tower in New York flanked by members of his family and his tax lawyer, on a stage festooned with flags. It was explained that the piles of manila folders on a table to his right contained the paperwork transferring business assets to a trust run by his sons. The stage-managed event was intended to indicate that Trump had divested himself of his business interests to ensure no conflict of interest once he assumed the office of president. A Freedom of Information Act request subsequently revealed the disjuncture between that image and the content of the files (Craig and Lipton 2017). It appears that the incoming administration was more concerned with producing an image that purports to show this happened, than a paper trail that demonstrates it was achieved. Likewise, on 27 January 2017, now President Trump called a press conference for the media to witness his signing of a range of executive orders, including one calling for 'extreme vetting' of individuals travelling from seven predominantly Muslim countries. The signing of the so-called travel ban took place in the Hall of Heroes at the Department of Defense in Arlington, Virginia. No matter that the ban was quickly mired in legal wrangling, photographs by Olivier Douliery were put in circulation, of the President signing the order and then, to emphasise how projected image amounts to action, holding up the order with his signature on it for the assembled cameras.

The photo-opportunity's success is measured by how widely it is reported. As Boorstin remarked, 'The question, "Is it real?" is less important than, "Is it newsworthy?"' (1961: 11). Such disingenuousness is central to analyses of how the public image of political figures is manufactured in the Trump era. Containing, if not controlling, claims and counterclaims about accuracy or integrity are not the primary concerns of such an image-focused media strategy; rather, this 'packaging' of news becomes a self-fulfilling prophecy at the heart of a 'post-truth' media strategy. Truth, in other words, is not just relative, it is incidental; perception carries the burden of representation. What is different in the age of digital communications catering for the illusion of spontaneity in a swirl of social media sharing is the dominance of the photo-op as news event in its own right, notwithstanding its disconnect from verifiable facts. The images produced from photo-ops are a key structuring principle in public debate. Issues, by this logic, are secondary to images.

THE INOPPORTUNE PHOTOGRAPH

This dominance of the photo-op is similarly rendered evident in the column inches devoted to its discursive repair following a failure in execution. These are inopportune photos in the sense that they miss their mark despite a successful staging, possibly because an aspect of the performance is off-key or, even worse, off-message. Trump's first visit with UK Prime Minister Theresa May produced a flurry of discussion after a photograph by Christopher Furlong emerged of the two holding hands as they walked to a press conference at the White House on 27 January. Likewise, the President's global tour in May 2017 produced a number of visual miscues poured over by media commentators. For instance, *Vanity Fair* (Bryant 2017; Weaver 2017) analysed apparent snubs to the President from his wife Melania (who appeared to be unwilling to hold his hand) and Agata Kornhauser-Duda, wife of the Polish President (who seemed to snub Trump's proffered hand, shaking the First Lady's instead). *Time*, in turn, scrutinised the imagery of the First Family taken during a meeting at the Vatican: 'One image in particular, of a grinning Trump next to a stone-faced Pope Francis, has gone viral,' it reported (Katz 2017). Indeed, one could be forgiven for thinking the only legacy of the whistle-stop tour of five countries in seven days was a series of inopportune photos, from the opening of the Global Center for Combating Extremist Ideology in Saudi Arabia (where Trump was photographed next to the Egyptian President and the Saudi King, each with their hands placed on an illuminated model of the globe) to the 43rd G7 Summit (where Trump had a tense, 25-second handshake with French President, Emmanuel Macron).[5]

In addition to the failed photo-op, there is the less common phenomenon of the deconstructed photo-op. These are inopportune photos in the sense that they reveal something other than what was intended in the envisaged script, thereby undermining—and at times symbolically reversing—its ideological impact. A scene captured by Drew Angerer in the Oval Office on 28 January had, by the summer of 2017 when it was recirculated by BBC News, CNN, and other news outlets, become illustrative of turmoil in the White House (BBC News 2017b; Cillizza 2017). It depicted President Trump receiving 'a congratulatory phone call from Russian President Vladimir Putin following his inauguration,' as well as five close (white, male) members of staff. Of the five, Vice President Mike Pence was the only one still in post seven months later. Earlier in the year, *The Washington Post* also used the same photo to address the lack of gender diversity (Nakamura and Phillip 2017). *The Guardian*, in turn, ran a picture by Evan Vucci of the President signing executive orders in the Oval Office on 23 January 2017 with the caption, 'This photograph is what patriarchy looks like.' He was flanked by five men: Reince Priebus, Peter Navarro, Jared Kushner, Stephen Miller, and Steve Bannon. The article addressed 'Trump's assault on women's rights' as a consequence of an order 'removing US funding to any overseas organisation that offers abortions' (Cosslett 2017).

When inopportune photographs become the story, opined reactions reverberate across the newscape to the detriment of fact-based reporting. What was once fodder for the 'and finally' segment of broadcast news is all too often elevated to the top of the story order and, in online contexts, serves as shimmering 'click-bait' attracting quick and easy 'hits' on websites. The handshake photo-op (a microcosm of political power-play with its subtle stratagems, like the hand on the shoulder or in the small of the back as you enter the building last of all) is now a central facet of the confected public image of politicians. Perhaps this is because so much of political action and impact (from trade agreements to diplomatic talks) cannot be captured in the frame of a single photograph. Perhaps it is because one's handshake, like the signature, is taken to be representative of one's character—such images being projected as validating signifiers of authentic personality. Certainly, the quasi-obsessive reproduction of handshake photographs highlights the consistent efforts taken to sustain the 'illusions which flood our experience,' to borrow another phrase from Boorstin. More than a matter of shadow becoming substance, their significance for Trump's media team lies in their value as infotainment which distracts and diverts. Again, even when the photo-op fails, images trump issues.

THE ACTION SHOT

Related to the photo-op is the image of the President conducting the business of his office—what we might call the action shot, to distinguish it from the practice of appearing in front of assembled media, as with the photo-op. The action shot may be the result of a photojournalist's working for a picture agency or news organisation, but often it will be taken in-house by a photographer attached to the administration.[6] One of the most significant action shots in the early days of the Trump presidency was the image of the command room at the Mar-a-Lago resort taken by Shealah Craighead (Chief Official White House Photographer for the Trump presidency) and distributed through Associated Press. It shows the President surrounded by advisers and administration members during air attacks against Syria's Assad regime on 8 April 2017. It was widely circulated, often alongside surveillance imagery taken after the attack released to the press (e.g. Awford et al. 2017). This action photo closely resembles another, as remarked on at the time by BBC News and others: 'A quick glance at the Trump team photo,' it surmised, 'instantly recalls what was perhaps the most memorable modern "war room" image, from 2011, when President Barack Obama and his national security team clustered around a monitor to watch the raid to kill Osama Bin Laden unfold' (Zurcher 2017).

As well as being considered as in dialogue with one another, both shots were considered to be inviting inter-textual references with earlier imagery. The Obama Command Room photograph, some commentators maintained, deserved to be read as a response to the images of the 11 September 2001 attacks. It proffered, at least in their view, both narrative and ideological closure. The Trump Command Room photograph was frequently typified in the ensuing news coverage in similar terms. The military action was framed as retaliation in response to the shocking images of victims of the chemical attacks in Idlib Province on 4 April 2017, in which 20 children were amongst the 72 casualties, according to the Syrian Observatory for Human Rights. It was widely reported that Trump's daughter, moved by the images of children who had died during the gas attack in Northern Syria, appealed to her father to intervene (e.g. Wood 2017b). The al-Shayrat airfield in Homs province was held to be the source of the attack and it was reported that US forces launched 59 Tomahawk missiles against the base. This sort of 'war of images' (to use W J T Mitchell's terminology) or 'iconoclash' (to use Bruno Latour's phrase) is an ever-present feature in twenty-first-century international relations, whether it be conflict between nations or so-called asymmetric warfare with non-state actors.

CONCLUSION

Given the speed of the news cycle regarding the Trump administration and the crises it is facing, much of the imagery under scrutiny here may soon fade from view. Nonetheless, we hope that the typology and critical reflection outlined here will serve to inform discussion of the prominent role of photographs in contemporary political communication. This chapter has simply sought to categorise the symptoms engendered by the condition. More research and debate is needed to determine appropriate treatments. With this in mind, we offer three observations.

First and most obvious, cynicism and satire are not sufficient. Just as 'fake news' has been weaponised by the Trump administration (see Chaps. 3 and 4 by Paul Levinson and Douglas Kellner in this volume), satire risks being effectively deactivated. Alison Jackson's witty work with look-a-likes, for instance, pricks the bubble of the President's manufactured image by offering putatively candid shots behind the mask. Trump, however, has worked to deflate and defang such caustic critique. At a rally in Florida on 7 November 2016 the day before the election, for example, the presidential candidate seemed more than happy to be photographed by Getty-affiliated Chip Somodevilla and Reuters' Carlo Allegri holding a mask with the likeness of his face. He reputedly asked the crowd, 'Is there any place more fun to be than a Trump rally?' (Omar 2016). Sean Spicer similarly co-opted comedy when he appeared at the Emmys in September 2017. It would appear that we have entered not only a 'post-truth era' but also a post-satire one.

Second, greater analytical and linguistic precision is needed. Photographs and phenomena such as those discussed here are frequently the focus of journalism and news reporting, as we have highlighted (cf. Friedersdorf 2016; Maheshwari 2016). A wider debate is needed, however, with a sharper critical edge. A common, jargon-free vocabulary is required to facilitate broader discussion and critique of the ways in which photographs facilitate and frustrate, divert and dynamise political deliberation. Moreover, the revelation of specific instances of misappropriated and manipulated photographs must be called out. See, for example, the anti-Islamic comments alongside the photograph of a woman in a headscarf at the scene of the terrorist attack on Westminster Bridge, London, in March 2017—an image that subsequently appeared on both the *Daily Mail* and *Sun* websites in the UK—which was traced back to Russian involvement (see Booth et al. 2017). The deconstructed photo-op likewise offers a valuable model for critical engagement with the politicisation of visual content in contemporary newscape.

Finally, the debate about photography should be situated within a wider project of renewing political dialogue in democratic societies prompted on both sides of the Atlantic by the 'populist' surprises of recent years. Submissions to the original select committee inquiry into fake news by the UK government's Department for Culture, Media and Sport (concluded prematurely owing to the snap UK general election of June 2017) made next to no references to photography. This is as imprudent as it is understandable. In one sense, to focus on images is to fall into the trap set by the media strategy of political communicators. It is to play within the rules of the game prescribed by others, to be distracted from actions and transgressions, focusing instead on representations. In another sense, discussing the central role of photography in the current news ecology is fundamental to understanding the course of contemporary political debate. As has recently been argued regarding photojournalism and its position in public culture, 'healthy democracies are those in which citizens are accustomed to arguing thoughtfully about how they are influenced' (Hariman and Lucaites 2016: 24 and 28). Engaging with the role of photographic imagery in shaping public perceptions, we believe, should be a central tenet of any wider initiative to understand and reinvigorate a public interest ethos in the contemporary digital news ecology.

NOTES

1. See, for example, Rutenberg (2017).
2. At a rally in Florida on 18 January 2017, President-elect Trump appeared to refer to a terrorist attack that did not take place: 'You look at what's happening last night in Sweden. Sweden? Who would believe this? Sweden!' (Bloom 2017).
3. The original tweet and subsequent comments by Schwartz are reproduced on camera and photography website PetaPixel (Zhang 2017).

4. See also William J. Mitchell, *The Reconfigured Eye: Visual Truth in the Post-photographic Era* (MIT Press, 1992).
5. May gave her version of events ('I think he was actually being a gentleman') in an interview with *Vogue* for which she was photographed by Annie Leibovitz (Wood 2017a, b). Macron too was quizzed on the images resulting from his photo-op with the President (Henley 2017).
6. The template for this sort of in-depth coverage was provided when Cornell Capa photographed the first 100 days of John F. Kennedy's presidency for Magnum Photos in 1961.

REFERENCES

Awford, J. et al. (2017) One Step from War, 8 April 2017 [Online]. Available at: https://www.thesun.co.uk/news/3275613/donald-trump-us-attacks-syria-chemical-attack-sarin-latest-news/ [Accessed: 21 November 2017].

BBC News (2017a) Trump claims media 'dishonest' over crowd photos, 22 January 2017 [Online]. Available at: http://www.bbc.co.uk/news/world-us-canada-38707722 [Accessed: 21 November 2017].

BBC News (2017b) The photo that highlights White House turmoil, 18 August 2017 [Online]. Available at: http://www.bbc.co.uk/news/world-us-canada-40982305 [Accessed: 21 November 2017].

Berry, S. (2016) Physician: Mainstream Media 'Strangely Silent' About Hillary Clinton's Health, 10 August 2016 [Online]. Available at: http://www.breitbart.com/big-government/2016/08/10/physician-strangely-silent-mainstream-media-fitness-hillary-clinton/ [Accessed: 21 November 2017].

Bloom, D. (2017) Donald Trump refers to incident 'last night' in Sweden that didn't happen and blames it on migrants, 19 Feb 2017 [Online]. Available at: http://www.mirror.co.uk/news/politics/donald-trump-refers-incident-sweden-9848299 [Accessed: 21 November 2017].

Boorstin, D. J. (1961) *The Image: A Guide to Pseudo-Events in America*. New York: Harper.

Booth, R. et al. (2017) Russia used hundreds of fake accounts to tweet about Brexit, data shows, 14 November 2017 [Online]. Available at: https://www.theguardian.com/world/2017/nov/14/how-400-russia-run-fake-accounts-posted-bogus-brexit-tweets [Accessed: 21 November 2017].

Bryant, K. (2017) Melania Trump and the Hand-Graze Seen Round the World, 22 May 2017 [Online]. Available at: https://www.vanityfair.com/style/2017/05/melania-trump-donald-slap-swat-saudi-arabia-israel-trip [Accessed: 21 November 2017].

Bump, P. (2017) No, the White House didn't Photoshop an image of the president's hand, 27 January 2017 [Online]. Available at: https://www.washingtonpost.com/news/politics/wp/2017/01/27/no-the-white-house-didnt-photoshop-an-image-of-the-presidents-hand/?utm_term=.fc24181720cd [Accessed: 21 November 2017].

Cillizza, C. (2017) 1 picture that explains the remarkable White House staff turnover, 19 August 2017 [Online]. Available at: http://edition.cnn.com/2017/08/18/politics/trump-bannon-white-house-chaos/index.html [Accessed: 21 November 2017].

Cosslett, R. L. (2017) This photo sums up Trump's assault on women's rights, 24 January 2017 [Online]. Available at: https://www.theguardian.com/commentisfree/2017/jan/24/photo-trump-womens-rights-protest-reproductive-abortion-developing-contries [Accessed: 21 November 2017].

Craig, S., and Lipton, E. (2017) Trust Records Show Trump Is Still Closely Tied to His Empire, 3 February 2017 [Online]. Available at: https://www.nytimes.com/2017/02/03/us/politics/donald-trump-business.html [Accessed: 21 November 2017].

Friedersdorf, C. (2016) Donald Trump, Master of the Pseudo-Event, 8 December 2016 [Online]. Available at: https://www.theatlantic.com/politics/archive/2016/12/all-the-president-elects-pseudo-events/509630/ [Accessed: 21 November 2017].

Grundberg, A. (1990) Ask It No Questions: The Camera Can Lie, 12 August 1990 [Online]. Available at: http://www.nytimes.com/1990/08/12/arts/photography-view-ask-it-no-questions-the-camera-can-lie.html?pagewanted=all [Accessed: 21 November 2017].

Hariman, R. and Lucaites, J. L. (2016) *The Public Image: Photography and Civic Spectatorship*. Chicago: University of Chicago Press.

Henley, J. (2017) Emmanuel Macron: My handshake with Trump was 'a moment of truth', 28 May 2017 [Online]. Available at: https://www.theguardian.com/world/2017/may/28/emmanuel-macron-my-handshake-with-trump-was-a-moment-of-truth [Accessed: 21 November 2017].

Hill, J., and Schwartz, V. R. (2015) *Getting the Picture: The Visual Culture of the News*. London: Bloomsbury

Howley, P. (2016) Internet Melts Down over Photos of Hillary Clinton Getting Helped Up the Stairs, 7 August 2016 [Online]. Available at http://www.breitbart.com/2016-presidential-race/2016/08/07/hillary-clinton-needs-help-getting-stairs/ [Accessed: 21 November 2017].

Katz, A. (2017) The Story Behind the Viral Photo of Pope Francis and Donald Trump, 24 May 2017 [Online]. Available at: http://time.com/4792245/pope-francis-donald-trump-viral-photo/ [Accessed: 21 November 2017].

Kellner, D. (2019) Trump's War Against the Media, Fake News, and (A) Social Media in Catherine Happer, Andrew Hoskins, and William Merrin, eds. *Trump's War on the Media*. Basingstoke, UK: Palgrave Macmillan, pp.47–68.

Krasodomski-Jones, A. (2016) *Talking To Ourselves? Political Debate Online and the Echo Chamber Effect*. London: Demos.

Levinson, P. (2019) Turning the Tables: How Trump Turned Fake News from a Weapon of Deception to a Weapon of Mass Destruction of Legitimate News in Catherine Happer, Andrew Hoskins, and William Merrin, eds. *Trump's War on the Media*. Basingstoke, UK: Palgrave Macmillan, pp.33–46.

Maheshwari, S. (2016) How Fake News Goes Viral: A Case Study, 20 November 2016 [Online]. Available at: https://www.nytimes.com/2016/11/20/business/media/how-fake-news-spreads.html [Accessed: 21 November 2017].

Mallonee, L. (2016) How photos fuel the spread of fake news, 21 December 2016 [Online]. Available at: https://www.wired.com/2016/12/photos-fuel-spread-fake-news/ [Accessed: 21 November 2017].

Nakamura, D., and Phillip, A. (2017) Trump's administration isn't very diverse. Photo ops make it glaringly obvious, 5 February 2017 [Online]. Available at: https://www.washingtonpost.com/politics/trumps-administration-isnt-very-diverse-photo-ops-make-it-glaringly-obvious/2017/02/02/a0353e28-e956-11e6-bf6f-301b6b443624_story.html?tid=a_inl&utm_term=.7262884e3712 [Accessed: 21 November 2017].

Omar, M. (2016) Donald Trump Lifts Donald Trump Mask At Rally Because Nothing Makes Sense Anymore, 7 November 2016 [Online]. Available at: http://www.huffingtonpost.ca/2016/11/07/donald-trump-holds-trump-mask_n_12846332.html [Accessed: 21 November 2017].

Rutenberg, J. (2017) The Massacre That Wasn't, and a Turning Point for 'Fake News', 5 February 2017 [Online]. Available at: https://www.nytimes.com/2017/02/05/business/the-massacre-that-wasnt-and-a-turning-point-for-fake-news.html?_r=0 [Accessed: 21 November, 2017]

Segarra, L. M. (2017) Read the Transcript of President Trump's 'Blame on Both Sides' Comments on Charlottesville, 15 August 2017 [Online]. Available at: http://time.com/4902144/donald-trump-charlottesville-blame-both-sides-kkk-nazi/ [Accessed: 21 November 2017].

Weaver, H. (2017) The First Lady of Poland Smoothly Avoided Shaking Donald Trump's Hand, 6 July 2017 [Online]. Available at: https://www.vanityfair.com/style/2017/07/first-lady-of-poland-avoided-donald-trump-handshake [Accessed: 21 November 2017].

Williams, R. (1961) *The Long Revolution*. London: Chatto and Windus.

Wood, G. (2017a) U.K. Prime Minister Theresa May on Leading Britain Post-Brexit, 20 March 2017 [Online]. Available at: https://www.vogue.com/article/british-prime-minister-theresa-may-interview-brexit-political-views [Accessed: 21 November 2017].

Wood, V. (2017b) Donald Trump carried out Syria missile strike 'after being convinced by daughter Ivanka', 9 April 2017 [Online]. Available at: https://www.express.co.uk/news/world/789399/Donald-Trump-Ivanka-Trump-Syria-Missile-Strike-Assad-US-Russia-Tomahawk [Accessed: 21 November 2017].

Zhang, M. (2017) Fake Photo of Trump's 'Photoshopped' Hand Fools the Internet, 28 Jan 2017 [Online]. Available at: https://petapixel.com/2017/01/28/fake-photo-trumps-photoshopped-hand-fools-internet/ [Accessed: 21 November 2017].

Zurcher, A. (2017) Decoding the Trump 'war room' photograph, 7 April 2017 [Online]. Available at: http://www.bbc.co.uk/news/world-us-canada-39486617 [Accessed: 21 November 2017].

PART III

Reporting Trump: Building the Brand

'Authentic' Men and 'Angry' Women: Trump, Reality Television, and Gendered Constructions of Business and Politics

Lisa W. Kelly

'Every system of cruelty requires its own theatre' states Nick Couldry (2008: 3), referring to the relationship between neoliberalism and reality reality television, the latter of which he argues draws on the rituals of everyday life to legitimise the norms, values, and social practices on which neoliberalism depends. In Trump, then, we could say we have found our villain, both in his role in *The Apprentice* (NBC 2004–2017) and now as President of the United States. With regards to television, however, this casting process has a long tradition. Engagement with business and entrepreneurship within factual programming has historically been limited to news and current affairs, resulting in relatively sober journalistic content with an authoritative voice aimed at a niche audience. Fictional television, on the other hand, has regularly featured entrepreneurs and businessmen (and it has traditionally been *men*) in key comic and dramatic roles (see Lichter et al. 1994; Williams 2004). This has resulted in largely negative portrayals in which such characters are presented as 'suspect, untrustworthy or figures of fun' (Boyle and Magor 2008) or 'crooks, conmen and clowns'

L. W. Kelly (✉)
University of Glasgow, Glasgow, UK

© The Author(s) 2019
C. Happer et al. (eds.), *Trump's Media War*,
https://doi.org/10.1007/978-3-319-94069-4_6

(Theberge 1981). While Trump has segued from something of a 'clown' character in the public's imagination to an altogether more dangerous figure, these descriptions also call to mind earlier fictional representations such as JR Ewing of *Dallas* (CBS 1978–1991) in the US context or, in the United Kingdom, *Minder*'s (ITV 1979–1994) Arthur Daley and Del Boy in *Only Fools and Horses* (BBC 1981–2003).

In many ways, these representations changed with the development of reality television from the 1990s onwards, and it was this shift that formed the basis of our research project examining the rise of the 'business entertainment format' and the resultant 'celebrity entrepreneurs' that it produced (Boyle and Kelly 2010, 2012; Kelly and Boyle 2011). It should be noted that while recognising the global circulation of such formats (e.g., *The Apprentice* has been adapted in 29 countries), our original empirical research was primarily concerned with the UK context. As such, we interviewed channel controllers, commissioners, and producers operating within the United Kingdom's public service broadcasting landscape (e.g., BBC and Channel 4) before conducting audience focus groups with UK-based viewers in Glasgow and London. This means that we did not analyse Trump's performance within *The Apprentice* in detail and, given the limitations of this chapter in terms of length, I do not attempt to do so here. Instead, what I aim to do is return to some of the findings of the project to re-evaluate them within the context of Trump. Specifically, this includes gendered constructions of both reality television and business and entrepreneurship, alongside networks of (political) power more widely.

The importance of television as a medium to the construction of Trump's celebrity persona and his resultant presidency is, I feel, absent from much journalistic and academic discourse, which tends to be concerned with print and social media through a focus on 'fake news' and Trump's late-night tweets. I argue, however, for the continued centrality of reality television in shaping understandings of Trump and political culture within what is often considered to be a 'post-TV' age. To do so, I offer an overview of the ways in which reality television (or factual entertainment more widely) has impacted on representations of business and entrepreneurship onscreen, with a specific focus on how 'work on the self' is presented as a requirement for success in the flexible economy (Ouellette and Hay 2008). I also examine the gendered construction of this in relation to both the 'feminisation of TV' (Ball 2012) and the shift towards self-entrepreneurship, before exploring the dichotomy between 'authentic' men and 'angry' women within the spheres of business and politics.

Heather Hendershot (2009: 244) argues that reality television is a 'genre obsessively focused on labour', from the task-based structure of the international format *Big Brother* (Veronica 1999) to the more explicit business framework of *The Apprentice*. This focus has resulted in a wider range of business and entrepreneurial representations onscreen, particularly in terms of the types of sectors involved and the 'ordinary' people taking part (Bonner 2003). For example, in her analysis of US reality programming, Hendershot (2009) looks at the different kinds of labour carried out by celebrity socialites Paris Hilton and Nicole Richie in *The Simple Life* (Fox 2003–2005) and contrasts it with the weekly tasks set for the (unknown) budding fashion designers competing in *Project Runway* (Bravo 2004–2008). While both these shows sit firmly within the US tradition of constructed reality series, business entertainment programming more widely 'can be placed within a continuum that features lightly-constructed documentaries at one end of the scale through to highly-formatted reality television at the other' (Boyle and Kelly 2012: 47).

The programmes examined in our own research ranged from what we term 'business gameshows', in the form of the UK versions of *The Apprentice* (BBC 2015) and *Dragons' Den* (BBC 2015), to 'troubleshooter' formats, which feature 'experts' attempting to turn around failing businesses within specific industry sectors, such as retail (*Mary Queen of Shops*, BBC 2015), hospitality (*Ramsay's Kitchen Nightmares*, Channel 4 2004–2014), and property (*Property Ladder*, Channel 4 2001–2009). In each instance, participants tend to reflect the diverse make-up of the United Kingdom more broadly with regards to gender, ethnicity, socio-economic background, and geographical location (the latter falling under a general north/south divide rather than the more complex make-up of the nations and regions). However, it is only gender diversity that regularly extends to the business professionals featured, with many women placed in the role of judge/investor or troubleshooter/expert. While I will discuss this later in the chapter, it should be noted that women who inhabit these positions tend to adopt a more nurturing approach that places them in the position of encouraging 'mentor' rather than ruthless 'judge'. On interviewing Sarah Beeny, the host of *Property Ladder* who provides advice and guidance to prospective developers on the series, she explained that her own personal style was to shy away from confrontation, as 'you don't have to go in with the old size tens and kick ass to be taken seriously' (quoted in Boyle and Kelly 2012, 128).

This opening up of business and entrepreneurship to a broader range of participants and sectors ties in with wider debates around the 'feminisation of TV' which, Vicky Ball (2012: 254) argues,

> is characterized through the production of "softer" programming, such as reality, lifestyle, talk shows and makeovers, [and] narratives that privilege personalization and affectivity. It is also associated with the "dumbing down" of television in the 1990s, as it is regarded as eroding the medium's public service values in its address to the consumer over that of the citizen.

Ball (ibid: 251) positions this shift to 'softer programming' in relation to the deregulation or 'casualisation' of TV as an industry, alongside the 'feminisation of employment more widely' through the growth in terms and conditions often associated with 'women's work', which include low pay and job insecurity. At the same time, reality television works to translate and legitimise the demands of neoliberalism for the wider audience, specifically the ways in which it places responsibility on the individual to continually transform in order to survive within the flexible economy:

> From programs that teach people how to improve their looks, personality and social skills to makeover competitions that transform raw human potential into the next top model, multimillionaire or American Idol, reality television presents work on the self as a prerequisite for personal and professional success. (Ouellette and Hay 2008: 100)

In the precarious neoliberal landscape, Richard Sennett (2006) has noted how change and flexibility are now privileged over the mastery of a particular skill, and we can see this in the task-based structure of most reality television. In this environment, 'the individual is no longer an "employee", "staffer", "worker" or "human resource" but has become his/her own branded commodity' (Ouellette and Hay 2008: 105). To this list, we can now add 'public servant', as Trump (and his family) seeks to brand, and profit from, the presidency.

Ultimately, reality television works to encourage viewers to become 'entrepreneurs of the self', or 'CEOs of Me, Inc.' (Du Gay 1996; McGee 2005), in order to bring about what Ouellette and Hay (2008: 103) describe as 'personal advantage in a competitive marketplace... [viewers are] managers of their "greatest assets" – themselves'. This is the type of discourse exhibited by both Trump and reality show contestants. For example, in Series 6 of *The Apprentice UK*, one candidate styled himself as Stuart

Baggs: The Brand, while for contestants of *America's Next Top Model* (UPN 2003–2006; The CW 2006–2015; VH1 2016–present; and the various international versions around the world), their product is literally their physical selves. This is something that Tyra Banks, creator of the show, consistently reminds them of, as she carries out her multiple roles of host, mentor, and judge onscreen. Banks is herself a model, entrepreneur, television executive, and business CEO and, in an acknowledgement of the importance of personal branding beyond the fashion industry in the neoliberal era, was invited to deliver a guest lecture at Stanford University entitled 'Project You: Building and Extending Your Personal Brand' (Sandler 2017).

For Ouellette and Hay (2008: 118), however, the shift towards self-entrepreneurship tends to be constructed according to a 'deeply gendered moral divide between honest work (male) and crafty self-promotion (female)'. Drawing on Valerie Walkerdine's (2003) research, they go on to highlight how 'it is easier for men to perform an entrepreneurialized, stylized version of self-reinvention, than it is for women to legitimately acquire and project attributes such as brilliance and competency, which have historically been coded as inherently male' (Ouellette and Hay 2008: 123). It is perhaps significant then that Tyra Banks (a woman of colour) established herself within an 'image industry' (McRobbie 1998) before experiencing success as a businesswoman following her move into reality television. Women in the public sphere continue to face criticism about their appearance rather than their professional capabilities and, in the case of female politicians, their policies. This discriminatory practice is something that Scottish First Minister Nicola Sturgeon has consistently highlighted, not least after the *Daily Mail* (2017), a UK tabloid, published a front-page photo of her and Prime Minister Theresa May meeting to discuss Brexit negotiations under the headline 'Never mind Brexit, who won Legs-it!'.

Trump's own carefully cultivated image is also central to his appeal, with his self-reinvention taking him from brash 1980s playboy to stern judge of *The Apprentice* and now President of the United States. Biographer Gwenda Blair (2016) considers Trump's hair to be a critical part of his personal brand, working as a highly effective trademark that makes him the perpetual centre of attention, either through humanising the wealthy tycoon or positioning him as nothing more than the entertaining clown mentioned earlier. Rachel Dubrofsky's (2016: 664) analysis takes this further, as she notes how during the election campaign, Trump's 'florid face framed by similarly glowing orange strawberry-blond hair' was often 'captured [by photographers] in motion, as if he can never be still'. In doing so, he is depicted as 'unruly', a term usually reserved for women whose bodies (or voices) are deemed excessive (see Rowe 1990). While such transgressive behaviour positions women as a source of danger (and is historically permitted only within the comic sphere), it serves to highlight the apparent 'authenticity' of white men such as Trump or, indeed, UK Foreign Secretary Boris Johnson and his similarly unruly mop. It is also worth noting that another similarity between both men is their vast inherited wealth. Thus, while the structures and discourses of reality television suggest that 'work on the self' is the key to success (or survival) within the neoliberal economy, they fail to account for wider structural inequalities relating to gender, ethnicity, and socio-economic status that ensure such success is limited to the few.

Gender is, of course, key when examining both Trump and his opponent Hillary Clinton's 2016 presidential campaigns and subsequent voter engagement. Returning again to Ouellette and Hay's (2008: 123) work, they argue that 'when women attempt to 'perform' intelligence and authority, they are more apt to be perceived as pathological than self-entrepreneurial'—a critique often aimed at Clinton. Anne Helen Petersen (2016, online) argues that Clinton ultimately suffered at the polls, not from necessarily being seen as a 'soft' woman or even a 'shrill' woman, but rather a 'sneaky' woman, a perceived duplicitousness directly related to her 'unrepentant ambition':

> [T]he constant reminders of Clinton's intellect, ambition, experience, and self-worth served to stoke the fires burning her effigy. Such attributes are only valued by this country [America], after all, when they apply to men. (ibid)

This resonates with one of the significant findings to arise from our own audience research with viewers of business entertainment formats. Focus group respondents demonstrated their complex relationships to this kind of programming, as they constantly negotiated between what they found to be 'perceived authenticity' or 'cynical performance' with regard to the motivations of the entrepreneurs featured (Boyle and Kelly 2012). They were also aware of the constructed nature of factual entertainment and the resultant 'stereotypes' or 'caricatures' it produces; an understanding that is at odds with traditional perceptions of 'masses of indiscriminating reality TV viewers' (Ouellette 2016: 647). Despite this, however, female entrepreneurs were more likely to be judged in relation to their apparent 'cynical performance' while men were continually perceived as 'authentic'.

This only differed for women who were positioned as the nurturing, mentor figure I highlighted earlier, and thus were considered 'more constructive rather than destructive' due to their supposedly 'female way of dealing with problems' (quoted in Boyle and Kelly 2012: 128). In stark contrast, respondents were highly critical of successful women who either inhabited the role of judge/investor onscreen or were clearly ambitious and competitive within the business gameshow format. For example, at the time of our research, Deborah Meaden was the sole woman on a panel of wealthy investors assembled for *Dragons' Den*, the UK version of a Japanese format in which budding entrepreneurs pitch their business ideas with the aim of securing start-up investment. Meaden was regularly described by respondents as 'stern' or 'scary', 'aggressive' rather than 'feminine', and therefore not a suitable 'role model' for women in business (ibid: 130). The title of the show highlights, of course, the ways in which the business term 'angel' investor is reworked into a 'dragon' for entertainment purposes. Yet, it was Meaden, rather than her male contemporaries, who was singled out for criticism. When she was later joined on the panel by Hilary Devey, a woman from the north of England who built a successful business within the macho haulage industry, media discourse also reduced Devey to her perceived ruthlessness and distinctive personal style, 'like Cruella de Vil with shoulder pads' as one headline described her (Wollaston 2011).

In general, respondents equated masculine terms, such as 'strong', 'dynamic', 'arrogant' and 'aggressive', with business activity and entrepreneurship. However, aggressiveness was only considered desirable within a male context. As a result, both male and female respondents tended to absolve men, such as Alan Sugar (the UK host of *The Apprentice*) and Gordon Ramsay (the eponymous chef of *Ramsay's Kitchen Nightmares*), for the bullying behaviour exhibited with their respective programmes, as this was attributed to their 'passion' for business and entrepreneurship; it's ok because they genuinely 'care'. This echoes some of the reasons given by Trump supporters for backing him. In an article published the morning after the election result, BBC News (9 November, online) reflected on the wide-ranging reasons put forward by supporters canvassed by the broadcaster over the course of the campaign. In addition to supporting specific policies, such as those relating to the economy or immigration, for example, many comments highlighted how Trump appeared 'real' and 'sincere' in comparison to traditional politicians and that he didn't 'hold back' due to political correctness but rather 'you get what he really believes in'. His specific business credentials (despite numerous reported bank-ruptcies and lawsuits) were not only regarded as an asset but were held up by one supporter as evidence that he was 'passionate, driven, confident, motivated [so] I'd like to see how he'd be as leader of the United States' (ibid).

In her analysis of Trump, Dubrofsky (2016: 664) argues that within reality television there is a

> tension between privileging authentic-seeming self-expression and curated displays: one appears most authentic when one is unable to stop oneself from breaking the expected conventions of a particular space with strict parameters for behaviour.

Reality show participants who either appear to forget about the cameras or are so overcome with emotion that they do not care about the presence of cameras 'are articulated as authentic, no matter how unlikeable' (ibid). This presents difficulties for women in the public sphere, due to prevailing gendered stereotypes that 'characterize women as possessing *likeable* qual-ities and men as possessing *competent* ones' (Harkins et al. 2017; my emphasis). Eric Guthey (2016: 668) also discusses Trump's supposed authenticity and relates it to the ways in which his supporters feel that they have 'direct access to his very real emotions – specifically to his blind rage, which many of them are happy to share'. Higgins (this volume) notes that Trump's continual breaking of political conventions, often discarding them in highly critical ways, plays into this too. While the public display of 'rage' may be acceptable for wealthy white men such as Trump (or the aforementioned Alan Sugar and Gordon Ramsay), Rowe (1990: 7) reminds us that 'anger remains the most unacceptable of emotions for women'. As one of our respondents acknowledged, 'women are still expected to act in a certain way. Aggression or anger [is] seen as negative [so] they can't be as bold as the men as it becomes a character flaw' (quoted in Boyle and Kelly 2012: 131).

This is a key point that Clinton (2017) draws attention to in her book *What Happened*, which is described as an account of what she was think-ing and *feeling* over the course of the election. Discussing the second televised election debate, which took place two days after Trump's 'pussy grabbing' comments had been revealed, she describes how he was 'looming' behind her, following her closely around the stage and making her feel uncomfortable by 'literally breathing down my neck' (Clinton: 136). Through his actions, Trump made visible on live TV the predatory behaviour he had been captured on tape bragging about. While Clinton (ibid: 136) acknowledges that her 'skin crawled', she nevertheless felt restricted in her capacity to respond and positions this not as an individual failing but as a result of the demands placed on her as a woman in the public sphere:

> It was one of those moments where you wish you could hit Pause and ask everyone watching, "Well, what would *you* do?"
> Do you stay calm, keep smiling, and carry on, as if he weren't repeatedly invading your space?
> Or do you turn, look him in the eye, and say loudly and clearly, "Back up, you creep, get away from me, I know you love to intimidate women but you can't intimidate me, so *back up*".

Clinton (ibid: 136–137) chose the former, acknowledging that although the latter may have made for 'better TV', presumably by providing dramatic confrontation or a moment of 'authentic' self-expression, ultimately 'people recoil from an angry woman'. Michelle Obama experienced this at a heightened level when she was positioned as an 'angry *black* woman' during Obama's first election campaign (see McGinley 2009; my emphasis).

Trump, on the other hand, continues to display his rage in a variety of forms following his election and, while the focus is often on his late-night tweets (which range in targets from the North Korean dictator Kim Jong-un to Carmen Yulín Cruz, the Mayor of Puerto Rican city San Juan which was devastated by Hurricane Maria), his rage is most pronounced when it is captured on television. For example, during a speech in Alabama with cameras present, he launched an attack on NFL players who 'took a knee' during the National Anthem in protest at police brutality against people of colour (Reid 2017). Significantly, he not only used a gendered insult during his outburst but also his catchphrase from *The Apprentice*: 'Wouldn't you love to see one of these NFL owners, when somebody disrespects the flag, to say, "Get that son of a bitch off the field right now. Out! He's fired. He's fired!"' This was accompanied by finger-pointing hand gestures that have traditionally come from behind his desk as part of the boardroom set of *The Apprentice* but are now positioned behind a lectern imprinted with the Seal of the President of the United States. Such performances can continue to be viewed through the prism of reality television however. For example, while critics highlight their constructed nature, a spectacle designed to distract from other (more important) issues (Edkins 2017), for Trump's supporters they demonstrate his seemingly authentic display of self-expression by transgressing social and behavioural norms—an indulgence that is not extended to female politicians, entrepreneurs, or reality show participants.

To conclude, I will return to the business entertainment format to emphasise the ways in which regular television exposure has been converted into broader political capital in recent years. According to the Centre for Public Impact in the United Kingdom (Brown 2016),

> versions of *The Apprentice* have been produced in 29 countries around the world and there have been 33 presenters in total including Donald Trump. Of these, a total of 12 have gained political office of some sort which means the chances of making the transition are greater than one in three.

While Trump may be the most high-profile, he is not the first presenter of *The Apprentice* to make the transition to president. This title is reserved for career banker Lado Gurgenidze, who hosted the show in Georgia in 2006 before becoming Prime Minister of the country the following year for a short term. Similarly, just six weeks before Trump's election in November 2016, John Doria Jr., former host of *The Apprentice* in Brazil, was voted in as mayor of São Paulo after just one round, while outspoken Canadian businessman Kevin O'Leary, who has appeared on both Canada's *Dragons' Den* (CBS 2006) and the resultant US version *Shark Tank* (ABC 2009), launched a bid to lead Canada's Conservative party in 2017. Of these, only one woman is on the list: Nora Mojskejová, who starred in the Czech Republic's version of *The Apprentice* (titled *Boss*) before becoming the leader of the Slovak political party SSS-NM. Mojskejová has also founded her own fashion label.

This is part of a wider trend we found in our own research (Boyle and Kelly 2010, 2012). For example, Conservative Prime Minister David Cameron hired Mary Portas, *Queen of Shops*, to carry out a review of the British high street and appointed Karren Brady, of *The Apprentice*, as his Business Ambassador. Brady has since become a Baroness, joining Alan Sugar in the House of Lords, after Labour Prime Minister Gordon Brown appointed him as 'Enterprise Czar', a role that apparently came with a 'peerage attached' (Finch 2009). Sugar has since quit the Labour party (but not the Lords), only to reprise his role for the Conservatives. Duncan Bannatyne of *Dragons' Den*, a Labour supporter, had been making donations to the party since 1997 and was a prominent businessman in the North East. Yet, it was only after he started regularly appearing on TV that he found himself invited to Downing Street and asked to play a role in shaping policy around encouraging entrepreneurship (Boyle and Kelly 2012: 140). In our earlier research (Boyle and Kelly 2010), we argued that these appointments reveal the networks of power that exist between political and media elites, alongside the perception, amongst professional or career politicians who supposedly lack 'real-life' experience and 'personality', that celebrities are better placed to reach out and connect with the public on a range of issues. As I have demonstrated, this is bound up with the perception that they are more authentic, passionate and willing to speak their mind, as a result of what is actually a carefully cultivated TV persona. Following the election of Trump then, and the wider 'Apprentice Phenomenon' (Brown 2016) around the world, it appears that personality politics rooted in the structures and discourses of reality television is here to stay—just not if you're a woman.

References

Ball, V. (2012) 'The "Feminization" of British Television and the Re-Traditionalization of Gender.' *Feminist Media Studies*, 12 (2), pp. 248–264.

Blair, G. [Online] (2016) 'Inside the mind of Donald Trump.' *The Guardian*, 12 November. Available at: http://www.theguardian.com/us-news/2016/nov/12/inside-the-mind-of-donald-trump-biographer-gwenda-blair

Bonner, F. (2003) *Ordinary Television: Analyzing Popular TV*. London: Sage.

Boyle, R., and Kelly, L.W. (2010) 'The Celebrity Entrepreneur on Television: Profile, Politics and Power.' *Celebrity Studies*, 1 (3), pp. 334–350.

Boyle, R., and Kelly, L.W. (2012) *The Television Entrepreneurs: Social Change and Public Understanding of Business*. Routledge: London.

Boyle, R., and Magor, M. (2008) 'A Nation of Entrepreneurs? Television, Social Change and the Rise of the Entrepreneur.' *International Journal of Media and Cultural Politics*, 4 (2), pp. 125–144.

Brown, A. [Online] (2016) 'The Apprentice Phenomenon.' *Centre for Public Impact*, 19 December. URL: http://www.centreforpublicimpact.org/the-apprentice-phenomenon/

Clinton, H.R. (2017) *What Happened*. New York: Simon & Schuster.

Couldry, N. (2008) 'Reality TV, or the secret theater of neoliberalism.' *Review of Education, Pedagogy, and Cultural Studies*, 30 (3), pp. 3–13.

Daily Mail [Online] (2017) 'Never mind Brexit, who won Legs-it!' 28 March.

Dubrofsky, R. (2016) 'Authentic Trump: Yearning for Civility.' *Television and New Media*, 17 (7), pp. 663–66.

Du Gay, P. (1996) *Consumption and Identity at Work*. London: Sage.

Edkins, B. (2017) 'Trump's Attacks on the NFL Distract the Press.' *Forbes*, 24 September. Available at: https://www.forbes.com/sites/brettedkins/2017/09/24/trumps-attacks-on-the-nfl-distract-the-press/#2ba6319d1402

Finch, J. (2009) 'Profile: Sir Alan Sugar.' *The Guardian*, 5 June. Available at: http://www.theguardian.com/politics/2009/jun/05/alan-sugar-profile-peerage-enterprise-tsar

Guthey, E. (2016) 'Don't misunderstand the Donald (Like We Did).' *Television and New Media*, 17 (7), pp. 667–670.

Harkins, S.G., Williams, K.D., and Burger, J. M. (2017) *The Oxford Handbook of Social Influence*. New York: Oxford University Press.

Hendershot, H. (2009) 'Belabored Reality: Making it Work on *The Simple Life* and *Project Runway*.' Eds Murray, S. and Ouellette, L. *Reality TV: Remaking Television* Culture. New York and London: New York University Press, pp. 243–259.

Kelly, L. W. and Boyle, R. (2011) 'Business on Television: Continuity, Change and Risk in the Development of Television's "Business Entertainment Format".' *Television and New Media*, 12 (3), pp. 228–247.

Lichter, S.R., Lichter, L.S., and Rothman, S. (1994) *Prime Time: How TV Portrays American Culture*. Washington, DC: Regnery.

McGee, M. (2005) *Self-Help, Inc: Makeover Culture in American Life*. Oxford: Oxford University Press.

McGinley, A.C. (2009) 'Hillary Clinton, Sarah Palin, and Michelle Obama: Performing Gender, Race, and Class on the Campaign Trail.' *Scholarly Works*. Paper 171.

McRobbie, A. (1998) *British Fashion Design: Rag Trade or Image Industry?* London: Routledge.

Ouellette, L. (2016) 'The Trump Show.' *Television and New Media*, 17 (7), pp. 647–650.

Ouellette, L., and Hay, J. (2008) *Better Living Through Reality TV: Television and Post-Welfare Citizenship*. Malden, MA: Blackwell.

Petersen, A.H. [Online] (2016) 'This is How Much America hates Women.' *BuzzFeed*, 9 November. Available at: http://www.buzzfeed.com/annehelenpetersen/america-hates-women?utm_term=.uuPYX44aR#.pkjxO884n

Reid, E. [Online] (2017) Why Colin Kaepernick and I decided to take a knee.' *New York Times*, 25 September. Available at: https://www.nytimes.com/2017/09/25/opinion/colin-kaepernick-football-protests.html?mcubz=0

Rowe, K.K. (1990) '*Roseanne*: Unruly Woman as Domestic Goddess.' *Screen*, (31) 4, pp. 408–419.

Sandler, E. [Online] (2017) 'Supermodel Teaches At Stanford: How To Learn About Personal Branding With Tyra Banks.' *Forbes*, 12 June. Available at: http://www.forbes.com/sites/emmasandler/2017/06/12/tyra-banks-talks-teaching-at-stanford/#180165ec6965

Sennett, R. (2006) 'What do we mean by talent?' *The Political Quarterly*, 77 (1), pp. 163–167.

Theberge, L.J. (1981) *Crooks, Conmen and Clowns: Businessmen in TV Entertainment*. Washington, DC: Media Institute.

Walkerdine, V. (2003) 'Reclassifying Upward Mobility: Femininity and the Neo-Liberal Subject.' *Gender and Education*, 15 (3), pp. 237–248.

Williams, J. (2004) *Entertaining the Nation: A Social History of British Television*. Stroud: Sutton.

Wollaston, S. (2011) 'TV Review: *Dragons' Den*.' *The Guardian*, 31 July.

CHAPTER 7

Covering Trump: Reflections from the Campaign Trail and the Challenge for Journalism

Peter Geoghegan

In late October 2016, about a week before the US presidential election, I found myself in a wealthy neighbourhood on the outskirts of Cleveland, Ohio. The Buckeye State has long been "the bellwether" in American politics. In the previous 13 presidential elections, Ohioans backed the winning candidate every time.

A few weeks earlier, a colleague and I had decided to drive as far across the United States as we could before the vote itself to try to get a sense of the race on the ground. By the time we reached Cleveland, we had been on the road well over a week. On a bright autumn afternoon, a trio of pensioners was sitting outside a Whole Foods supermarket. Cleveland has a reputation as working class city. But these elderly voters were not veterans of the gas industry or the once sprawling auto factories. One was a retired doctor, the other an accountant, the third a former solicitor.

Cleveland has long been a Democratic stronghold, but all three shook their heads when I asked if they would be voting for Hillary Clinton.

P. Geoghegan (✉)
Open Democracy, Glasgow, UK

© The Author(s) 2019
C. Happer et al. (eds.), *Trump's Media War*,
https://doi.org/10.1007/978-3-319-94069-4_7

"Hillary Clinton supports abortion at 40 weeks," the solicitor told me solemnly.

The doctor nodded his head. "Yeah, they crush the baby's head and suck out the brains with a tube."

On the road I had got used to hearing bizarre factoids presented as truth, particularly where the Democratic nominee was concerned. But I had not heard this one before.

"Abortion at 40 weeks," I replied, clearly taken aback. "But that's a fully formed child. That would be murder."

"It's true," the accountant said, with a rueful shake of his head. He passed me his mobile phone. On the screen was a story from a website I had never heard of, ostensibly confirming Clinton's commitment to the right to abort foetuses at full term. The headline was full of words like "truth" and "baby killer."

"Trump even mentioned it in the debate," the man said, taking the phone back so he could find another story. The next report was from the final presidential debate, which had taken place a couple of weeks earlier. In one exchange during the debate Trump had said Clinton supported ripping babies out of the womb in the ninth month of pregnancy. At the time, journalists pointed at seeming non sequitur as yet another instance of Trump's lack of understanding. I had watched the debate myself but did not even register the abortion comment amid the general hubbub.

The article on the Clevelander's mobile phone reporting Trump's remarks was from a website called the Washington Examiner. The masthead font was the same as the Washington Post. So was the layout. In the news report, Trump's comments were presented as evidence that Clinton supported termination at 40 weeks. For all three men, the Republican nominee was simply backing up a story they had seen floating around their news feeds for months. Trump was validating the news they read, which at the same time validated Trump.

I was only vaguely aware of the Washington Examiner before the US election. The website actually began life as a physical newspaper, as a free tabloid distributed in DC from 2005. It was always conservative but since going online-only in 2013 it tacked further to the right, with some success. During the presidential election, the Washington Examiner was the third most popular right-wing platform on Twitter (Faris et al. 2017).

Ahead of the presidential election, some media outlets declared that Ohio had lost its bellwether status. *The New York Times* said that the state was "decreasingly representative of contemporary America." On

November 8, 2016, Donald Trump won Ohio by more than eight percentage points. This result combined with much narrower wins in key swing states such as Pennsylvania, Michigan, Wisconsin, and Florida was enough for the GOP candidate to take the Electoral College, despite winning almost three million votes fewer than Hillary Clinton.

On Election Day, abortion was the second most searched policy term in connection with Donald Trump, according to analysis from Google News. Abortion was the most common word in searches for Hillary Clinton.

Fear and Disinformation on the Campaign Trail

In the weeks running up to polling day, the widespread view among political commentators on both sides of the Atlantic was that Hillary Clinton would become the 45th president of the United States, possibly by a wide margin. Journalists often noted Trump's historically low approval ratings, but they often ignored the Democratic nominee's own unpopularity. That left Clinton particularly vulnerable to negative media stories that could dent her support. As pollster Nate Silver noted in a series of post-election analyses, "with a large fraction of voters not firmly committed to either candidate—no doubt in part because of the historic unpopularity of both Clinton and Trump—it didn't take much to move them from one candidate to the other, and so news events had more impact on the polls in 2016 than they did in 2012" (Silver 2017a, http://fivethirtyeight.com/features/the-invisible-undecided-voter/).

The most significant of those news events came in late October, when FBI Director James Comey—in an unprecedented letter to Congress—announced that he was examining thousands of Hillary Clinton's emails for possible violations of classification laws. A few weeks earlier, WikiLeaks began publishing thousands of emails from the private email account of the chairman of Hillary Clinton's presidential campaign, John Podesta. Emails had been a recurring theme of the election campaign. The FBI had originally conducted an investigation into Clinton's use of a private email server during her tenure as secretary of state. In July 2016, Comey declared Clinton's handling of classified information "careless" but not criminal. His announcement that he was looking again at Clinton's emails just days before the election was widely perceived as a turning point (for discussion of the gendered nature of these processes see Kelly, this volume).

Many of the late-deciding voters—who would swing the election for Trump—were mainly swayed by "an unfavorable news environment for Clinton in the shadow of the James B. Comey letter to Congress and the Wikileaks dumps" (Silver 2017b).

That's exactly what I found on the road. From the Rust Belt city of Youngstown, to suburban Ohio, to rural West Virginia, the main issue for every voter, of every hue, seemed to be the same—Clinton's emails. "I don't like Trump much, but Clinton is so corrupt. Just look at the thing with her emails," was a common refrain.

Voters were not the only ones talking about emails. Throughout the campaign, the majority of mainstream media coverage largely followed Donald Trump's agenda. "When reporting on Hillary Clinton, coverage primarily focused on the various scandals related to the Clinton Foundation and emails," as Faris, Roberts, Etling, Bourassa, Zuckerman, and Benkle (2017) note. This tendency to represent Clinton as "Crooked Hillary"—Trump's words—was shared across right-wing media, particularly cable news.

As we travelled across the United States, my colleague and I had a single rule: watch Fox News Channel wherever we stayed. So we heard how "the blacks" were going to steal the vote in Philadelphia. How Democrats were fraudulently registering legions of voters. How established media could not be trusted. But more than anything else we heard about emails. Morning, noon, and night, it seemed someone was on Fox News talking about Hillary Clinton and her emails. I never heard anybody ever asked how WikiLeaks acquired the Podesta emails. Subsequent analysis suggests Russian government hackers tricked Podesta into disclosing his Gmail password (Kellner 2017).

Fox News has long been a mainstay of the conspiratorial right. Founded by Rupert Murdoch, Fox News was launched in 1996 with an avowedly conservative agenda. Over time, the station's connection with the further reaches of the Republican Party deepened. The idea that Barack Obama was not born in the United States was regularly propagated on Fox News. (The most famous birther? Donald Trump.)

During the election, Fox took an avowedly pro-Trump line. But it was more than just a sympathetic outlet for the Republican nominee; it was a platform that buttressed the Republican candidate's entire worldview—and that of his supporters. The three elderly gentlemen I met outside that Cleveland supermarket got most of their news from two main sources: social media and Fox News. When I asked voters in places like Ashland—a rural town in the middle of Ohio—where they got their information mainly simply said, 'the internet.'

The internet was not a bi-partisan news space. While centre-left outlets, such as CNN and the *New York Times* dominated the liberal media ecosystem, the most popular outfits for Republican voters were extremely conservative. Popular websites such as Breitbart and InfoWars often displayed an active disregard for the central tenets of traditional reporting. As Faris, Roberts, Etling, Bourassa, Zuckerman, and Benkle (2017) argue in a paper entitled "Partisanship, Propaganda and Disinformation: Online Media and the 2016 US Presidential Election," "traditional media accountability mechanisms—for example, fact-checking sites, media watchdog groups, and cross-media criticism—appear to have wielded little influence on the insular conservative media sphere. Claims aimed for "internal" consumption within the right-wing media ecosystem were more extreme, less internally coherent, and appealed more to the "paranoid style" of American politics than claims intended to affect mainstream media reporting."

Right-wing news sites were not only adept at spreading propaganda; they often did so while looking *like* traditional news outlets. Telling the Washington Examiner and the *Washington Post* apart is not always easy for inconsistent news consumers, especially if both look so similar online, especially mobile phones. Media literacy, and the lack of it, is part of the story of media coverage of the 2016 election. So was the proliferation of what is often called "fake news"—an unhelpful catchall term but which must include the consciously inaccurate information spread online that was, more often, favourable to Trump and damaging to Clinton.

But the story of Donald Trump and the media during the presidential campaign is more than just the white heat of technology put to nefarious ends. If it was the internet that won it, why was Clinton unable to win that fight? Or at least put up a better contest? Let us look again at our Cleveland pensioners. All three said they did not trust the media. That view is hardly unusual, on both sides of the Atlantic (see also Torrance this volume). In 2016, just 32 per cent of Americans told Gallup they have faith in the media. Among Republicans, that figure was just 14 per cent.

This lack of trust in media is not unexplainable. Many mainstream outlets in the United States—as in the United Kingdom—have been guilty of what could be most kindly described as selective biases, most glaringly for some in the run-up to the invasion of Iraq in 2003. The reliance on insider briefings and anonymous sources has often contributed to a sense—rightly or wrongly—that mainstream media fits the facts to suit an agenda. This disenchantment with established media was evident not just on the right but also among some supporters of prospective Democratic nominee Bernie Sanders.

At the same time, Trump and his boosters were able to take advantage of media conventions around the framing of narratives to gain credence for their agenda. Just as in the United Kingdom, traditional US outlets frequently relied on "he said, she said" stories during the campaign. Headlines like "Trump says build a wall, Clinton disagrees" were common. As George Lakoff argues, this approach to reporting makes it relatively easy to capture a debate by framing a narrative, even if what is being reported has little factual basis, or is even outright untrue. In the wake of Trump's election, a number of established media outlets changed their approach, actively calling out the president's dissembling. (*The New York Times* even has a page called "Trump's Lies" that it regularly adds to.) But in the weeks and months before polling day, almost all mainstream media still cleaved to the "Trump claims"-style of reporting, which allowed the candidate and his supporters to set the news agenda regardless of the veracity of the claims being made.

Right-wing activists were also able to take advantage of traditional media framing to gain credibility for their messages. This was most obvious in the case of a book entitled *Clinton Cash: The Untold Story of How and Why Foreign Governments and Businesses Helped Make Bill and Hillary Rich*. Published in May 2015, *Clinton Cash* was written by Peter Schweizer, who at the time was described as "Breitbart Senior Editor at Large," and focused on the Clinton Foundation's financial dealings. The book's claims were widely covered in the US media, most prominently in the *New York Times* which, in an advance of publication, published an extensive piece headlined "Cash Flowed to Clinton Foundation Amid Russian Uranium Deal." Reports of the revelations in *Clinton Cash* in the mainstream media opened up Breitbart's agenda to a whole new audience that would not normally read the site or listen to talk radio. Also, alt-right outlets such as Breitbart were then able to report these anti-Clinton stories in exaggerated ways but link to original coverage in respected titles such as the *New York Times*. It was no coincidence that many of the main lines of these stories—Clinton's financial probity, her links to Wall Street—became the main thrust of the Trump campaign. The narrative was framed.

But mainstream media often did little investigation into the background of *Clinton Cash* itself. The research for the book was published by the

Government Accountability Institute (GAI), a body founded by Schweizer, the book's author, and Steve Bannon, then head of Breitbart and later part of Trump's inner circle. The GAI was funded by Robert Mercer, an investor in Breitbart and a super PAC donor to the Trump campaign (Faris et al. 2017). Rather than publish these juicy stories on Breitbart—which would be the traditional media approach—Bannon brokered a series of the deals with the *News York Times*, the *Washington Post*, and Fox News for exclusive access. These stories in established media leant credibility to the book's claims, even if the underlying evidence was often less than watertight. Despite its bombastic headline about Clinton's links to a Russian uranium deal, the *New York Times*' story based on Schweizer's book, for example, acknowledged that "whether the donations played any role in the approval of the uranium deal is unknown." Nevertheless, the story—originally published in April 2015—became one of the *New York Times*' most popular on Twitter during the summer of 2016. The article was also heavily shared in the right-wing media sphere on sites such as Breitbart, Free Beacon, the Washington Examiner, and Fox News itself (Faris et al. 2017).

Clinton Cash and the reporting of the Clinton Foundation "represents a classic instance of a disinformation and propaganda campaign mediated through a network of allied media sources" (Faris et al. 2017). The story did not depend wholly on invented stories but rather mixed "bits and pieces of facts, often anchored in partial readings of concrete documents that lend validity to the claims, with false insinuations, leaps of logic, and flat-out false statements. The influence of the propaganda depends on repetition and validation within a network of sites" (Faris et al. 2017). Major right-wing media such as Fox News and Breitbart often linked to smaller, less well-known sites' coverage of the Clinton Foundation, building repetition and enhancing the status of obscure right-wing outlets. Faris, Roberts, Etling, Bourassa, Zuckerman, and Benkle (2017) term this process "network propaganda." In effect, Schweizer and Bannon had hacked traditional media outlets to gain traction for the decidedly partial claims made in *Clinton Cash*. This was achieved not by computer hackers but by taking advantage of established mainstream media norms to produce propaganda effects.

Such disinformation can have profound effects on voters, effects that traditional journalists often struggle to pick up because they cannot even know what they should be looking for. When Trump talked about abortion in the ninth month in a live presidential debate, reporters scratched their heads and decried the latest Trump "gaffe." But the millions who had read dubious stories about Clinton's support for killing young children nodded alone. What Trump was saying confirmed what they had read online.

A Media Problem Bigger than Trump

Framing a narrative alone does not win an election, or even a media election battle.

Trump was also able to take advantage of systemic problems within the American news industry, particularly in print. The decline of the traditional US metro papers over the last decade has been stark. Newspapers such as the *Baltimore Sun*, the *Cleveland Plain Dealer*, or the *Philadelphia Inquirer* once had a national reach and a formidable roster of beat reporters. Now most struggle to survive. Local newspapers were often too resource-strapped to commission the kind of in-depth swing state polls that could have captured the micro-moves that eventually won Trump the presidency (Silver 2017c).

At the same time, national titles often failed to pick up on the showing political mood on the ground—rather than visit, say, Youngstown, Ohio, on an average weekday, as we did, the press pack often arrived only for political rallies. Such theatre makes easy copy but rarely elucidates the reality of daily life. As readers see themselves reflected less and less in the stories that they read, trust in the media drains even further. The insider nature of so much political reporting only adds to this disconnect. As Nate Silver notes, the day after Trump's election, *New York Times* Executive Editor Dean Baquet said that the biggest flaw in his paper's 2016 coverage was in not having enough reporters "on the road, out in the country, talking to different kinds of people."

The media's tendency to privilege voices from within the Beltway, and to focus on political machinations rather than personal stories, predated Trump's candidacy. They also feed into a wider problem for media, and for politics—how to engage with the lived complexities of what Frederic Jamieson calls "late capitalism." Somewhat ironically, journalists should have been perfectly placed to understand the economic insecurity that underpinned at least some of the Trump vote, particularly in Rust Belt states such as Ohio and Michigan. Over the last 40 years, about as many journalists have lost their jobs as coal miners. But journalists have often struggled to see their travails as emblematic of society-wide economic shifts. The cost-cutting, the endless rounds of voluntary redundancy, are blamed—often correctly—on poor management from faceless head offices. But journalists are at the coal face—metaphor intended—of what was a pivotal issue of the election, the death of the American middle class.

Thomas Frank touched on the failure of journalists to see their industry's problems as part of a wider economic insecurity in a long piece in Harper's, criticising the *Washington Post*'s overwhelmingly negative coverage of Democratic challenger Bernie Sanders. Frank's words are worth quoting at length:

> ...no group knows the story of the dying middle class more intimately than journalists. So why do the people at the very top of this profession identify themselves with the smug, the satisfied, the powerful? Why would a person working in a moribund industry compose a paean to the Wall Street bailouts? Why would someone like *Post* opinion writer Stephen Stromberg drop megatons of angry repudiation on a certain Vermont senator for his "outrageous negativity about the state of the country"? For the country's journalists—Stromberg's colleagues, technically speaking—that state is pretty goddamned negative. (Frank 2016)

The reporters covering the presidential election were disproportionately well-educated, liberal, white and living in major cities. Many would have known nobody who intended to vote Trump. I spent the days immediately before the presidential election in Washington, DC, and New York City. There I visited colleagues in some of the famous news outlets in the world. Nobody I met talked about who would win. Everyone assumed a Clinton victory, to the point where they seemed bored with the campaign. Over a beer in Manhattan, a *New York Times* editor did, however, ask, "What's it like in the country? Sitting in my office I really don't know what's really going on."

The scope for traditional media to influence elections through their political preferences is often overstated. The oft-repeated assumption that it was "*the Sun* wot won it" for the Conservatives in the 1992 general election has been called into question (Curtice 1999). During the 2016 US presidential election, 59 major newspapers endorsed a candidate. Only two backed Donald Trump (Silver 2017d). And yet Trump was—and is—very much a creation of the contemporary media landscape. A businessman whose only truly successful venture has been his own brand (for a fuller discussion of this see Kelly, this volume). A man more famous for his bouffant hair than his policies becomes a reality-TV star and then president.

Trump also understands the demands of modern, 24–7 media in a way that arguably no other politician has. During the 2016 campaign, Trump dominated media coverage—even though much of this reporting was critical. Throughout his candidacy, Trump was remarkably successful at grabbing free media coverage, a skill honed during his time as a real estate developer in New York. In March 2016, the *New York Times* reported that Trump had earned close to $2 billion worth of media attention. More than six months before Election Day, Trump had already garnered twice the value of the most expensive presidential campaign in history—and had only spent a fraction of that sum himself. In all, Trump only spent $600 million on his campaign—barely half of what Clinton burned through on the road to defeat. This discrepancy was obvious on the ground. Save the occasional Trump window sticker or Correx board, there really was no sign of a Trump campaign in the weeks I spent driving around the Midwest. In Bethlehem, the largest town in Northampton County, Pennsylvania, the Clinton campaign was so large that they had to set up a second office. There was no Trump equivalent save the odd garden sign declaring "Make American Great Again." In Bethlehem, I spent an afternoon with Clinton campaigners, many of whom had volunteered from out of state. They chatted freely but when I asked if I could interview them on mic they demurred. "We would have to check that with head office," one told me. "We could let you know in a few days." By then I would be long gone, but the accusations that Clinton had a run an overly centralised campaign online and off remain (Enli 2017). Northampton County was one of the top ten swing counties in the whole of the United States. In 2008 and 2012, Northampton backed Obama. But in 2016, the county voted Trump by a margin of over 10,000.

Conclusion

The US media has learnt lessons from the 2016 presidential campaign. In the wake of Trump's victory, quality titles such as the *New Yorker*, the *New York Times* and the *Washington Post* have produced some remarkable, in-depth reporting. Reports from the flyover states—particularly the white working class posthumously identified as the secret of Trump's unexpected success—have abounded. But Trump still sets the news agenda with his Twitter account—regardless of the veracity of his comments.

In office, Trump has called the media the "enemy of the American people" (Kellner 2017). Once venerable outlets such as CNN have been dismissed as "fake news." Trump's public declarations—often riddled with factual inaccuracies and outright lies—have given rise to a frightening new vista of deception as an emerging trend in American politics and public discourse, with potentially seismic repercussions. As journalist and prominent public radio host Brooke Gladstone writes, "It is not the lies that pose the existential danger to democracy. It's the lying, the kind of thoroughgoing lying that gives rise to a whole new reality or, better still, to no reality at all" (Gladstone 2017).

The challenge for professional journalists in the age of Trump—and Brexit—is to perforate the echo chambers that have built up in the digital space. Analysis of the US presidential election has found that the news sphere was dominated by media characterised as centre-left or far-right. The centre-right—once the bastion of the Republican Party—barely got a look in (Faris et al. 2017). At the same time, partisans, particularly within the Trump campaign, were able to effectively game traditional media outfits to run certain storylines. Post-hoc journalistic excuses that "we were only reporting claims" fail to acknowledge the power that framing narratives has on audiences. Facts don't matter, stories do.

Stripped of legitimacy by the Commander-in-Chief, and many others, the media faces a challenge to be heard. A succession of revelations about Trump's ties to Russia and his clientelistic White House administration has done little to blunt the president's appeal. Around four-fifths of Republican voters still back Trump.

I haven't kept in touch with the three old guys I met in Cleveland, but I am still in contact with some of the Trump supporters I met in October and November. All have kept the faith. "The media are out to get Trump," one wrote to me about six months into the new president's term in office. "But they won't succeed. Trump's too smart for the media."

References

Curtice, J. (1999) Was it the Sun wot won it again? The influence of newspapers in the 1997 election campaign. http://citeseerx.ist.psu.edu/viewdoc/downlo ad?doi=10.1.1.570.64&rep=rep1&type=pdf (accessed June 5th 2018).

Faris, R. M. et al (2017) 'Partisanship, Propaganda, and Disinformation: Online Media and the 2016 U.S. Presidential Election'. Berkman Klein Center for Internet & Society Research Paper. https://dash.harvard.edu/bitstream/ handle/1/33759251/2017-08_electionReport_0.pdf?sequence=9 (accessed 4th June 2018)

Frank, T. (2016, November) 'The media's extermination of Bernie Sanders, and real reform', Harper's Magazine. https://harpers.org/archive/2016/11/swat-team-2/7/ (accessed 5th June 2018).

Gladstone, B. (2017) 'Why Trump Lies', Slate. http://www.slate.com/articles/news_and_politics/politics/2017/05/why_trump_lies_it_s_not_to_hide_the_truth_it_s_to_alter_reality.html?via=gdpr-consent (accessed 5th June 2018).

Enli, G. (2017) Twitter as arena for the authentic outsider: exploring the social media campaigns of Trump and Clinton in the 2016 US presidential election. European Journal of Communication, 32 (1), 50–61.

Kellner, D. (2017) The American Horror Show: Election 2016 and the Ascendency of Donald J. Trump. Rotterdam, The Netherlands: Sense Publishers.

Silver, N. (2017a) 'The Invisible Undecided Voter', FiveThirtyEight. http://fivethirtyeight.com/features/the-invisible-undecided-voter/ (accessed 4th June 2018).

Silver, N. (2017b) 'The Comey Letter Probably Cost Clinton The Election', FiveThirtyEight. https://fivethirtyeight.com/features/the-comey-letter-probably-cost-clinton-the-election/ (accessed 6th June 2018).

Silver, N. (2017c) 'Ohio Was A Bellwether After All', FiveThirtyEight. https://fivethirtyeight.com/features/ohio-was-a-bellwether-after-all/ (accessed 6th June 2018).

Silver, N (2017d) 'There Really Was A Liberal Media Bubble', FiveThirtyEight. https://fivethirtyeight.com/features/there-really-was-a-liberal-media-bubble/ (accessed 5th June 2018).

CHAPTER 8

The Scottish Provenance of Trump's Approach to the Media

David Torrance

INTRODUCTION

The day before the 2017 US inauguration, I found myself in Washington DC's Arlington Cemetery. After joining the expected throng at the grave of the 35th president, I fell in with a smaller crowd which had gathered further up the hill. It became clear this was in anticipation of seeing the 45th president (elect) drive by en route to a traditional pre-inaugural wreath-laying ceremony. Sure enough, the motorcade swept by and he waved, reducing those present to near apoplexy.

Noticing that I hadn't joined in, a man standing behind me asked, a little suspiciously, if I was a 'Trump man'. Unthinkingly I said no, I was a journalist. He looked away with chilling disdain. 'From the UK!' I added, pathetically. With that, I scuttled off, keen not to experience any more anti-media hostility, although I'd encountered plenty during a six-week tour of the US prior to the 2016 presidential election, and indeed would again at the inauguration itself.

During that extraordinary political 'fall', I'd got used to hearing pejorative references to the 'mainstream media' (MSM), the 'failing' *New York Times* and the 'Clinton News Network' (CNN), and also became conscious of

D. Torrance (✉)
London, UK

© The Author(s) 2019
C. Happer et al. (eds.), *Trump's Media War*,
https://doi.org/10.1007/978-3-319-94069-4_8

low- (and high-) level conspiracy theories and, of course, numerous examples of what was becoming known as 'fake news'. Often, I would speak to American friends (and more cerebral acquaintances) who assumed I'd be shocked by the deteriorating public discourse and constant war of attrition between politicians and journalists.

In fact, I found much of it familiar, not only from the UK's European Referendum that'd taken place a few months before but also from the Scottish independence debate of 2011–14. It struck me that while the protagonists in each case differed on points of policy, the *approach* was remarkably similar, particularly when it came to ad hominem attacks on the 'mainstream media'.

But while scholars and commentators have frequently drawn a line between Brexit and Trump (see Mair et al. 2017) few, if any, have traced that back to Scotland, although Ian Katz, the editor of BBC *Newsnight*, rightly believed the 'howls of outrage from first SNP supporters, then Corbynistas, over alleged BBC bias' had anticipated 'the rising anti-media mood' we later saw in the US (Katz 2017; also Geoghegan this volume).

BACKGROUND

There were, of course, political connections between all three. The first to engage with Donald Trump was the then First Minister Jack McConnell on a visit to New York City in 2005. It was at that point the future President told McConnell and representatives from Scottish Development International about his intention to invest in a multimillion-pound golf and leisure complex in Scotland. 'In the early years, successive Scottish governments were ardent suitors', observed journalist Dani Garavelli, 'constantly cajoling and flattering, bending the knee and maybe even the rules, in the hope that Trump would bestow his blessings on them' (Garavelli 2015).

Robert Gordon University gave Trump an honorary degree and the Scottish Government appointed him a 'GlobalScot', while Alex Salmond first met the Trump a year before he succeeded McConnell as First Minister, at the 'Dressed to Kilt' fashion show, again in Trump's home city of New York. But it was a little later the Salmond/Trump relationship reached its apex, when a committee of Aberdeenshire Council voted to reject Trump's £750 million leisure complex plan. The Scottish Government then took the unprecedented step of 'calling in' an application Trump had made clear he would not appeal, with ministers granting approval for construction work to begin (on a Site of Special Scientific Interest) a year later.

What happened next has been well documented, particularly by documentary-maker Anthony Baxter (see Baxter 2012). In short, Trump bulldozed the beach and harassed local residents, calling farmer Michael Forbes (who refused to move) 'an embarrassment to Scotland' and someone who 'lives like a pig'. If Alex Salmond, now First Minister and a local MSP, considered this or several other incidents unacceptable, then he kept such concerns to himself. Only when the Scottish Government accepted plans for an 11-turbine wind farm off the north-east coast near the Menie development did the relationship turn sour. Trump turned against Salmond, accusing him, ironically, of destroying the environment (Schreckinger 2016).

For the next few years, in interviews and in private correspondence, Trump—well-known for harbouring long-standing grudges—rarely missed an opportunity to denounce 'Mad Alex' (Brooks 2016). In the US, meanwhile, he had lent public legitimacy to the 'birther movement' (which doubted Barack Obama's birth on US soil) and generally geared up to launch his bid for the White House. Still he remained a 'GlobalScot', despite a petition by Scottish Green Party co-leader Patrick Harvie to have him removed. 'Perhaps the SNP's reluctance to dump Trump', speculated journalist Dani Garavelli, could 'be explained by Salmond's attraction to men with big wallets and bigger egos; men like Rupert Murdoch, Brian Souter and Fred Goodwin, who can prove powerful allies, but come with baggage' (Garavelli 2015).

ALEX SALMOND AFTER 2011

Following the 2011 Scottish Parliament elections, meanwhile, Alex Salmond began to display proto-Trumpian characteristics now he led a majority, rather than a minority, administration. Having impressed even his critics with an ecumenical, statesmanlike approach to politics between 2007 and 2011, the Scottish National Party (SNP) leader reverted to the previous form, a highly partisan, shoot-from-the-hip, take-no-prisoners approach.

That summer, for example, was dominated by a series of attacks on the authority of the UK Supreme Court and the competence of its two Scottish judges after it and they ruled that the Scottish legal system had twice breached the European Convention on Human Rights in significant criminal cases. Justice Secretary Kenny MacAskill suggested that most

Supreme Court Justices' only knowledge of Scotland came through attending the annual Edinburgh festivals, while Salmond spoke of Scots law being replaced 'by Lord Hope's law', a personal attack on a widely respected Scottish legal figure (Carrell 2011).

The purpose of the attacks was mostly likely fears that the UK Supreme Court might, in future, overrule Scottish Parliament attempts to introduce a bill to hold an independence referendum in Edinburgh, legislation that would be ultra vires under the 1998 Scotland Act. Thus, the First Minister intended to delegitimise the Supreme Court, framing it as an enemy of Scottish interests and, of course, independence.

When this row eventually died down, Salmond then launched a further series of ad hominem attacks—often from the Scottish Parliament chamber—on public figures, including the economist John McLaren and Dave Scott, head of the anti-bigotry organisation Nil by Mouth. Both had expressed (legitimate) concerns about Scottish Government statistics or legislation, but were denigrated on the tribal basis that they had once been associated with the Scottish Labour Party.

The deteriorating tone was reflected on social media, hardly surprising considering Salmond—SNP leader and First Minister—had given the nod to an enthusiastic group of Nationalists that such behaviour was acceptable. The outgoing Scottish Labour leader Iain Gray even claimed the SNP had injected what he called a 'vile' poison into Scottish politics, warning those jostling to succeed him that

> you will be attacked, you will be smeared, you will be lied about, you will be threatened. The cybernats and the bedsit bloggers will call you traitor, quisling, lapdog and worse. They will question your appearance, your integrity and your sexuality. They will drag your family and your faith into the lies and the vitriol. It will be worse if you are a woman. (Gray 2011)

Indeed, feelings often ran high, particularly after 2012, when the Scottish and UK governments formally agreed an independence referendum would take place in the autumn of 2014. In mid-2013 someone spray-painted the word 'TRAITORS' on the *Scotsman* newspaper's Edinburgh headquarters (HQ), while Salmond began personally to attack certain news outlets. When, for example, *The Economist* depicted Scotland as 'Skintland' in an irreverent cover story (the article itself was more serious), the First Minister stormed that it would 'rue the day'. 'This is Unionism boiled down to its essence', he added, 'and stuck on a front page for every community in Scotland to see their sneering condescension' (hereafter all references, unless otherwise noted, from Torrance 2015).

This was a significant departure, for since becoming leader of the SNP (for the first time) back in 1990, not only had Salmond made a point of cultivating the media, but he had generally enjoyed positive write-ups in the Scottish and UK press, journalists and commentators admiring his turn of phrase, tactical prowess and eye for a potential headline. Broadcast journalists even got used to the clearly self-confident SNP leader turning up at TV studios on the off chance they might require a comment on the story of the day.

The shift, therefore, seems to have been a deliberate strategy on Salmond's part, one that had its origins in the first elections to the Scottish Parliament in 1999. Then, frustrated by a lack of media support for the SNP, the party had attempted to bypass the press by publishing its own 'newspaper'—*Scotland's Voice*—although that had ended up being little more than a poorly produced (not to mention costly) propaganda sheet. Fifteen years later, however, the means of bypassing the Fourth Estate was much more effective, a combination of social media, sympathetic bloggers and, crucially, a high-profile campaign of delegitimisation.

There was undoubtedly also a personal element. Salmond had been irritated by Freedom of Information requests from certain newspapers, including one concerning a trip to Chicago during the 2012 Ryder Cup during which the First Minister and his wife had accumulated a £3000 bill at the five-star Peninsula Hotel. This Salmond dismissed as 'ridiculous frippery', although typically he went to extraordinary (costly, and ultimately unsuccessful) lengths to prevent such information from reaching the public domain.

Naturally, once an independence referendum had been confirmed, this amount of scrutiny, not only of Salmond and the Scottish Government but the SNP's 'prospectus' for independence, significantly increased, and in response certain newspapers, particularly the *Scotsman*, and broadcasters, most notably the BBC, found themselves at the receiving end of First Ministerial broadsides and even more vitriolic online commentary. This reached its height in 2014, as the referendum on 18 September approached.

In May that year, when the anti-European United Kingdom Independence Party (UKIP) won one of Scotland's five European Parliament seats, Salmond (whose party had expected to gain a third MEP) blamed the BBC for having 'beamed' UKIP's message 'into Scotland'. The *British* Broadcasting Corporation was thereafter a frequent target. Asked directly if its reporting was biased, the First Minister replied, 'Yes, absolutely, of course it is…but they don't realise they're biased. It's the unconscious bias, which is the most extraordinary thing of all.' Some academics, for example John Robertson, attempted to quantify this perceived bias, although the methodology rested upon the questionable premise that the 'Yes' and 'No' campaigns each produced an equal number of credible news stories worthy of 'positive' coverage (see Robertson 2016, 59–69).

And when the BBC was not being 'biased' it was, in Salmond's view, guilty of 'incompetence', with Salmond repeatedly telephoning its director-general Lord (Tony) Hall to complain of its 'near-colonial attitude', or it being 'a disgrace to public service broadcasting'. It was, Salmond told Hall in one exchange, 'difficult to tell where the network BBC stops and the NO campaign begins'. In his referendum diary, Salmond acknowledged that such a comment would not achieve anything, but he 'really enjoyed saying it'.

In retrospect, Salmond was displaying a very Trump-like obsession with, and sensitivity about, what he took to calling—like the future president—the 'mainstream media'. He believed the *Scotsman*, as he wrote in his referendum diary, was 'on a suicide mission', *The Times* regularly displayed 'anti-Scottish bias' (pointing this out to its editor gave him 'considerable pleasure'), while he was incredulous when the *Sunday Post* splashed on another hotel expenses story. 'It would be possible to meet company CEOs or international dignitaries at the local Holiday Inn', he mused indignantly, 'but I'm not sure how well that would work for Scotland's benefit'.

Salmond's referendum diary also recorded for posterity his attempt to offer a young *Telegraph* journalist 'a packet of liquorice allsorts for good attendance at every press event'. When, inexplicably in Salmond's eyes, Ben Riley-Smith took 'exception' to such a condescending gesture, Salmond put his 'tetchiness' down to low morale at the *Telegraph*, which was, after all, 'a subdivision of the NO campaign' (Salmond 2015a).

At the same time, and again anticipating Trump's contradictory approach, Salmond attempted to play down the Fourth Estate's importance in political terms. 'If having the bulk of press on side was a determination of success in elections', Salmond had remarked in July 2013, 'then I wouldn't be First Minister', a comment that conveniently ignored the support he had enjoyed in 2007, and particularly 2011, from several Scottish newspapers and columnists.

The final few weeks of the referendum campaign saw a further intensification of Salmond's attacks on the media and individual journalists. Followed a televised debate in which Salmond was widely seen to have beaten the former Chancellor Alistair Darling, leader of the 'Better Together' No campaign, the SNP leader resented repeated questioning from 'metropolitan' journalists about his proposals for a currency union with the rest of the UK should Scotland become independent. Sky News' Faisal Islam, for example, was told he shouldn't 'play at being Alistair Darling' or 'impersonate the No campaign' (Johnson 2014). Other reporters, usually from the BBC, got similar treatment for asking perfectly legitimate questions.

The nadir came during a press conference in Edinburgh for international journalists (though, unusually, 'Yes' campaigners filled many of the seats) a week before polling day. Nick Robinson, the BBC's political editor, pressed Salmond about the threat of Scotland-based banks to move south should a majority of voters back independence, and was accused of 'heckling' by the First Minister (Robinson was, in turn, heckled by the non-journalists present).

Robinson's broadcast report wasn't perfect—it implied Salmond hadn't answered his questions—but the response from certain Yes supporters illustrated how febrile the atmosphere had become. In the following days, several hundred gathered outside BBC Scotland's Pacific Quay HQ to protest at the broadcaster's 'bias' in general and Robinson in particular, demanding he be sacked. Strikingly, when asked to comment, Salmond appeared to endorse the protest, which reports suggested many journalists had found intimidating. 'We must allow people to express a view in a peaceful and joyous fashion', he said, adding that the referendum had been 'a joyous empowering campaign; a lesson, a model in the exercise of true democracy'. Significantly, the Robinson affair became widely cited as conclusive evidence of BBC 'bias', although of course it took place long after such accusations began to enter political discourse.

The Corporation insisted it had been 'balanced and impartial' in its reporting while Paul Holleran, the National Union of Journalists' Scottish organiser, spoke of his members having been 'on the receiving end of a range of abuse and intolerance on social media, some of which has been logged and may be reported to the police'. 'Robust debate is fine', he added. 'Pointing out when journalists get their facts wrong is expected and welcomed. But NUJ members believe in a free press, a fair media, with journalists allowed to do their jobs free of intimidation. What is totally unacceptable is the use of threats of violence' (Carrell 2014). At the Yes campaign's eve-of-poll rally in Perth, meanwhile, Robinson was booed like a pantomime villain when he was sighted standing on the venue's balcony.

At that point, Salmond, the SNP, and broader independence 'movement' believed it was on the cusp of a historic victory, but it was not to be. Scots self-determined in favour of the Union by 55–45 per cent (on an unprecedentedly high turnout) and the First Minister announced his intention to step down. Even his resignation statement at his official residence provoked accusations that certain journalists had been purposefully excluded from the press conference, although Salmond and his aides strenuously denied this, citing lack of space. 'If you look at the people that were there', Salmond commented later, 'you'll find plenty of candidates who would not be among my journalist of the year'.

THE REFERENDUM AND AFTER

Having appeared to give credence to some popular Nationalist conspiracy theories during the campaign—'secret' oil fields, for example, under the River Clyde—in the wake of the referendum result, Alex Salmond continued to lash out, telling the BBC's Andrew Neil that certain voters had been 'misled', 'gulled', and effectively 'tricked' into voting No by the promise of more powers for Holyrood. And even before a cross-party commission (which included the SNP) had been convened to deliver that 'Vow', Salmond accused the Unionist parties of 'cavilling and reneging' on their pre-referendum Vow.

This curious behaviour continued over the next few weeks. Salmond took the unusual step of attacking a commentator in the letters pages of the *Herald* (this writer, as it happens) while also phoning the BBC's Morning Call programme and getting into an on-air argument with local councillor Jim Gifford about councils pursuing old Poll Tax debts. To admirers this was 'vintage' Salmond, although to others it sounded like hectoring populism.

Over the next few years, Salmond—after May 2015 back at Westminster as the MP for Gordon—would return again and again to accusations of BBC 'bias'. One year on from the referendum, for example, he declared that this had been a 'significant factor' in the referendum result, blasting the BBC for what he called 'institutional bias'. The Nick Robinson incident, meanwhile, was reignited when the now former political editor commented that protests outside BBC Scotland had been 'Putin-like'. Responding in his column for the *Courier* newspaper, the former First Minister said the BBC's coverage of the referendum had been 'a disgrace', while Robinson ought to be 'both embarrassed and ashamed' of his own reporting (Salmond 2015b).

In early 2017, meanwhile, Salmond accused what he called the 'yoon media' ('yoon' had become pejorative shorthand for 'Unionist') of presenting an 'alternative reality' to Scots following a row about business rates. Commenting in a video blog, he seemed conscious that his language and arguments might invite comparison with his old sparring partner Donald Trump:

> Now, I won't call it the fake facts media, or the fake media, or the alternative facts media, because that would be to quote the President of the United States, and you don't have to be a racist or a misogynist to know when stories are being distorted. So I like to call it in Scotland the yoon media. That's that element of the Scottish press who interprets any story, any issue, and makes it an attempt to either attack or discredit the SNP...So it does provide a fantastic example of, not what we're going to call fake facts in Scotland, but the alternative reality which is presented by elements of the yoon media. (Gordon 2017a)

On that occasion, a Scottish Government source made it clear that Nicola Sturgeon, who had succeeded Salmond as First Minister in late 2014, did not believe there was a 'yoon media', and indeed she went to great lengths to take a different approach to the press than her increasingly belligerent predecessor. Where Salmond attacked Nick Robinson, Sturgeon invited him for dinner, while at SNP events the new SNP leader diligently avoided invitations from activists to echo Salmond's accusations of BBC 'bias'. Sure, she might not like what some journalists wrote, she often admitted, but in her view a free press was central to any democratic society. The new First Minister even expressed doubts as to the reliability of increasingly popular online news outlets (Torrance 2016).

With the Scottish Government's record under heightened scrutiny and the SNP, after a decade in which it had dominated Scottish politics, beginning to lose support, in tweets, interviews, and one-on-one encounters, Sturgeon increasingly questioned independent experts and even the methodology used by bodies like Audit Scotland. As the *Herald* journalist Tom Gordon observed, 'cynical Trump-lite trash' was 'becoming the norm' for an increasingly tired Scottish Government (Gordon 2017b). Appearing at the Edinburgh International Book Festival, Sturgeon admitted to experiencing 'a little bit of envy' as she watched President Trump shout 'wheesht, fake news' at reporters in the US. 'I have fantasies', she joked, 'about doing that at press conferences' (Sturgeon 2017a).

A SHARED APPROACH

For more than a year after the European Referendum of 2016—which itself had seen 'Leave' campaigners mount attacks on the BBC and other 'liberal' 'mainstream media' outlets—there existed a curious alliance between Scottish Nationalists, Brexiteers, and, latterly, supporters of Trump, all of whom believed that much of the media was irredeemably hostile to their respective political projects.

A few weeks in the summer of 2017 neatly illustrated the overlap. Across the Atlantic, President Trump appalled even some of his most loyal supporters with a series of intemperate (and misogynistic) tweets directed at critical journalists, while in the UK the Cabinet minister Andrea Leadsom responded to some difficult questioning from the BBC's *Newsnight* programme by telling an astonished interviewer that it 'would be helpful if broadcasters were willing to be a bit patriotic' (Leadsom 2017). Shortly after that, the International Trade Secretary Liam Fox accused the BBC of failing to report Brexit 'positively' while Alex Salmond, uncharacteristically quiet since losing his Commons seat at the 2017 general election, accused the BBC and 'deadwood press' of wanting Scotland to enter recession so it could attack the SNP (Schofield 2017).

A common theme among this trio of attackers was nationalism, be it American, British, or Scottish. This is not to say that all three posited an identical political agenda—far from it—but the driving force in each case was a deep-rooted belief in national superiority and the necessity of constitutional change in order to protect and extend it. Thus, a critical media was framed as unpatriotic or 'anti' Scottish, British, or American. In an otherwise thoughtful book called *Demanding Democracy: The Case for a Scottish Media*, Christopher Silver returned again and again to the idea that Scotland lacked its 'own' media, much of its ownership and editorial control resting either in London or overseas. So, during the independence referendum campaign, instead of 'the Scottish press playing an active role in the development of the independence cause', it 'sacrificed much of its credibility and influence, not on the altar of Scottish statehood, but in an effort to preserve union' (Silver 2015).

This, of course, confused journalists with political campaigners, while the oft-stated Silver critique contained a multitude of contradictions. 'Bias' had been redefined to describe any piece of news or commentary, no matter how strong its empirical basis, that cast doubt on the desirability of Scottish independence, while certain outlets were somehow regarded as beyond reproach. Vehemently pro-independence websites such as Wings over Scotland, for example, were rarely criticised (even by Scottish Government ministers) despite lacking any balancing pro-Union voices. While the *Scotsman* and *Herald* newspapers, which both hosted a balance of pro- and anti-independence voices, were dismissed as 'biased', pro-independence titles such as the *Sunday Herald* and *The National,* which carried only sympathetic columnists, were generally seen as fair and balanced.

Like Trump, Alex Salmond's approach was both hypocritical and inconsistent. He spent years, for example, cultivating the controversial media mogul Rupert Murdoch in the hope that the Scottish edition of his *Sun* newspaper would support not only the SNP (as it did in the 2011 and 2016 Holyrood elections) but also independence in 2014. Even when it did not, instead adopting a neutral stance, Salmond rarely criticised it (though many Nationalists disliked the *Scottish Sun* intensely), while Murdoch's publishing empire paid him a handsome advance for his poorly-received referendum diary.

Salmond also had no qualms about accepting a generous weekly rate to write a column in the *Press and Journal* and *Courier* newspapers, which he presumably exempted from the 'deadwood press'. Similarly, on returning to the House of Commons in May 2015, LBC—presumably not part of London's 'metropolitan' media—provided the former First Minister with his own weekly radio phone-in slot, something upgraded to a three-hour *Salmond on Sunday* show in the autumn of 2017. A few months later, meanwhile, Salmond attracted widespread criticism after unveiling a weekly television show on the Kremlin-backed RT (formerly Russia Today). Even his successor, Nicola Sturgeon, made it clear that 'his choice of channel would not have been [her] choice' (Sturgeon 2017b).

Indeed, in an unconscious echo of President Trump's pre-presidency showbiz career (he presented *The Apprentice* for 14 seasons in the US), out of Parliament following the June 2017 general election, Salmond turned performer, presenting himself 'unleashed' at the Edinburgh Fringe Festival during August 2017. This, too, provided an outlet for even more anti-media rhetoric. In a *Big Issue* interview publicising his new show, the former First Minister said he understood that everyone had to 'earn a crust' but said (of journalists) that 'there are some things you just shouldn't do and running down your country is one of them. I don't know how they live with themselves' (Salmond 2017b). This characterisation of some reporters as unpatriotic was, of course, shared by Brexiteers and supporters of the US president.

And during the run itself, Salmond declared that members of the press were 'largely despised not just because of what they write, but also because of what they don't write and the ignorance, the prejudice that that displays', a comment that earned a rebuke from the UK director of Reporters Without Borders, an international organisation that promotes press freedom. 'Alex Salmond has unfortunately become the latest in a long line of public figures displaying a hostile attitude towards the press', remarked Rebecca Vincent, 'such as Theresa May, Boris Johnson, and Andrea Leadsom in the UK, and, globally, figures like Donald Trump. Comments like these only serve to erode the climate for free expression' (Vincent 2017).

CONCLUSION

In any case, Salmond et al. had achieved their broader aim. So large was the gap between the rhetoric and reality of their respective independence, Brexit and 'make America great again' projects that the media was always bound to fill that gap with an unwelcome—and electorally unhelpful—level of scrutiny and sceptical coverage. Thus, the protagonists had two options: improve their prospectuses and seek to win over the 'mainstream media', or alternatively to delegitimise it and therefore weaken its impact. In other words, they chose to shoot the messengers rather than improve the message.

And while Brexiteers and supporters of Trump were content to be lumped together as part of the same phenomenon, particularly in their disdain for the 'mainstream media', Nationalists were not, preferring to see themselves as occupying a superior moral plane. Once, on Twitter, I asked with faux innocence what precisely differentiated Salmond's criticism of the press from that of Trump and was told, in all seriousness, that while the Scottish media deserved it, the US equivalent did not.

There was, therefore, often a striking lack of self-awareness. 'The problem with Donald, of course, is a character problem', Salmond told the *Today* programme. 'It's what happens when somebody disagrees with him or somebody says no to him' (Salmond 2017a). For many on the receiving end of years of invective—not all of, it should be noted, unjustified—that was also a pretty good description of his own approach as First Minister.

Had Salmond detected the populist tide before any of his contemporaries, domestic or international? Or had a combination of events made journalists an inevitable target during a polarising referendum? Whatever the case, it was more accurate to view Donald J. Trump as the culmination, rather than the origin, of the ongoing anti-media atmosphere. But rather than starting with Brexit, it happened in Scotland first.

REFERENCES

Baxter, A. (2012), http://www.youvebeentrumped.com/youvebeentrumped.com/THE_MOVIE.html [accessed: 9 July 2017].

Brooks, L. (2016), https://www.theguardian.com/us-news/2016/dec/21/mad-alex-donald-trump-letters-abuse-ex-scottish-first-minister [accessed: 9 July 2017].

Carrell, S. (2011), https://www.theguardian.com/uk/2011/jun/01/alex-salmond-scotland-supreme-court [accessed: 9 July 2017].

Carrell, S. (2014), https://www.theguardian.com/politics/2014/sep/15/alex-salmond-bbc-protest-nick-robinson [accessed: 9 July 2017].

Garavelli, D. (2015), 'Insight: How Scots leaders fell for Donald Trump', *Scotland on Sunday*, 13 December 2015.

Gordon, T. (2017a), 'Alex Salmond accused of acting like Donald Trump after attacking "yoon media"', *The Herald*, 21 February 2017.

Gordon, T. (2017b), 'Sturgeon needs to be bold to revive her tired government', *The Herald*, 1 July 2017.

Gray, I. (2011), 'Iain Gray attacks "vile poison" of SNP politics, *Scotland on Sunday*, 30 October 2011.

Johnson, S. (2014), 'Alex Salmond criticises leading political journalist during heated interview', *Daily Telegraph*, 27 August 2014.

Katz, I. (2017), 'Media culpa: journalists are losing the public's trust', *The Spectator*, 8 July 2017.

Leadsom, A. (2017), https://www.theguardian.com/politics/2017/jun/24/andrea-leadsom-patriotic-brexit-coverage-newsnight-eu-negotiations [accessed: 9 July 2017]

Mair, J., Clark, T., Fowler, N., Snoddy, R. and Tait, R. (eds.) (2017), *Brexit, Trump and the Media*, Bury St Edmunds: Abramis Academic Publishing.

Robertson, J. (2016), 'Scottish TV Coverage of the Referendum Campaign from September 2012 to September 2014', in Blain et al. (eds.), *Scotland's Referendum and the Media*, Edinburgh: Edinburgh University Press.

Salmond, A. (2015a), *The Dream Shall Never Die: 100 Days that Changed Scotland Forever*, London: William Collins.

Salmond, A. (2015b), http://www.independent.co.uk/news/people/alex-salmond-claims-nick-robinson-should-be-ashamed-as-he-condemns-bbcs-scottish-referendum-coverage-10469119.html [accessed: 9 July 2017].

Salmond, A. (2017a), *Today*, BBC Radio 4, 20 January 2017.

Salmond, A. (2017b), https://www.bigissue.com/interviews/alex-salmond-regret-daft-early-resignation-snp-leader/ [accessed: 14 September 2017].

Schofield, K. (2017), https://www.politicshome.com/news/uk/political-parties/snp/alex-salmond/news/87324/alex-salmond-savages-dead-wood-press-and [accessed: 9 July 2017].

Schreckinger, B. (2016), http://www.politico.eu/article/how-donald-trump-wore-out-his-scottish-welcome-aberdeen-golf-us-presidential-election-2016-america/ [accessed: 9 July 2017].

Silver, C. (2015), *Demanding Democracy: The Case for a Scottish Media*, Edinburgh: Word Power Books.

Sturgeon, N. (2017a), https://www.edbookfest.co.uk/press-release/scotland-s-first-minister-admits-nationalism-a-difficult-word-at-edinburgh-international-book-festival [accessed: 14 September 2017].

Sturgeon, N. (2017b), http://www.bbc.co.uk/news/uk-scotland-scotland-politics-41941359 [accessed: 13 December 2017].

Torrance, D. (2015), *Salmond: Against the Odds* (third edition), Edinburgh: Birlinn.

Torrance, D. (2016), *Nicola Sturgeon: A Political Life* (second edition), Edinburgh: Birlinn.

Vincent, R. (2017), https://www.sundaypost.com/fp/trump-like-salmond-told-to-grow-up-after-scots-press-attacks/ [accessed: 14 September 2017]

PART IV

The Politics of Performance

The Point of Reform

CHAPTER 9

The Donald: Media, Celebrity, Authenticity, and Accountability

Michael Higgins

INTRODUCTION

This chapter discusses the consequences of US President Donald Trump for our understanding of media and politics. We offer a particular focus on the interplay between Trump and celebrity politics while looking at his persona and use of social media. The chapter sets out by discussing the mediatisation of politics, highlighting the importance of political conditions and the development of celebrity politics. In discussing the particular instance of Trump, the chapter highlights aftermath of the 2007 economic crash and the consequent rise of anti-government populism. In Trump's pursuit an anti-establishment discourse, the chapter stresses the stigmatisation of specialist knowledge and links this with developments in media affordances and the flow of information. The chapter argues that the subjective discourse usurping expertise forms a part of a broader emergence of discourses around authenticity and sincerity. In conclusion, the chapter suggests that Trump's media-centred politics amounts to a "pseudo-presidency", which escapes conventional forms of accountability.

M. Higgins (✉)
University of Strathclyde, Glasgow, UK

© The Author(s) 2019
C. Happer et al. (eds.), *Trump's Media War*,
https://doi.org/10.1007/978-3-319-94069-4_9

Media, Political Celebrity, and Trump

Much scholarly attention has been directed towards understanding the "mediatisation" of political culture, and this seems likely to increase during the presidency of Donald Trump. Mediatisation refers to the influence of what Mazzoleni and Schulz (1999) term "media logic" in the conduct of political affairs. While not necessarily assuming that media has a negative or positive impact on political culture, the study of mediatisation analyses the extent to which the political and media realms develop and draw upon common principles of selection and representation. Studies show the active internalisation of media styles amongst politicians, but also how politicians have come to show their understanding of media form and logic by engaging tactically with media, in pursuit of such performative goals as trustworthiness and authenticity (Esser and Strömbäck 2014; Higgins 2018).

There is, however, still scope for more attention to be given to the variety of factors and agents that intervene in the relationship between politics and media. One such factor is the prevailing political mood and how this is reflected in how government enters into the experience of the everyday. Understanding such shifts—often constructed as "public opinion" (Lewis 2001)—helps determine those news values to become most readily associated with political coverage. In particular, periods of crisis, including economic depression and the threat of terrorism, engage news in what Richards (2007) describes as an appropriately pitched emotional reach to the audience, manipulating a more seemingly profound relationship between the coverage of the political realm and the perceived concerns of the audience, and opening the political realm to those politicians adept in producing suitably emotive forms of engagement.

This leads to another set of components in the relationship between media and politics, which are the personalities of those involved and the scope these offer for coverage. In setting this in context, Thompson (1995: 121) points to previously fast-held distinctions between public and private existence, where "public" referred to an "activity or authority that was related to or derived from the state", and this could be set against those "private" activities insulated within the boundaries of the domestic or private realms. Thompson (1995) argues that we had moved into an age of "mediated publicness" in which the personal has become an element of public life. This forms part of a longer-term "transformation of visibility", recasting the conduct of private and public accountability. For Thompson

(1995), it is "information flow" combined with a reordered relationship between space and time that has altered the terms and implications of being visible.

The gradual breach of these boundaries between public and private conduct has impacted upon few more than those that hold prominent office in public life. Thompson (1995: 120) notes that "whether they wish to or not, political leaders today must be prepared to adapt their activities to a new kind of visibility" which demands willingness and competence in public exposure. In a manner that chimes with the presidency of Trump, Thompson (2000) describes an intensified media fixation on political scandal. New techniques of political visibility, such as we see in Trump's use of Twitter, enable the institutions of news gathering and composition to exploit the "symbolic power" of actions and statements ascribed as inconsistent with public duty. Such scandals range in their character from business-related maleficence to sexual misconduct. At the same time as they satisfy a perceived appetite for personalised news, scandals figure within the overall media discourse as a way of inscribing the currencies of "reputation and trust" into political coverage (Thompson 2000: 246). In the case of Trump, scandal has extended to the release of statements that can be interpreted as offensive, as well as breaches in political decorum.

Wheeler (2013) uses the notion of "celebrity" to describe how new forms of political professionalism have emerged to adapt to this realm of media visibility, with all its promotional opportunities and scandalous pitfalls. In Wheeler's assessment, in informing the priorities of political activity, the expectations of visibility have overtaken more idealistic performance criteria such as scrupulous devotion to service and responsibility; concerns raised by Boorstin (1962) in the 1960s through to Postman (1985) in the 1980s. Boorstin (1962) in particular is interested in "pseudo-events", by which he means activities that are conceived for the sole purpose of mediation, including press conferences, photo opportunities, and certain types of public speech. Alluding to a sense of ritual in the processes of newsgathering that Tuchman (1978) was later to find in newsroom activities, Boorstin argues that gathering news has become a cooperative endeavour between the journalists and politicians. Extending from collusion in the organisation and recording of these pseudo-events to using social media to maintain news attention, as the reach and affordances of media expand, so do the range of activities of media-savvy politicians, anxious to attract coverage (Wheeler 2013; Higgins 2017).

Street (2004), however, offers a key distinction in the developing relationship between politics and celebrity. Most commonly, discussion of political celebrity looks to how activities associated with celebrity culture have been appropriated and adapted by politicians for public approval. As we have seen, from a critical perspective, the implications of this are that the forms and priorities of entertainment are introduced into political culture, to the detriment of seriousness and rigour (Postman 1985; Wheeler 2013). However, Street (2004) describes a second and increasingly common type of celebrity politician: that of the existent celebrity figure moving into the political realm. A key distinction between the two types—styled by Street (2004) as CP1 and CP2—is that whereas the politician deploying celebrity tactics is obliged to construct a sellable "persona", the established celebrity enters the political realm with a public personality and an established performative repertoire. Drake and Higgins (2006) illustrate this using the example of Arnold Schwarzenegger, and his use of various aspects of his filmic persona in his role as Governor of California, from self-depreciating references to his limited actorly range to the punning nickname "The Governator" (a reference to his celebrated role as "The Terminator"). As Kelly notes in this volume this process is a highly gendered one: the transition is one that is for the most part made successfully by public *men*.

TRUMP AS CELEBRITY POLITICIAN

Donald Trump therefore falls into the latter category of celebrity politician, such that he was an established personality before standing for President. As well as co-writing of a best-selling book on business dealings—*The Art of the Deal* (Trump and Schwartz 1987)—Trump was a long-standing property magnate who actively courted publicity, including posed photographs for several magazine covers. With varying degrees of success, Trump also lent his renown and self-asserted image of high-quality and success to a number of consumer products, including Trump-branded vodka and steaks. In general terms, Trump's image exemplifies the category of television personality that Boyle and Kelly (2016) refer to as the "new rich", with ruthless guile in pursuit of success taking the place of old-world culture and civility. Trump's media image is also based on a bombastic persona that has little in common with the artful self-awareness of Schwarzenegger. Trump's combination of conspicuous self-regard with foregrounded ruthlessness has entered into the popular canon in his role as chief judge and host of reality game show *The Apprentice* (Higgins and Smith 2017).

Trump's fixation on image is as every bit as important to his political identity, as is apparent in the preface to his book *Crippled America*:

> Some readers may be wondering why the picture we used on the cover of this book is so angry and mean looking. I had some beautiful pictures taken in which I had a big smile on my face. I looked happy. I looked content. I looked like a very nice person. My family loved those pictures and wanted me to use one of them. The photographer did a great job. But I decided it wasn't appropriate. In this book we're talking about Crippled America. Unfortunately, there's very little that's nice about it. So I wanted a picture where I wasn't happy, a picture that reflected the anger and unhappiness that I feel, rather than joy. Because we're not in a joyous situation right now. (Trump 2015: ix)

The book is intended as a manifesto of Trump's intentions for government. In this passage, Trump asserts that his vision for government and his performance of personality are bound together. In writing of the constructed and projected "idiolect" of the political personality, Street (2003) emphasises these judgements concerning the appropriateness of persona and the profit in using demeanour as a way of emphasising the earnest nature of the matters at hand. In Trump's simplistic assessment, contemplation of a bleak political environment calls for an austere disposition; and the anticipation of a serious undertaking is necessarily reflected in an unsmiling countenance.

While it is therefore clear that Trump is a yet further example of a celebrity politician, there are a number of factors that make him an especially interesting case study. For one thing, in winning office Trump outperformed the great majority of the early electoral expectations. While some of this success may be a symptom of this particular "populist zeitgeist" (Mudde 2014), from which Trump draws support and rhetorical inspiration, we should also consider longer-term shifts in the democratisation of information and its implications. It is also essential to consider the performative qualities that Trump presents, and the implications these may have for the conduct of public discourse, particularly in his flaunted disregard for expressive consistency and the value of professional and research expertise.

THE 2007 CRASH AND THE RISE OF POPULISM

The first factor we wish to highlight, which we have alluded to at several points, is Trump's association with populism. While Trump's attachment to populism is opportunistic and often superficial in its opposition to state intervention (Higgins 2017), his rise is consistent with a pattern of populist success worldwide (Badiou 2008; Niemi 2013; Chakravartty and Roy 2015). In the classic definition, populism is a doctrinal view of political relations that places the concerns of a virtuous people at odds with the interests of an inherently corrupt and exploitative elite (Canovan 1981). According to Burack and Snyder-Hall (2012: 440), the current swell in populism from which Trump has benefited is rooted in the economic crash of 2007, and specifically the subsequent US government intervention. The state-directed use of economic mechanisms, while fiscally responsible, enabled the redirection of blame for the subsequent economic remedy away from the responsible banks and mortgage providers and towards the government itself, easily cast as the intrusive state.

Insisting that it reflects a popularly-held perspective on these remedial actions of government, *Dissent* magazine argued that the most important experience of the Obama years "was one of austerity" (Konczal 2017). In the US and beyond—with the notable exception of Iceland—the response to economic crisis was retained within the purview of state responsibility, thereby side-lining sustained critical discussion, far less fundamental reconfiguration, of the finance sector. Accordingly, policy and subsequent media coverage were focused on the aftermath of the crash, and in particular the consequences of the government implementation of financial repair and austerity. Even as the austerity project remains ideologically driven in its own terms (Kelsey et al. 2015), allied with the support of a considerable pro-business and anti-state media sector led by Fox News in the US, resulting anti-government sentiments provide fertile ground for a declaredly pro-private sector political figure such as Trump.

THE DEFLATION IN THE VALUE POPULARLY ACCORDED TO KNOWLEDGE

The second factor is the popular depreciation in the value accorded to knowledge, and the implications this has for expertise and political competence. Many of Trump's public pronouncements have been directed towards stressing his contempt for the virtues of expertise, opting instead for his personal instinct and experience. Before his election to the presidency, Trump's offences against research-based knowledge included answering a Scottish parliamentary committee on the impact of wind farms by asserting "I am the evidence" (BBC 2014), as well as claiming greater insight into terror group ISIS than intelligence-led US generals

(Baron 2017). Since his election, his battle against the restrictions of conventional knowledge has included the practical steps of "deskilling the bureaucracy" (Rocco 2017) by replacing specialist advisers with supporters, and has shaped his public discourse, including the use of his @RealDonaldTrump Twitter account to engage in climate change denial.

While predecessor President Obama did not hide his scholarly credentials, even criticising Trump for his wilful ignorance, there is a longer history of disassociation between conventional policy-related research and presidential governance. Williams's (1990) study of Ronald Reagan's terms in office describes an "anti-analytical" presidency, where government philosophy would be determined more by the president's style of delivery and gut instinct than by specialist evidence. Rocco (2017) suggests that Trump's approach has taken this further, evolving into a celebration of whimsical inconstancy: an "adhocracy" in which all specialist input can be dismissed as fake.

While expertise is crucial, Trump's abuse of knowledge is partly reliant upon its cultural shifts. In his assessment of postmodernity, Lyotard (1984) argues that we are witness to the increasing commodification of knowledge, the possession of which would be an increasingly important mechanism for the exercise of power. In ways that now resonate with US election-related discussions over the intervention of foreign hackers, Lyotard (1984: 5) anticipates that nation-states would contest control and ownership of knowledge. He also suggests that the increasing ubiquity of knowledge of different types and to varying purposes will result in increasingly sharp determinations between forms of knowledge as useable currency (Lyotard 1984: 6).

We can highlight two lines of attack on the place of knowledge in the popular realm that are exploited by Trump. The first draws upon Lyotard's (1984: 53) warning that as the exchangeability of knowledge increases, this will diminish the value of specialist knowledge providers. Our increased shared capacity to share information—the democratisation of knowledge—also democratises the means to impart knowledge and engage in informed discussion. However, as well as increasing the circulation of erroneous knowledge, this diminishes the material exchange value popularly attached to knowledge, and to some extent its cultural prestige. Where Lyotard (1984: 27) points to the dominance of scientific knowledge over more outwardly culturally contingent forms, exemplified by him as "narrative knowledge", the example of Trump shows that even expert knowledge is subject to this deflation in value. As we will explore in the next section, this contingency between legitimate and illegitimate knowledge leaves a space which more confident assertions of the subjective and performances of authentic spontaneity can claim dominance.

As the earlier analysis of Reagan's presidency by Williams (1990) would lead us to expect, expertise has been under attack for some time and from a number of directions. Hofstadter (1964), for example, writes of an extended history of anti-intellectualism in America, suggesting that this draws upon assorted myths associated with the US's Founding Fathers and the pragmatic life and experiences of the western frontier. As well as according with the instinctive anti-establishment attitudes characterised in Trump's dalliance with populism, our analysis of Lyotard (1984) recalls that where access to participatory media gives us easy access to the facts, these are often no match for the uniqueness and vivaciousness of subjective expression.

The Recasting of Sincerity and Authenticity

This fight against intellectualism and expertise, a struggle in which we include Trump, takes sustenance from the development of sincerity and authenticity as outcomes of media performance. Central to Trump's appeal is his success in seeming to "tell it like it is", while citing personal experience and material standing in warranting any outbursts. In mainstream broadcast news, this takes a more benign form in what John Durham Peters (2011) calls "media witnessing". This refers to the discursive power accorded within media of "being there" and speaking from the scene, with the attendant implications of experience and embodied investment. Less benignly, an emphasis on presence and the personal engenders another form of truth, where passion, spontaneity, and opinion bear the mark of a new popular authenticity. Enli (2015) refers to constructions of "mediated authenticity" founded on appearances of spontaneity and groundedness, and where seeming "real" becomes a gauge of political judgement. Montgomery (1999) discussed such performative markers of sincerity amongst politicians speaking in public, predominately around these displays of unscripted hesitancy and emotional involvement.

We have already examined Trump's pitch for sincerity in the management of his demeanour. In Trump's case, however, this link between unscriptedness and authenticity is manifest less through hesitancy of speech than in the "off-message" character of his @RealDonaldTrump Twitter account. This claim to sincerity offers Trump considerable freedom to disavow reason and verifiable truth. Oborne and Roberts (2017: ix–x) write that Trump "exploited Twitter's ability to express raw sentiment instantly, without nuance or subtext, and its ability to blur- even extinguish the boundary between sentiment and fact". In the latitude it enjoys, the conduct of Trump's own Twitter account partially contrasts with the more controlled @POTUS official presidential account and diverges wildly from the conventionally controlled informational practices of the pre-Trump White House press office.

Some argue this should be seen alongside a lack of willingness to challenge untruths in selected media organisations, as they relate to the Trump presidency. *Wall Street Journal* editor Gerard Baker says in relation to Trump that lies have to refer to "a deliberate attempt to mislead". That is to say, Trump produces a discursive repertoire that refuses any relationship with truth as we might understand it. While, outwardly, this is a reflection on a legal definition of intentional deceit, it betrays something of the complexity and hold of Trump's pretences of authenticity, set against consistency and rationality, in making sense of his public discourse.

SOCIAL MEDIA AND THE DEMOCRATISATION OF COMMUNICATION

Another crucial factor in the expressive power and popular conceit of Trump is his use of media platforms that are available to all, in terms of both access and participation. Indeed, he concedes of his political success "I think I maybe wouldn't be here if it wasn't for Twitter" (quoted in Oborne and Roberts 2017: vii). In offering what Ausserhofer and Maireder (2013) refer to as a "networked public sphere", social media, and Twitter in particular, has enabled the circulation of opinions of all stripes and from all levels of credibility (as Geoghegan discusses in this volume, this is aided by erosion of trust in the mainstream media). Allied with the rise of a non-conventional approach to facticity sanctioned by the discursive activities of Trump, the prevailing tone of Twitter has taken a component of this public sphere beyond the boundaries of agonistic dispute, giving prominence to bogus claims and personalised abuse. As it provides an exchange of fanciful opinion and vitriol, it is also necessary to consider research suggesting Twitter operates as densely populated "echo chamber" between like-minded co-followers (Colleoni et al. 2013). In this vision, politically oriented discourse on Twitter rallies support and consolidates existent opinion, rather than testing contrary views or sustaining the circulation of information.

In political terms too, Elmer, Langlois, and McKelvey (2012) argue that the constant access to communication platforms has obligated an attitude of "permanent campaign" amongst politicians, driven on by political commentators, pollsters, and bloggers, producing a style of government dedicated less to sound administration than to maximising ongoing support for forthcoming elections. Trump has moved beyond even Elmer et al.'s (2012) vision, joining the ranks of the political bloggers with his own short-form Twitter presence, all the while continuing to commission campaign-style rallies of supporters. Elmer et al. (2012) suggest that the commitment to never-ending promotion surrenders political control to the proprieties of speech-writers and advisers: government navigated by communicative style and audience response.

TRUMP AND ACCOUNTABILITY

Of course, the terms of populism we referred to earlier are not just political, but also stylistic. As Leo Braudy (1997) shows in his history of fame, politicians in search of approval have long had the motive to call upon those styles and media platforms that become associated with popular engagement, and Trump's Twitter feed and campaign-style pseudo-events are a contemporary manifestation of this. In a study of the relationship between politics and popular culture, Street, Inthorn, and Scott (2013: 85) concede that the popularisation of politics maintains a distance from those forms of understanding associated with the political realm, but note that this does at least facilitate "collective deliberation about the exercise of public power" in accessible ways. Emphasising more the critical possibilities of the popular, Jones (2010) highlights the activities of entertainment media, and especially satiric television, and use of politicians' performative characteristics to hold them to ridicule, thereby emptying those very qualities of the aura of spontaneity on which they depend.

Contrarily, if Trump is to be held to account and improved through political and media scrutiny, this depends on him being held to conventional standards by determined questioners. The celebrated checks and balances of the US system are robust in principle, but can be partially circumvented by the politicisation of the wider executive support network referred to above. There is also the impact of Trump on the media's coverage of the relative power of the US political institutions. For example, Farnsworth and Lichter (2006) look to a decades-long shift in media focus from the US legislature to the office of the president, occasioning more of the personality-driven politics described above. While, owing to his difficulty in getting early bills such as the repeal of the Affordable Care Act through, the legislature has featured heavily in the early part of his presidency, Trump's continued alienation from the US party establishment further intensifies this focus on the individual with all his media-friendly, capricious qualities.

CONCLUSION

Pessimistically, the concentration of Trump's communicative activities may excuse him from the normal terms of political accountability: celebrating inconsistency and valorising spontaneity over purpose. In the kindest analysis, Trump moves us towards what we may call a "discursive presidency": one that will be defined by the success of communicative acts in their own terms, valuing visibility and publicity above facticity and real-world implications. From sympathetic media, in particular, Trump may be judged by popular measures of success, valorising his style and attitude to the extent that his becomes a "pseudo-presidency", serving only the attention it generates.

Yet, we have shown that Trump is not a paradigm shift in political culture. On the contrary, the Trump presidency is a mutation of longer-term developments in political visibility and of the shifting relations between politics and media. However, the example of Trump does intensify a number of debates over the directions in which these developments lead. In understanding the success of Trump, the norms and proprieties of mediatisation, including the successful projection of his own persona, might produce the more realistic measure: less a presidency than an enterprise in celebrity image management.

REFERENCES

Ausserhofer, Julian and Maireder, Axel (2013) "National politics on Twitter: Structures and topics of a networked public sphere", *Information, Communication and Society* 16(3): 291–314.

Badiou, Alain (2008) *The Meaning of Sarkozy*. London: Verso.

Baron, Kevin (2017) "Trump and the generals", *The Atlantic* March 1.

BBC (2014) "Donald Trump tells MSPs: 'I am the evidence'", at: http://www.bbc.co.uk/news/av/uk-scotland-20463092/donald-trump-tells-msps-i-am-the-evidence

Boorstin, Daniel J. (1962) *The Image: or, what happened to the American Dream.* New York: Athenaeum.

Boyle, Raymond and Kelly, Lisa W. (2016) *The Television Entrepreneurs: Social Change and Public Understanding of Business*. Abingdon: Routledge.

Braudy, Leo (1997) *The Frenzy of Renown: Fame and its History*. New York: Vintage.

Burack, Cynthia, and Snyder-Hall, Claire (2012) Introduction: Right-wing populism and the media. New Political Science 34(4): 439–454.

Canovan, Margaret (1981) *Populism*. Junction: London.

Chakravartty, Paula and Srirupa Roy (2015) "Mr Modi goes to Delhi: mediated populism and the 2014 Indian Elections", *Television and New Media* 16: 311–322.

Colleoni, Elanor, Rozza, Alessandro and Arvidsson, Adam (2013) "Echo chamber of public sphere? Predicting political orientation and measuring political homophily in Twitter using big data", *Journal of Communication* 64(2): 317–332.

Drake, Philip and Higgins, Michael (2006) "I'm a celebrity, get me into politics: the political celebrity and the celebrity politician", in Sue Holmes and Sean Redmond (eds) *Framing Celebrity: New Directions in Celebrity Culture*. London: Routledge, pp. 88–100.

Elmer, Greg, Langlois, Ganaele and McKelvey, Fenwick (2012) *The Permanent Campaign: New Media, New Politics*. New York: Peter Lang.

Enli, Gunn (2015) *Mediated Authenticity: How the Media Constructs Reality*. New York: Peter Lang.

Esser, F. and Strömbäck, Jesper (eds) (2014) *Mediatization of Politics*. Basingstoke: Palgrave.

Farnsworth, Stephen J. and Lichter, Robert (2006) *The Mediated Presidency: Television News and Presidential Governance*. Lanham: Rowman and Littlefield.

Higgins, Michael and Smith, Angela (2017) *Belligerent Broadcasting: Synthetic Argument in Broadcasting*. Abingdon: Routledge.

Higgins, Michael (2017) "Mediated populism, culture and media form", *Palgrave Communications*.

Higgins, Michael (2018) "Mediatization and political language", in Ruth Wodak and Bernhard Forchtner (eds) *The Routledge Handbook of Language and Politics*. Abingdon: Routledge, pp. 383–397.

Hofstadter, R. (1964) *Anti-intellectualism in America*. London: Jonathan Cape.

Jones, Jeffrey P. (2010) *Entertaining Politics: Satiric Television and Political Engagement* (2). New York: Rowman and Littlefield.

Kelsey, Darren, Mueller, Frank, Whittle, Andrea and KhosraviNik, Majid (2015) "Financial crisis and austerity: interdisciplinary concerns in critical discourse studies", *Critical Discourse Studies*, at: https://doi.org/10.1080/17405904.2015.1074600.

Konczal, Mike (2017) "The austerity of the Obama years", *Dissent Magazine*, 17 January https://www.dissentmagazine.org/online_articles/austerity-obama-years.

Lewis, Justin (2001) *Constructing Public Opinion*. New York: Columbia University Press.

Lyotard, Jean-François (1984) *The Postmodern Condition: A Report on Knowledge*. Manchester: Manchester University Press.

Mazzoleni, Gianfranco and Schulz, Winfried (1999) "Mediatization of politics? A challenge for democracy", *Political Communication* 16(3): pp. 247–261.

Montgomery, Martin (1999) "Speaking sincerely: public reactions to the death of Diana", *Language and Literature* 8(1): 5–33.

Mudde, C. (2014) The populist zeitgeist. *Government and Opposition* 39(4): 541–663.

Niemi, Mari K. (2013) "The True Finns: identity politics and populist leadership on the threshold of the party's electoral triumph", *Javnost-The Public* 20(3): 77–92.

Oborne, Peter and Roberts, Tom (2017) *How Trump Thinks: His Tweets and the Birth of a New Political Language*. London: Head of Zeus.

Peters, John Durham (2011) "Witnessing", in Paul Frosh and Amit Pinchevski (eds) *Media Witnessing: Testimony in the Age of Mass Communication*. Basingstoke: Palgrave, pp. 23–40.

Postman, Neil (1985) *Amusing Ourselves to Death: Public Discourse in the Age of Show Business*. London: Methuen.

Richards, Barry (2007) *Emotional Governance*. Basingstoke: Palgrave.

Rocco, Philip (2017) "Most presidents rely on expertise. Trump treats experts like the enemy", *Washington Post*. At: https://www.washingtonpost.com/news/monkey-cage/wp/2017/07/24/most-presidents-rely-on-expertise-trump-treats-experts-like-the-enemy/?utm_term=.4800f8e431c3

Street, John (2003) "The celebrity politician: political style and popular culture", in John Corner and Dick Pels (eds) *Media and the Restyling of Politics: Consumerism, Celebrity and Cynicism*. London: Sage, pp. 85–98.

Street, John (2004) "Celebrity politicians: political culture and representation", *British Journal of Politics and International Relations* 6: 435–452.

Street, John, Inthorn, Sanna and Scott, Martin (2013) *From Entertainment to Citizenship: Politics and Popular Culture*. Manchester: Manchester University Press.

Thompson, John B. (1995) *The Media and Modernity: A Social Theory of the Media*. Cambridge: Polity.

Thompson, John B. (2000) *Political Scandal: Power and Visibility in the Media Age*. Cambridge: Polity.

Trump, Donald J. (2015) *Crippled America: How to Make America Great Again*. New York: Threshold.

Trump, Donald J. and Schwartz, Tony (1987) *The Art of the Deal*. New York: Baker and Taylor.

Tuchman, Gaye (1978) *Making News: A Study in the Construction of Reality*. New York: Free Press.

Wheeler, Mark (2013) *Celebrity Politics*. Cambridge: Polity.

Williams, Walter (1990) *Mismanaging America: The Rise of the Anti-Analytic Presidency*. Lawrence: Kansas University Press.

CHAPTER 10

The Big Standoff: Trump's Handshakes and the Limits of News Values

Ben O'Loughlin

After an Obama administration committed to 'unclenching fists' in diplomatic affairs, global media in 2017 reported President Trump using his hands to greet leaders with renewed American vigour. These diplomatic encounters can be conceptualised as standoffs: moments of uncertainty when nobody quite knows what will happen, including the people shaking hands. These are subjunctive moments: we audiences look on *with feeling* as the leaders' hands come together. There is something at stake, and it matters to us. As Trump grabbed the hands of Canadian President Trudeau, Chinese Premier Xi, and even catching UK Prime Minister Theresa May off-guard by taking her hand as they walked down some steps, global audiences can look on and feel an affective charge that seems to have geopolitical implications.

While each of President Trump's handshakes with foreign leaders has taken the form of a standoff, the significance of these standoffs is that they

Thank you to Andrew Chadwick and Cristian Vaccari for feedback on an earlier draft, and to the editors for their comments and suggestions.

B. O'Loughlin (✉)
Department of Politics and International Relations, Royal Holloway, University of London, Egham, UK

© The Author(s) 2019
C. Happer et al. (eds.), *Trump's Media War*,
https://doi.org/10.1007/978-3-319-94069-4_10

signal, together, Trump's standoff with international relations per se. Trump's win-lose, zero-sum handshakes offer a visual presentation of isolationism that produces a jarring effect; they are a shock to long-established and near-universally shared norms of diplomatic conduct as well as policies that ostensibly maintain a liberal, multilateral world order made up of plural but largely cooperative governance mechanisms. The rest of the world can refuse to play Trump's game here, or play the game by enduring the handshakes while otherwise sustaining multilateral order themselves and making deals without Trump—as was case in 2017 when Trump's administration opted out of climate change and trade deals.

Analysis of news coverage of each handshake standoff teaches us three things about media and international relations. First, news values bring some order to how international relations are presented. News values privilege personalisation, calibration to powerful actors, and drama. Trump's handshakes meet these criteria. This led news reporting to amplify these standoffs into geostrategic moments. News reports suggested that these moments signalled power relations in an uncertain global order; the subjunctive mood leads us to anticipate World War III if a handshake goes wrong (especially if it goes wrong for Trump), or a harmonious alliance if the handshake goes well. Through global media, the handshakes act as a divining rod for audiences to detect which way international relations will flow.

Second, in a digital media ecology in which audiences consume and produce footage and remediation of Trump's handshakes, these *multisensorial* mediums allow *communication to return to gesture*. In the modern era, written political communication limited gestural opportunities, while risk-averse leaders carefully managed any television appearance. Trump extends and then bypasses that, firmly anchoring us in tactile communication; his bodily gesture is felt, at a distance. He may have no control over *how* his gesture is felt, but the analysis below will show that he presented a measure of glee in enjoying his own anarchic actions.

Third, while Trump's vigorous grabbing shook news coverage for some months, journalists learnt to *contain* his standoffs and *normalise* his encounters. Yet in doing so, this forced news media reflection on their complicity in publicising Trump and a degree of realisation about the *limits of news values*. Let us begin with containment. Television and diplomatic handshakes have an entwined history; each new handshake can be framed through the lens of prior handshake standoffs. Once Trump's handshakes were compared to previous leaders' encounters, the handshake could be dissected, scrutinised, and understood. Indeed, while Trump's handshakes exemplified the potential to use standoffs to gesture globally, digitally, in a disruptive way, the handshakes also demonstrated the capacity of news media soon learn to contain and ritualise—to the extent Trump's opponents have learned to turn these standoffs to their advantage.

The *manner* of this containment also indicates something important, however. By winning the US presidency by exploiting mainstream news values, Trump forced professional journalists to assess the risks and limits of those news values. Efforts to impose a tone *on* the Trump presidency—seriousness or mockery—provoked Trump to either attack mainstream media or seek to keep exploiting those news values. Trump's foreign policy conduct appeared to keep journalists in a perpetual state of shock and a 'new normal' of constant outrage or anxiety. Yet foreign policy reporting ultimately focuses on matters of substance: national security and war and peace. By pointing to a lack of tangible policy outcomes and the role of journalism in exposing the difficulties of foreign policymaking in the Trump administration, news media seem able to contain Trump. This also allows journalists to demonstrate to readers that, stepped back from the brink, they are not led by the worst excesses of news values. However, mainstream media are not the only media. Trump's outrageous gesture politics is perfect for viral GIFs, videos, and user commentary. These often function best by pushing at the very limit of the news values that foreign policy correspondents have stepped back from. There are tensions across media ecologies, then, as different media organisations and platforms enable contradictory dynamics of amplification and containment through different registers. Foreign policy correspondents cannot control how Trump's gestures are remediated and interpreted even on matters of war and peace.

Once we see that process in the round, from disruption to containment, then the bigger argument of this chapter takes form. I argue that Trump's many handshake standoffs add up to one single standoff with the entire not-Trump world: with mainstream media, with other world leaders; in short, a standoff with the way things had been done until Trump became president. This is not a standoff Trump can win, but it is one he can sustain because of the chaotic media ecology. Diplomacy is careful for a reason, has evolved over millennia (Neumann 2011), and has contained leaders more brazen and outlandish than Trump. All other states and leaders base their interactions on those norms because those norms are most likely to increase the collective good while minimising immediate risk to the countries and leaders involved in any encounter. The analysis below even suggests that in Trump's expression of shame when he is caught breaking norms by German Chancellor Angela Merkel (which has happened twice), it may be, that Trump himself knows he cannot win the larger standoff. And yet, he knows another gesture an hour later will be amplified through GIFs and outrage. Since the contradiction has not fully played out, for the moment his show goes on.

WHY ANALYSE DIPLOMATIC HANDSHAKES AS STANDOFFS?

The moment of diplomatic encounter has a colourful history. When meeting Merkel before the cameras in 2007, Russian Premier Vladimir Putin, knowing Merkel's fear of dogs, released before her his large black Labrador, Koni (Nehring 2017). A press photo shows the two leaders sitting in chairs in front of a mantelpiece with the dog before them roaming freely, Merkel with hands clasped together. Putin had earlier sent Merkel a toy dog (Hounsell 2007). Famously, the signing of the Arab-Israeli peace accord in Washington DC in September 1993 allowed global media coverage of a handshake between the Palestinian National Authority's President Yasser Arafat and Israel's Prime Minister Rabin. As US President Bill Clinton stood behind them, his arms encircling the two leaders, the moment came for Arafat and Rabin to shake hands. However, Arafat moved a second quicker than Rabin. This resulted in widespread media speculation about the meaning of Rabin's slight hesitation. As Boden and Hoskins noted, 'in conventional clock time, it is less than a second', but still photographs in the next day's newspapers allowed the reader to witness the sequence frame by frame (Boden and Hoskins 1995: 5). In the context of one of the world's most intransigent conflicts, gesture produces symbolism ripe for interpretation.

We cannot understand Trump's handshakes without understanding how strongly he is motivated to be the opposite of his predecessor, Barack Obama, in every possible way.[1] Obama himself had tried to distinguish his presidential approach from his predecessor, George W. Bush. According to one White House advisor, Obama liked to 'lead from behind' by nudging allies and sharing the burdens of solving collective international problems (Lizza 2011; see also Obama 2010: 18, 47). In his 20 January 2009 inaugural address, Obama tried to offer words that might begin to de-escalate tensions between the United States and Muslim and Arab audiences in the wake of the 2003 Iraq War and the war on terror launched by his predecessor:

To the Muslim world, we seek a new way forward, based on mutual interest and mutual respect. To those leaders around the globe who seek to sow conflict, or blame their society's ills on the West, know that your people will judge you on what you can build, not what you destroy.

To those who cling to power through corruption and deceit and the silencing of dissent, know that you are on the wrong side of history, but that *we will extend a hand if you are willing to unclench your fist*. (Obama 2009: no page, emphasis added)

For Trump, the logic of his own approach entailed restoring the clenched hand, coming from behind to put America First and thereby Make America Great Again. Diplomatic encounters offered Trump a stage to perform this. A *Financial Times* analysis in early 2017 stated, 'Handshakes combine the ritual of the truce (the hand-clasp first emerged as a signal that a right-hander was not about to draw his weapon) with the preamble of battle' (Hill 2017). Once this became a clear pattern for Trump in those early months of 2017, news media began publishing compilations of Trump handshakes, often presented as comedy (see e.g. Strachan 2017). On some occasions Trump shook the hand vigorously. In the case of encounters with Merkel and Israeli Prime Minister Benjamin Netanyahu, he ignored their offers of a handshake. On all occasions, Trump made the decision of how the situation would unfold, reconstructing a moment of friendly greeting into a confrontation, creating tensions with the foreign leaders he was meeting.

To gain analytical grip on these confrontations, we must treat them as instances of a standoff. Following Wagner-Pacifici (2000: 3, emphasis in original), I treat standoffs as *'action in the subjunctive mood'*: witnesses hypothesise about likely outcomes and their speculation is tinged with emotion—doubt, hope, fear. 'I dread that my leader will make a fool of himself'; 'I fear Trump will try to break my hand'; 'I hope I can show greater strength in this moment to Trump and to the world.' Standoffs are moments in which comparative sociologists and ethnographers have identified regularities and norms of behaviour. However, Trump violates these and hence we need to theorise his exceptionalism. We could rationalise these moments post-hoc, as if they are finished events; or we could approach them as prospective events, but each would lack a focus on what actually happens. Instead, there is a duration to these moments, when 'fate hangs in the balance', and we should focus on how actors respond to the contingency of that moment (ibid: 5).

Wagner-Pacifici analyses US domestic standoffs between public authorities and cults, rebels and insurgents at Wounded Knee in 1973, Ruby Ridge in 1992 and Waco in 1993. Her analysis shows that the duration of single moments is stretched across a series of encounters that together constitute 'the' standoff. Temporality is key to resolving standoffs. It becomes clear that some actors are operating towards a historical and even apocalyptic time horizon, while public authorities are more concerned by immediate news and electoral cycles. Given these disjunctures, 'What needs to happen' for these moments to avoid total conflict, Wagner-Pacifici writes, 'is a restructuring of the situation so that there is some, however small, place of overlap between the definitions of the situation on the part of the adversaries'. In Trump's handshakes we find that leaders largely acquiesce to his aggressive game, but this is unlikely to translate into influence for Trump because those leaders can work with each other.

Let us consider what Trump's handshake standoffs tell us about how media and international relations bear upon each other.

LESSON ONE: NEWS VALUES LEAD MEDIA TO AMPLIFY HANDSHAKES INTO GEOSTRATEGIC MOMENTS

News values—personalisation, calibration to powerful actors, and drama—lead reporting to amplify these standoffs into geostrategic moments signalling power relations in an uncertain global order. This significance for national identity and prestige reinforces why it is necessary to analyse standoffs in the subjunctive mood. Anticipation of possible antagonism around a Trump handshake premediates the worst—potentially World War III—yet a handshake passing without antagonism offers relief and the possibility for cooperation. We must also consider Trump's position as self-defined un-Obama and as president of a superpower who campaigned on an America First ticket: simply to have superpower status brings the anxiety of not being recognised *as* a superpower or of losing that status materially (Steele 2010). One must be seen to *be* a superpower. If Obama believed in multilateralism and power *with*, Trump's rhetoric suggested a belief in bilateral deals and power *over*. This entailed he had to enact observable demonstrations of primacy and strength.

Let us first locate this visually. The contingency intrinsic to Trump's handshakes in 2017 stemmed not only from uncertainty about how he would behave, but also because the control of images by Trump's White House team was slapdash; it was not always clear whether photographs were released with Trump's consent or the consent of any of his team. His team appeared to allow a Russian photographer into the Oval Office, widely reported as a security lapse (Graham 2017). However, it also signalled Trump's lack of control of the flow of images. Photographs emerged from the White House of men shaking hands behind Trump's back and with secret documents open before Trump and readable to the viewer, with Trump seemingly oblivious and unconcerned (Roa 2017). As he sought to project strength, it could never be fully anticipated what images of a Trump handshake would appear at all.

This anarchic, unscripted quality found mutual support in Trump's foreign policy making in 2017. If deals with Cuba, Iran, and attempts to reach out to 'the Muslim world' indicated that Obama's calculus was bound by long-term horizons, Trump appeared bound by immediate social and alt-right media reactions. In June 2017, when US Secretary of State Rex Tillerson called for an end to a blockade of Qatar by some of its Middle Eastern neighbours, Trump contradicted him within hours and renewed his support for a blockade because he had been told Qatar funded terrorism (Berenson 2017). It is not clear that Trump recognised the time horizons or historical legacies shaping the thinking of his interlocutors in these standoffs. For example, snubbing Merkel's handshake offer appeared to ignore or misrecognise that Germany has been the US' leading Western ally in securing the post-Cold War peace in Europe. However, in March 2017 during the exchange when Merkel offered her hand, Trump ignored her, studiously avoided her gaze as his hands pointed down at the floor, hinting at a note of shame. He may realise he is doing something that appals the rest of the international community and, in such moments, we find him visibly embodying non-cooperation. In the moment, Merkel seemed amused by this, but Trump's policy positions on NATO, climate change and trade were directly opposed to Merkel's and, consequently, the handshake rejection is the expression of Trump's injection of disorder into international relations.

In contrast to the lightly controlled chaos of Putin's Labrador roaming around Merkel within a larger Russia-German relationship of interdependence, then, there is a genuine unpredictability in Trump's conduct of foreign policy. Media-enabled moments of geopolitical importance reflect that; form and content align in radical disorder.

Lesson Two: The Global Digital Gesture Is Possible

That disorder is *felt*. The digitally enabled return to multisensorial mediums allows communication to return its focus to gesture. Decades of written political communication limited gestural opportunities, while risk-averse leaders carefully managed any television appearance. It is a tradition of US presidents to use assertive *rhetoric* about US primacy and to project Manichean good/evil, us/them identities. Trump bypassed that, firmly anchoring us in tactile communication; his bodily gesture is felt, at a distance, without control (on Trump's use of physical demeanour, see Higgins in this volume). Certainly, undiplomatic words in international affairs can feel rammed down your throat—what Bially Mattern calls 'representational force' and what novelist Tom McCarthy notes is our tendency to 'gag' on some words (Bially Mattern 2005: 48; McCarthy 2015: 142). There is also the discomfort triggered from the force of watching Trump squeeze a leader's hand until the victim visibly winces. This was the case when Trump met Japan's Shinzo Abe in February 2017. It is equally uncomfortable viewing Trump attempting to wrestle a leader's arm out of its socket, as seemingly was the case with France's Emmanuel Macron. Upon feeling that bodily gesture we audiences can then freeze, replay, zoom in, share, offer commentary. How do journalists frame it?

Rolling news offers repetition, but soon analysis kicks in: What does the gesture mean? The *Independent* called on body language expert Darren Stanton, who told the newspaper that Trump's handshake was 'all about the assertion of power and control' (cited in Shugerman 2017). The *Huffington Post* interviewed various psychology professors. They suggested that for Trump it was about alpha maleness. They found this odd because handshakes had traditionally been a gesture of goodwill and of sealing cooperation (Stein 2017). The *Telegraph* offered a Trump 'handshake tracker' in which readers were invited to study various Trump handshakes and analyse three phases: the clasp, the yank, and the release (Blagburn 2017). Interestingly, this was in its Lifestyle section, not politics, suggesting a lack of seriousness.

The handshake became a primary Trumpian gesture because it allows a zero-sum relation, a win, and because he has not always prospered amid the ambiguities and delicacies of hugs and kisses (c.f. Kellner 2016: 46). It is also, like much Trump public display, outrageous. It confuses the 'art of the deal' back-stage protocol of intimidating the other and establishing dominance with the front-stage setting of diplomacy and the ritualised representation of one's country. Like his tweets or some of his campaign speeches, he steps outside normal political discourse. How would a leader expect to get away with embarrassing another national leader? This adds another layer of news value—it has a dramatic unexpectedness: we have never seen a leader act this way.

Lesson Three: News Media Can Contain These Standoffs, but Not Entirely

Television and diplomatic handshakes have an entwined history; each new handshake can be framed through the lens of prior handshake standoffs. Hence, while Trump's vigorous grabbing shook coverage for some months, news media learned how to contain his standoffs and normalise his encounters.

The first leader to try to take control of these moments back from Trump was Canadian Trudeau, who, according to *Newsweek*, 'approached Trump with speed, grabbed his shoulder and got in close before the president had a change to tug at his arm' (Marcin 2017). *Vice* news reported this as 'the first shot in a bloodless war' and suggested Trudeau had prepared for 'Every possible move, every possible contingency' for that moment when Trump would be outside his car door waiting to shake his hand (Brown 2017). Again we find the subjunctive mood: anticipation of the affective charge of an encounter and its outcome.

In May 2017 Trump appeared to suffer his first handshake defeat at the hands of French President Emmanuel Macron in Brussels ahead of a NATO summit. A pool report from White House press correspondents said:

> The two presidents, each wearing dark suits and blue ties (Trump's was thick and royal blue; Macron's was skinny and navy) sat in antique cream-upholstered arm chairs, with two American and French flags behind them. They shook hands for an extended period of time. Each president gripped the other's hand with considerable intensity, their knuckles turning white and their jaws clenching and faces tightening. (Rucker, cited in Crowther 2017)

For the *Financial Times*, 'It was the handshake felt around the world' (Hill 2017). Macron later said his handshake with Trump was 'not accidental'; he added: 'It's important to show one won't make small concessions, even symbolic ones' (cited in Pedder 2017). It was, he said, a 'moment of truth' (ibid). But what truth? To show he is a true leader, or that France is truly an equal sovereign power to the US? Even *GQ* magazine was moved to write, 'it should go without saying that macho displays of peacocking and penis measuring are stupid and should have no place in international diplomacy' (Moore 2017). Not long after, Trump failed again to get the upper hand, as Tajikistan President Emomali Rahmon pulled Trump towards him as they shook hands (Marcin 2017). In June 2017, Polish First Lady Agata Kornhauser-Duda took control. At a meeting in Warsaw she refused Trump's offer of a handshake, turning away from his hand to offer Melania Trump a handshake instead, before finally turning again to shake Trump by the hand (Abramson 2017).

The international community has shown patience in the standoff and can now re-impose its order. This is partly cultural, perhaps. Wagner-Pacifici writes, 'In the action-oriented culture of the United States, there is an exaggerated *horror vacui* – the horror of nothingness, of doing nothing – that exerts pressure on the standoff. Nobody wants to do nothing' (Wagner-Pacifici 2000: 80). Merkel's lack of concern, and even amusement, when Trump failed to accept her offer of a handshake is precisely the patient, you-will-come-round-to-our-ways stance that unsettles a leader who positioned himself as *especially* American.

Did Trump remain a danger, nevertheless? After his 'moment of truth' with the US president, Macron faced Trump again later that day in Brussels. News footage shot from behind Macron shows him walking along a blue carpet towards a crowd of NATO leaders, with Angela Merkel and Donald Trump in the leading row. Macron appears to begin walking directly towards Trump, who begins to open his right hand in readiness, only for Macron to bend his path and 'swerve' in Merkel's direction (*Washington Post* 2017). Trump mildly shrugs as he waits for five or six seconds while Macron greets two other leaders. As cameras flash, Macron finally turns to Trump, who takes his hand and pulls his arm aggressively. After two seconds of meaty shaking, Trump evidently thinks he 'wins' the encounter. Trump breaks into a broad smile, faces the cameras, and then turns to pat Macron on the shoulder—a pat of consolation. However, Trump catches the eye of Merkel, who is smirking. Trump is immediately downcast; he has been caught, and his eyes turn to the ground. As the cameras flash, the line of leaders moves forward together and the moment has passed.

Through the combination of news media repetition and re-assertion of diplomatic rituals, it appears Trump's handshakes are contained. This would attest to the 'modulation' model of news reporting that indicates journalists can contain or amplify the emotional significance and political salience of events (Hoskins and O'Loughlin 2007). However, there are certain factors that complicate the model in this case. First, US news media in particular appear to have used Trump to re-assert their legitimacy and the legitimacy of 'serious' journalism, as part of a wider claim about journalism's role in a democratic culture. Since the Trump presidency began, the *Washington Post* and *New York Times* have competed to hold that administration to account and to demonstrate rising readership figures. Meanwhile, the mythology of Watergate returns in *The Post*, the 2017 film directed by Steven Spielberg retelling the tale of *Post* editor Katherine Graham as she battled commercial and political pressures to give her investigate journalists scope to bring down the Nixon presidency. After the shock of enabling a Trump presidency by effectively offering free advertising to his campaign, Trump forced professional journalists to assess the risks and limits of those news values.[2] This constitutes a public re-assertion by the mainstream press of *the right to contain*.

Second, news media efforts to contain Trump are complicated of the distinct genre of presidential rhetoric and conduct—being 'presidential'. Mainstream journalists have sought instances in which Trump may at last be acting presidentially. This is especially the case for US journalists reporting on matters of foreign policy, in which national interests and matters of national security become paramount. Despite being locked in a bilateral, bitter standoff with Trump throughout 2017, the *New York Times* headlined Trump's Davos speech of January 2018 as 'A Sober Trump Reassures Davos Elite' (Baker 2018). The *Times* journalist pointed to inconsistencies in Trump's foreign and domestic economic policies, focusing on policy substance, but also appeared to be policing the line of appropriate behaviour, adding:

> Even during a later 10-minute session of questions and answers with Mr Schwab, Mr Trump generally stuck to the talking points, although he could not resist a jab at the "fake" media.

However, as much as mainstream journalists may position themselves as renewed arbiters of appropriate presidential style and policy substance, mainstream media are not the only media. Trump's outrageous gesture politics is perfect for viral GIFs, videos and user commentary. These push at the very limit of the news values that foreign policy correspondents have stepped back from and sought to contain again. This points to tensions across media ecologies that Trump can exploit to evade containment. Different media organisations and platforms enable contradictory dynamics of amplification and containment through different registers. Foreign policy correspondents cannot control how Trump's gestures are remediated and interpreted even on matters of war and peace. Trump can appear sober at Davos or contrite before Angela Merkel, but a few moments later he can return to outrageous conduct and reach an audience. Mainstream news media may assert a right to contain, but that is no longer how global media functions.

Conclusion: The Big Standoff

Trump's handshakes exemplify the potential to use standoffs to gesture globally, digitally, but also indicate how news media soon learn to contain and ritualise—so much so that Trump's opponents learned to turn these standoffs to their advantage. But that tactical adaptation masks a broader strategy in play. Trump's many handshake standoffs add up to one single standoff between Trump and the entire not-Trump world: a standoff with mainstream media, with other world leaders; in short, a standoff with the way things had been done until Trump became president.

Trump presents an impoverished form of diplomatic engagement. Diplomatic encounters must support sustainable communication so that leaders can maintain sufficient trust to keep talking (Ferrari forthcoming). This applies not only when bilateral relations are difficult but as part of an international community that must solve collective problems. For this reason, Trump does not gain influence in these moments. Other leaders can form alliances without the US.

As an academic who has taught international political economy to undergraduates since 2003, it has always been a struggle to convey the rise of economic nationalism in the 1920s and the sense of nations turning inwards, particularly to students who have only experienced a world of economic interdependence and global governance based on liberal values (albeit these values are not always practised). Trump's handshakes gave a flavour of what that turn against liberal interdependence looks and feels like. International news media initially had fun with Trump's handshakes, before re-framing the handshakes as 'a thing' in the cultural zeitgeist (Scott 2015), to be dissected. This limited their affective, status-quo challenging force. Hence, we see how media can amplify a startling return to isolationism but then contain and allow critique and, through other national leaders, ultimately measured responses. Those leaders side step the Trump grip while journalists can point to policy shortcomings. Yet journalists themselves cannot modulate Trump's affective charge as they would like. In a wider digital media ecology in which pushing traditional news values of visuality and immediacy to their limits gains virality and user-led remediation, there are always pathways for Trump to evade containment and go back on the attack.

In a standoff, time stops, allowing freeze-frame scrutiny, and yet time also moves too rapidly—leaders cannot react in time. Media make the site of the standoff permeable and visible, while also closed off. Yet because those leaders within the space can use media to learn how to adapt, to gain control of the moment that was initially both too fast and too slow but is now choreographed and unpacked for preparation. Wagner-Pacifici's analysis indicated that for a standoff to be resolved, there must be a restructuring of the situation so there is some overlap of meaning and time horizons. Certainly journalists restructured the situation by deconstructing it for audiences while audiences themselves played with handshake GIFs themselves. The handshakes were archived, compared, and mocked. Leaders then adapted to Trump's zero-sum collision and became playful and reflexive about it. While the second Macron handshake demonstrates Trump's gleeful drive to defeat other leaders, his shame at Merkel's amusement suggested he had been found out. Trump's strategy appeared unsustainable. Yet, paradoxically, the sheer excess and fluidity of digital media keep the standoff frozen because, while still at liberty in office, another Trump gesture is possible.

Notes

1. For an analysis of how Trump differentiated himself from Obama visually, see Roa (2017).
2. Despite spending far less on campaign advertising, Trump achieved $4.96 billion 'free media'—media coverage gained simply by hitting news values— compared to $3.24 billion for Clinton (Harris 2016).

References

Abramson, A. (2017). Watch Poland's First Lady Pass By President Trump's First Attempt at a Handshake. *Time*, 6 July. Available at: http://time.com/4847276/donald-trump-agata-kornhauser-duda-handshake/

Baker, P. (2018). A Sober Trump Reassures the Davos elite. *The New York Times*, 26 January. Available at: https://www.nytimes.com/2018/01/26/world/europe/donald-trump-davos-speech.html

Berenson, T. (2017). President Trump just directly contradicted his Secretary of State. *Time*, 9 June. Available at: http://time.com/4813247/donald-trump-contradict-rex-tillerson-qatar/

Bially Mattern, Janice (2005). *Ordering International Politics: Identity, Crisis and Representational Force*. New York: Routledge.

Blagburn, F. (2017). 'Clasp, yank, release': the great Donald Trump handshake tracker. *The Telegraph*, 26 May. Available at: http://www.telegraph.co.uk/men/the-filter/clasp-yank-release-great-donald-trump-handshake-tracker/?utm_content=buffer74fc6&utm_medium=social&utm_source=twitter.com&utm_campaign=buffer

Boden, D. and Hoskins, A. (1995). Time, Space and Television. Paper presented at Theory, Culture & Society conference, Lancaster University, 11 August.

Brown, D. (2017). The Definitive Analysis of 'The Handshake' Between Donald Trump and Justin Trudeau. Vice.com, 13 February. Available at: https://www.vice.com/en_ca/article/the-definitive-analysis-of-the-handshake-between-donald-trump-and-justin-trudeau?utm_source=vicenewsletterus

Crowther, P. (2017). Oh my. White House pooler @PhilipRucker's view of the Trump – Macron handshake in Brussels: knuckles turned white and faces tightened. @PhilipinDC, 25 May. Available at: https://twitter.com/PhilipinDC/status/867709667610374145

Ferrari, F. (forthcoming). *Metaphor and Persuasion in Strategic Communication: Sustainable Perspectives*. New York: Routledge.

Graham, C. (2017). White House 'misled over Russian photographer in Oval Office' amid security concerns. *The Telegraph*, 11 May. Available at: http://www.telegraph.co.uk/news/2017/05/11/white-house-misled-russian-photographer-oval-office-amid-security/

Harris, M. (2016). A Media Post-Mortem on the 2016 Election. mediaQuant, 14 November. Available at: https://www.mediaquant.net/2016/11/a-media-post-mortem-on-the-2016-presidential-election/

Hill, A. (2017). Why Donald Trump's weird handshake matters. *Financial Times*, 26 May. Available at: https://www.ft.com/content/ea244f6c-4219-11e7-82b6-896b95f30f58

Hoskins, A. & O'Loughlin, B. (2007). *Television and Terror: Conflicting Times and the Crisis of News Discourse*. Basingstoke: Palgrave.

Hounsell, B. (2007). Putin uses dog to intimidate Merkel. *Foreign Policy*, 14 June. Available at: http://foreignpolicy.com/2007/06/14/putin-uses-dog-to-intimidate-merkel/

Kellner, D. (2016). *American Nightmare: Donald Trump, Media Spectacle, and Authoritarian Populism*. Amsterdam: Sense Publishers.

Lizza, R. (2011). The Consequentialist. *The New Yorker*, 2 May. Available at: http://www.newyorker.com/magazine/2011/05/02/the-consequentialist (accessed 2 April 2015).

Marcin, T. (2017). Trump-Macron Handshake: White-Knuckled, Finger-Crushing Male Peacocking. *Newsweek*, 25 May. Available at: http://www.newsweek.com/trump-macron-handshake-awkward-615423

McCarthy, T. (2015). The CounterText Interview: Tom McCarthy. *CounterText*, 1(2): 135–153.

Moore, J. (2017). Donald Trump and Emmanuel Macron Used Their Handshake to Fight Over Who Has a Bigger Penis. *GQ*, 25 May. Available at: http://www. gq.com/story/donald-trump-handshake-emmanuel-macron

Nehring, H. (2017). Handshakes or Punches? What goes on behind closed diplomatic doors. *The Conversation*, 31 January. Available at: https://theconversation.com/ handshakes-or-punches-what-goes-on-behind-closed-diplomatic-doors-72017

Neumann, I.B. (2011). 'Euro-centric diplomacy: Challenging but manageable', *European Journal of International Relations*, 18(2), 299–321.

Obama, B. (2010). The National Security Strategy of the United States. May. Available at: http://nssarchive.us/NSSR/2010.pdf

Obama, B. (2009). Inaugural Address, Washington DC, 20 January. Available at: www.whitehouse.gov/blog/inaugural-address

Pedder, S. (2017). Macron's powershake with Trump was "not accidental", he says: "It's important to show one won't make small concessions, even symbolic ones". @PedderSophie, 28 May. Available at: https://twitter.com/PedderSophie/ status/868749939668639744?s=03

Roa, S. C. (2017). Watch: Key Pictures from Trump's First 100 Days: The Reading the Pictures Salon. *Reading The Pictures*, 11 April. Available at: http://www. readingthepictures.org/2017/04/trump-100-days-salon/

Scott, L. (2015). *The Four-Dimensional Human*. London: Penguin and Random House UK.

Shugerman, E. (2017). Psychologists break down the mysteries of Donald Trump's handshake. *The Independent*, 29 May. Available at: http://www.independent. co.uk/news/world/americas/donald-trump-handshake-emmanuel-macron-nato-psychology-a7762026.html

Steele, B. J. (2010). *Defacing Power: The Aesthetics of Insecurity in Global Politics*. Ann Arbor, MI: University of Michigan Press.

Stein, S. (2017). The Madness And Science Behind The Donald Trump Handshake. *The Huffington Post*, 31 May. Available at: http://www.huffingtonpost.com/ entry/donald-trump-handshake_us_592adb83e4b0df57cbfc23fd?ncid=engm odushpmg00000004

Strachan, M. (2017). Does Donald Trump Know How To Shake Hands? An Investigation. *Huffington Post*, 10 February. Available at: http://www. huffingtonpost.com/?icid=hjx004

Wagner-Pacifici, R. (2000). *Theorizing the Standoff: Contingency in Action*. Cambridge: Cambridge University Press.

Washington Post. (2017). Macron appears to swerve away from Trump at NATO summit. 25 May. Available at: https://www.washingtonpost.com/video/ politics/macron-appears-to-swerve-away-from-trump-at-nato-summit/ 2017/05/25/e2cadcd8-4186-11e7-b29f-f40ffced2ddb_video.html

CHAPTER 11

"Classic Theatre" as Media Against Trump: Imagining Chekhov

John Tulloch

This chapter explores the under-researched field of professional theatre's resistance to hegemonic power over the Trump presidential election and Brexit referendum. It focuses on three recent productions of Chekhov as live performances mediatized as "classical theatre" in the context of politicized "truth", "reality" and "fake news".

All three of these productions ostend, in the semiotic sense of creating dramatic macro- and micro-contexts (Elam 1989), death and living, despair and hope, collapse and endurance. Two of these plays, as adaptations of Chekhov's *Cherry Orchard*, address Trump either directly or as part of the Trump/Brexit risk equation; the other Chekhov play, the Sydney Theatre Company (STC) *Three Sisters*, acknowledges that, because this is great art, audiences may well find associations with Trump, Putin and WikiLeaks, but emphasizes that the writer-adapter and director wanted to foreground a personalized existentialism of death, that of Chekhov himself.

The concept of "story-teller" (as writer or director) emerges centrally for each of these plays as source of hope (or else its foregrounded absence in *Three Sisters*), and productions are mediatized by live performance and online review. So reflexivity about each of these agencies (including my

J. Tulloch (✉)
Charles Sturt University, NSW, Australia

© The Author(s) 2019
C. Happer et al. (eds.), *Trump's Media War*,
https://doi.org/10.1007/978-3-319-94069-4_11

own interpretation) is a necessary aspect of the discussion. In doing this the chapter explores different conjunctures of "history then" and "history now" as Chekhov is imagined as media against Trump.

An Australian journalist recently wrote that "Fake News" is shifting away from the notion of false stories about a US presidential candidate circulating on the internet. "These days, Donald Trump tends to apply the term to all legitimate news he doesn't like", concluding that "it is more important than ever for those of us in the business of #realnews to make sure our assertions are based on solid facts" (Fitzimmons 2018). This chapter takes the view that facts are social constructions, but that they are also real in the context of a critical realist epistemology (Lovell 1980; Tulloch and Blood 2012, pp. 199ff). Theoretically the chapter argues for an interdisciplinary-dialogical approach to avoid the silo risk of single-discipline studies. Methodologically it insists on evidential backing underpinning epistemology and theory in assessing dialogue between different versions of "Chekhov". Inevitably this raises the question: how equipped *are* academics (or theatre professionals) to resist "fake news" eras if scholarly data in their own fields are elided or forgotten?

"Classic Theatre" As Genre: Mediatized Shakespeare in the Park

In June 2017, a right-wing protester interrupted a Shakespeare-in-the-Park production in New York of *Julius Caesar*, shouting "this is political violence against the right". Even as some of the audience booed her off the stage, the incident was filmed by a well-known right-wing provocateur who shouted back at the audience, "You are Nazis like Joseph Goebbels... You are terrorists" (Wahlquist and Beckett 2017).

This 'live' but mediatized aggression was interpreted by the play's creative personnel as part of Donald Trump's war on the media; in particular targeting its performance in public theatre space. Director Oscar Eustis stated after the interrupted performance, "Free speech for all, but let's not stop the show". In a production where the assassinated Caesar looked very like Trump, the Public Theater commented on Twitter that it had expected this protest as "part of a paid strategy driven by social media" (Ibid).

Soon after this incident, two of the Public Theater's main corporate financiers announced that they were withdrawing their sponsorship, after Donald Trump Jr. tweeted that he was wondering "how much of this 'art' is funded by taxpayers' money" (Beckett 2017). Reporting this mediated theatrical controversy, *Guardian* journalist Lois Becket quoted an interview with a Public Theater spokeswoman who emphasized that

> Shakespeare's play, and our production, make the opposite point: those who attempt to defend democracy by undemocratic means pay a terrible price and destroy the very things they are fighting to save...[The play's] discourse is the basis of a healthy democracy (Ibid).

This Shakespeare-in-the-Park incident indicates two things which we should think more about as academics and media professionals.

(i) It demonstrates that live theatre professionals are actively resisting Trump's war on established media. Helmore, in his *Observer* piece from New York "Broadway v Trump" highlights "US divisions under Trump", focusing initially on "political provocateur" filmmaker Michael Moore's about-to-open Broadway play, *The Terms of Surrender*, with its "emblazoned posters... 'Can a Broadway show bring a president down?'". As well as the *Julius Caesar* event, Helmore quotes actor Tom Sturridge—who played Winston Smith in the Robert Icke and Duncan Macmillan Broadway production of *1984*—noting that 95% of the script was taken directly from George Orwell's novel, and adds he was struck by how Orwell's phrase "words matter" was precisely echoed in former FBI director James Comey's testimony to the Senate intelligence committee. "I could feel the audience gasp that what they saw on CNN is now, somehow, refracted back through time to the mind of George Orwell in 1949 and put back in Broadway" (Ibid, p. 23). Orwell's *1984* warning about "doublethink" and mediatized control was here, recognized by performers and audiences alike, consciously in the context of Trump's "fake news" war on media.

(ii) The Shakespeare-in-the-Park incident is important for the way in which theatrical events are communicated through the fusion of embodied public space and emergent social media. In their book, *Risk and Hyperconnectivity* (2016) Hoskins and Tulloch analysed the way in which media reporting of major risk events like the global financial crisis and its live street protests worked off each other. Similarly, they analysed the London riots and the 7/7 terrorism coronial inquest as mediatized assemblages, drawing on mainstream and emergent media as well as "theatrical embodiment in real embodied space" (Hoskins and Tulloch 2016, p. 203). It is clear from the mainstream media discussion of the Shakespeare-in-the-Park event—which foregrounds both twitter provocation and live-stage embodiment—that the logics of connectivity and memory are equally relevant to creative-professional agency in resisting Trump's war on media.

Hoskins and Tulloch define mediatization as "risk increasingly embedded in and penetrated by media, such that to understand, predict, assuage, employ, historicize, remember, forget, and imagine risk requires attention to that media (established and emergent) and its uses" (2016, p. 9). This chapter extends that "imagining", "historicizing", "remembering" and "forgetting" of risk across a configuration of established (live theatre) communication and emergent (online review) media by exploring the political aesthetics of professional story-tellers. The focus is on empirical case studies of live plays, watched by the author in the context of online reviewing, where shifting "classical theatre" assemblages of "war against Trump" are layered, ostended and remediated in different ways via mainstream ("classic theatre") and emergent medialities. Crucially, these resistances to Trump and Brexit each have their own creative and political aesthetic. In an interdisciplinary study of this nature, the analysis—like the theatrical event itself—needs to operate at the level of discursive academic debate, theatrical conventions, politically varying online responses, and social audiences.

CHEKHOV IN THE WAR AGAINST TRUMP: CARNIVAL, SONG, AND POLITICAL AESTHETICS

Central to Bakhtin's original formulation of "carnival" was the notion of turning social systems upside down, for a day or a performance, where ritualized, excessive parody reversed dominant socio-political order (see Alex Symons' "Trump and Satire" in this volume). Carnival is *symbolic* performance in public places (Hoskins and Tulloch 2016, p. 137). This was the case with Robert Icke's *1984* in London, New York and Sydney which turned Orwell's dystopic ending upside down by including *within* the play the novel's appendix on Newspeak, which audiences picked up as overt reference to Trump and "fake news" when the production was re-scheduled in 2017.

Hoskins and Tulloch emphasize "the relation of...emergent media technology to the performance in real public places that the carnival concept is all about" (2016, p. 153). Simon Cottle, writing in the field of risk and disaster studies about Global Summit sieges from Seattle to Gleneagles, argues that "the power of the Internet as well as the performative power of *carnivalesque* tactics deliberately designed for the known predilections of mainstream news media...can assume richly differentiated, often creative forms, but always with a reflexive eye on the media" (Cottle 2009, pp. 31, 34). Theatre, as an evolving public communication form, has become increasingly aware of carnivalesque connective power (as with *Julius Caesar*).

In October/November 2016 and February/March 2017 two major theatre writer/directors, Bonnie Greer and Trevor Griffiths separately repositioned Anton Chekhov's *The Cherry Orchard* to engage with the risk of Trump. At the same time, respected British theatre producer Sir Colin Callender said at the New York opening of Robert Icke's *1984*:

> When the social and political landscape is as vivid and turbulent as it currently is, all good drama and story-telling takes on a new resonance. The context informs the story, and the story responds to the context...– they've all taken new relevance since the election of Donald Trump. It's exciting that an art form as old as the theatre can continue to be a stimulus for debate. (Callender cited in Helmore 2017, p. 23)

But as well as being "Art", live-performance theatres are also communicative media, often combining virtualized and live agencies of resistance to power. This "upside down" intention was at the heart of Bonnie Greer's *Hotel Cerise* (*Cherry Hotel*) adaptation of Chekhov's *Cherry Orchard*. It was written to ostend

> a class that I know much about and which isn't written enough about: the upper class, the black elite...[which] working class folks like me ...[don't see as] victims of racism in the classic sense – they've insulated themselves from it through money and privilege. The drama of being black in America is so acute, so intense, that this class is often overlooked. (Greer 2016)

It was that "overlooked" black class that Greer displayed in *Hotel Cerise*'s narrative structure as she dramatized the differences between elite entertainers of the past serviced by the Cherry Hotel owners (during the era of Bessie Smith, Dinah Washington and Ella Fitzgerald) and contemporary Black Lives Matter servants (Tulloch 2018, pp. 423, 424). Her "Chekhov", Greer insisted to her audience (via programme notes) and to her reviewers (via interviews) was a *class* not a "black" reinterpretation. It was also a dramatization of current political risk that could, to re-use Sturridge's phrase, be refracted back to the aesthetics of Chekhov, "and then forwards again" to Trump's mediatized politics.

Likewise, socialist playwright Trevor Griffiths had already engaged during the 1970s and 1980s via Chekhov's *Cherry Orchard* with those specificities of local/general place, time and history that Cottle and Lester insist "clearly demands detailed empirical exploration and careful theorization" (2011, p. 7). In Griffiths' case these earlier adaptations of Chekhov had been at British historical moments just before and contemporary with the political emergence of Thatcher's neo-liberalism (Tulloch 2005, pp. 83–112; 2006, pp. 49–73). But now, in February/March 2017, Griffiths brought his "rediscovery" of Chekhov to a London stage for the first time with direct reference to Trump's politics and the Brexit debate.

Key to the political aesthetics of both Greer (in 2016) and Griffiths (in 1977, 1981 and 2017) was on-stage use of Brecht's alienation effect. Greer, coming to Chekhov anew, said she found politics, hatred, comedy, love and death in this "classic" text. Chekhov, for her, viewed death not just as natural termination, but also an *ongoing* narrative "template" to "push at" and interrogate on behalf of her political aesthetic, giving her the opportunity

> to do what I've dedicated the rest of my life in the theatre to doing: placing women of color and other minorities inside of classic works, to stretch, to push; and interrogate them…*Hotel Cerise* is…only the next step in the discovery of what makes a Great Work of the theatre. (Greer cited Tulloch 2018)

Great "classic" works of theatre are used by Greer both to re-embody women and "to stretch" current social-aesthetic templates by way of acting, lighting and song. That is her play's context as story-telling. Further, Greer believes that "there is a duty in a democratic society to make [culture] accessible to all…Culture is a nation talking to itself.…extending its humanity to others and … increasing it within itself" (Greer 2016, cited Tulloch 2018). Griffiths, too, speaks of "rediscovering" Chekhov for the widest possible audience; but for him the macro-context is ostended by revealing aspects which he argues Chekhov confined to a subtext because of 1904 Russian censorship (Tulloch 2006, p. 55). It was that censorship that Griffiths was turning upside down in his carnival "rediscovery" of Chekhov.

Griffiths interpreted Chekhov's much-debated "groaning" mine-cable sound and the servant Firs' words in declining "the Freedom" in Act 2 as specifically historical, class-based symbols threading through a sub-narrative that opened out to the "radical disjuncture" of the "vagrant". *Cherry Orchard's* Act 2 vagrant represented for Griffiths an historical figure "released by the French Revolution a hundred years previously and still wandering, still looking for social justice, equality, fraternity" (Griffiths 1990). This context of the under-class then exploded in his 1981 BBC televised *Cherry Orchard* into the era of Thatcher's early neo-liberalism (Griffiths "Preface" Tulloch 1990); and he would have liked the same "march through time" (see Tulloch 2006, pp. 169–179) to have occurred in the 2017 production. For Greer this vagrant "Passer-By" was also ostended on-stage: a black African slave mobile like a "ghost" from past oppression, and now appearing to *Hotel Cerise* owner Thimbutu to predict transformative risk with the advent of Trump.

In Griffiths' political aesthetic, Act 2 broke with the naturalistic performances and interior sets of all the other Acts: "It's like expressionism, the interior being turned outside, the subtext bursting through the text and the [naturalist] text getting washed away" (Griffiths cited in Tulloch 2006, pp. 54–5). Similarly, like *Hotel Cerise* online reviewer Julian Eaves, my immediate impression during Greer's production was of a "disjunctive alienating device" in Brecht's sense, where the regular use of "freeze-frame" lighting and the director's immobilization of other actors on-stage subverted the naturalist performance (Eaves 2016). Thus Greer's nineteenth century slave-woman burst from colonial oppression into the present class milieu of black celebrity, her plain white shift in stark contrast to the magnificently flamboyant couture of the African-American class elite, who derive their "insulating" wealth from white slave-owners of the past, and likewise separate themselves visually and experientially from Black Lives Matter African-American and other migrant under-classes (Tulloch 2018).

Clearly the live-stage fight-back against Trump by Greer and Griffiths was both a political *and* a theatrical event, the latter ostended via macro- and micro-contexts of character (ruling class vs. working/under-class), performance (live/immobilized), theatrical convention (alienation and expressionism against naturalism) and sound and music (the groaning cable, and the recorded songs of Ella Fitzgerald and Billie Holliday).

The point about Trump-critique in fiction is that this *is* fiction. It is *story-telling* in the sense that art and photography critic John Berger described himself. "If I am a story-teller it is because I *listen*. To me a storyteller is a passer-on – that is to say like someone who gets contraband across a frontier. Stories come to you all the time if you listen, if you listen, if you listen" (Jarman Lab 2016).

For Berger the fake but hegemonic nature of political and corporate language today has discredited prose in failing to describe the lives of the vast majority of the world's people. For Berger "words matter" too, but they have been co-opted, devalued politically and corporately. "By contrast, I think what people are living across the world today is very translatable and expressible and sharable in song. Maybe we live in a time when the truth is most easily told in song" (Ibid).

It is this "contraband" and "sharable" reality of song that Ken Loach drew on in his television documentary *Which Side Are You On? Songs and Poems of the Miners' Strike, 1984* about Thatcherite and police brutality; and it is song that Trevor Griffiths' threaded throughout his television drama *Food for Ravens* about the early death of British radical Labour Minister, Aneurin Bevan, after spearheading the British Welfare State.

Music was alive on Greer's stage. The songs of Fitzgerald and Holliday provided a haunting evocation of the exploitation of black people and their particular historical resistance as entertainers. But, in combination with the alienation technique of "freeze-frame" acting, lighting and costuming, the semiotic density of theatre as mediatization evokes both exploitation *of* African-Americans and *by* them. In Griffiths' *Food For Ravens* where he was, like Greer, in complete control of his story-telling as writer and director, he used the television form of camera, sound, song, and mix of naturalist, surreal, and expressionist style in a radical remembering *and* reimagining of class exploitation (Tulloch 2006, pp. 122–123). For the Left "hope" must always be a macro-context of fiction; and Trevor Griffiths would agree with the poet Ben Lerner (speaking about Berger as story-teller) that the Right has no new stories, since, as Griffiths argues, it is committed to pragmatism and a fake nostalgia. It is committed to telling and not listening to stories. Donald Trump tweets; he doesn't narrate stories.

HISTORICIZING CHEKHOV: ONLINE REVIEWS

"Classic theatre" as a genre engages not only with the "original" texts themselves, but also a long history of academic and theatre criticism as well (Tulloch 1985, pp. 185–206). "Classic theatre" writer/adapters *especially* are embedded in schemas of remembering, forgetting and reimagining stories told many times before. Productions like Greer's and Griffiths' (and STC's *Three Sisters*) aim to "stretch ...push...interrogate", "rediscover" or offer "a contemporary evolution" of those earlier schemata; while online reviewers offer audiences instant premediation and remediation of these live memories. As Brown and Hoskins argue, "The mediatization of memory involves a potentially continuous cycle of the premediation and remediation of schemata" (2010, p. 95) where they see premediation as the recycling of media schemas (like use of film of British people resisting the Blitz after the London terrorist attack of 2005, Hoskins and Tulloch 2016, pp. 209–210) to connect temporally different events, and provide emotional/cognitive focus and direction to audiences. But remediation can also take new radical paths, as in the case of Greer and Griffiths.

Most online reviewers of the Griffiths/Ergen *Cherry Orchard* recognized and articulated the relationship between Chekhov's time/space and our own. Gary Naylor speaks of the Arcola season's commemoration of the Russian Revolution, with *Cherry Orchard extra*-meaningful now that "revolutions of a kind have ripped through UK and US polity". Chekhov "finds a voice to communicate with an audience wrestling with new anxieties and new fears – and with new "orchards" being chopped down before their eyes" (2016). Claire Seymour says that it is hard to disagree with Ergen's point "that today we too face such revolution" as populations encounter "Brexit, Trump, a series of unpredictable elections to come in Europe" (2016). Theo Bosanquet opines "It's a strange thing watching Chekhov's masterpiece about a world on the brink of collapse when it feels the wheels of our own contemporary meltdown are firmly in motion" (2016) and Munotida Chinyanga notes that "Mehmet Ergen's interpretation implicitly explores ideas that relate to contemporary audiences, more specially class struggle, social conflict, displacement and the differences between younger and older generations which seem to fall within this environment post-Brexit and Trump's America" (2016).

But, as Hoskins and Tulloch note, "The first and/or dominant medium of representation can have an enduring effect on understandings and approaches to that being represented" (2016, p. 303). One dominant mediatization is that of writer/adaptors and directors (for Chekhov see Tulloch 1985). Equally important are online reviewers of Chekhov "then" and "now", particularly the *salience* they ascribe as potential *first audiences* of the play. These reviewers are, as Alasuutari (1999) framed it, a key part of the process of "audiencing": that is, mobilizing live texts and audiences together, in this case via immediate online response—not as discrete demographic facts "out there" but as discursive constructs located within multiple interpretive frames of remembering and forgetting Chekhov. Extending this notion of social audiences, Martin Barker emphasizes that "media and cultural encounters…have different degrees of salience for different viewers. The encounters that resonate the most with us, which we engage with richly, and maybe repeatedly, and which in some way connect with our sense of who we are…: these work differently from those that are more routine or quotidian, or which leave us critical or bored" (Barker 2011, pp. 110–11). Whether online reviewers are, in Barker's terms, "embracers" or "rejecters" of the production is as important as their recognition of contemporary "relevance". My point here is that this judgement of salience will, itself, be mediated by reviewers' social-aesthetic *memories* of the "classic" text in question.

Theatre reviewers self-project as "experts" in the semiotics of staging and performance (what Hoskins and Tulloch call their "mediality": the way that content is "posted, circulated, edited, and consumed", 2016, pp. 246–7); and this expertise generally structures the review's narrative. But reviewers also reveal significant *pleasure* as "embracers" or *dislike/boredom* as "rejecters", drawing on one or more aspects of the semiotic density of the multi-medial theatrical event in doing so. Where, as in our case, the target is "Chekhov against Trump", online critics mediatize live events and audiences. Matthew Lunn is one of Barker's "embracers", finding salience in the play's "vibrant" contemporaneousness by way of Ergen's "sense that something enormous is going to happen"; via Griffiths' "gorgeous translation"; and through key actors' "complexity" in performance (2017). In contrast Seymour is a "rejecter", despite recognizing the play's contemporary relevance. She had wanted to see "the glories" and "spatial majesty" of the cherry orchard in this production. But the "poetry" of the era was lost by the "unimaginative" lack of "grace and formality" in the sound design, and the "jazz inflected whirl with too much spangle and sparkle" of Act 3's half-hearted ball. Thus the "cherry orchard loses its symbolic potency and becomes just a verbal motif reminding us of Lopakhin's aspirations" (2017). It is the past of the gentry that Seymour wants remembered; and she doesn't find that memory in the Ergen/Griffiths production.

Seymour's review does more than offer its expertise in negatively elaborating the theatrical event's multi-layered mediality. It is also locked ideologically into the tragedy of this class, the gentry. Seymour is angry about Ranyevskya's infantilizing (even though not only Griffiths but Chekhov himself begin and end their plays in the nursery to offer this as, in part, an explanation for the gentry's fecklessness); and she is sold on "the glories of the cherry orchard", even though both Chekhov and Griffiths emphasize that the orchard is entirely unproductive.

In Seymour's online reviews the specific *historicity* of Chekhov's original play is a key tool in her rejecter's judgement of this 2017 *Cherry Orchard*. Trump-history plays no part whatsoever in the conservative reviewer's aesthetic equation, even though he is ostended in Seymour's opening remarks. Similarly, in a review titled "Chekhov stripped of its Russian soul", Julie Rank writes, "Mehmet Ergen's self-consciously gauche modern staging, nominally remains in Russia but feels like it's set in Surrey...[I]t fails to feel like a play for today due to the way in which so much of the tension is in relation to the fact that [Chekhov's is] a society in which serfdom had only been abolished for a generation" (2017).

In contrast, embracers of the Arcola *Cherry Orchard*, tended to enjoy the theatrical playing *between* different histories (as does Griffiths) rather than limiting it to one place and time. Thus Naylor blends Chekhov's historical moment with the Stalin period three decades later when the Soviet leader "saw off the kulaks with an unprecedented brutality", and then with Naylor's own biography when first seeing the play in the mid-1980s:

> when "The Orchard" was a Perestroika-era Russia...but also a post-industrializing Britain, its smokestacks being bulldozed literally by demolition men and metaphorically by the barrow-boys newly emboldened by The City's Big Bang switch to electronic, frictionless, borderless financial trading (and we all know how that fairytale ended).

Finally Naylor does move us on to the present time of Brexit and Trump:

> 30 years on – 103 years since it was written – the play's relevance is as sharp as ever... Lopakhin makes his move to purchase the estate and build his own dachas ...Jude Akuwudike...plays Lopakhin with a Cockney accent and white van swagger, insecure in his peasant past but convinced of his mon-eyed future. (Naylor 2017)

So Naylor's embracing response to *Cherry Orchard* is embedded in the production's particular *admixture* of history from Chekhov's time to our own; whereas in contrast, both Seymour's and Bosanquet's rejection finds Lopakhin inappropriately contemporary ("Cockney brazen"), with hardly a hint of the "inner turmoil" of the original Chekhov character. Chekhov's sense of time and place is lost for both online reviewers:

> Chekhov can withstand reinvention, and there have been some superb productions recently to prove it, including Robert Icke's *Vanya* and David Hare's *Young Chekhov* trilogy. But where others have made him feel startlingly contemporary, here he feels dully irrelevant. (Bosanquet 2017)

So if Chekhov "then" is locked in nostalgia, what does the "startlingly contemporary" mean for rejecters of the Arcola *Cherry Orchard* like Bosanquet. We can get some sense of this from highly positive reviews of Icke's *Uncle Vanya*.

Eleonor Turney's embracing review confirms "Icke's message that these people are not going anywhere as the world keeps turning" at the "heart of the human condition", where every character reaches out but then "realize that they are alone in an uncaring world" (2016). Even with its "eco-friendly doctor", *Variety* reviewer Matt Trueman says, this is "a study of inaction, the ways we waste time and the ways time wastes us". The slowly revolving wooded set "always moving, but going nowhere" keeps gathering useless clutter, "the exact opposite of Michael's beloved forests, disappearing bit by bit, year on year" (2016). Reviewer Holly Williams says of the doctor in this "incredibly faithful to the text version" that he is "more proto-lumbersexual than worthy eco-warrior – and his scenes with [Yelena] sizzle dangerously" (2016) with Icke's signature.

Nearly all the *Vanya* reviewers commented positively about its visceral theatricality: "This is what [Icke] gave us with his galvanic *1984*...This is what – less shatteringly but no less convincingly – he delivers with his finely scored, highly tuned *Uncle Vanya*" (Clapp 2016). But Icke's *Vanya* (like Kip Williams' *Three Sisters* we look at next) remediated Chekhov with "people not going anywhere as the world keeps turning" in its "human condition" *despite* its tree-planting "eco-warrior".

THE STC *THREE SISTERS*: DE-HISTORICIZING CHEKHOV

STC's Artistic Director Kip Williams says that adaptor Andrew Upton expands Chekhov's "grand experiment of naturalism" in their production:

> It's one of the things Chekhov helped bring to playwriting – capturing the way that people actually speak, the half thoughts, the change of direction of thought in mid-sentence. Andrew can capture that beautifully and offers a contemporary evolution of it. (Williams 2017, p. 5)

By setting his play in the early 1970s, at the end of the "1968" radical era, Upton was able to differentiate the three sisters, expanding them from the highly constrained upper-middle class domesticity of Chekhov's original Olga, Masha and Irina. In particular, the key role of Masha was liberated by Upton's text, becoming the owner of her own sensuality and eroticism, so that, if anything, it is the talkative Vershinin who is seduced by her. Masha's sexual agency is as overt as her use of F-word language. By way of subtext of song (as in Chekhov's original play, but in this case Bob Dylan chosen by Upton to "tie in with the bourgeois idea of getting to know the working class", Upton 2017, p. 14) we again see song rather than words play a theatrical role as existential alternative to the ritualized, domesticated, devalued prose of yearning and failure. Masha ignites this production like a flame as clearly as Olga deflates it with her comedic balloons in Act 1. So by *crossing between different time periods,* Upton expanded in a liberating way Chekhov's own huge influence on the history of theatrical language.

A second history that was engaged with powerfully on-stage was that of theatrical naturalism. In his edited book, *Naturalist Plays,* Megson speaks of Chekhov's *Three Sisters* balancing "the representation of surface reality in the Naturalistic mode with an expressivity and self-conscious theatricality that pushes towards the metaphorical, and, at times, overtly symbolic... In such moments, the illusionist credentials of Naturalism break down and Chekhov anticipates the preoccupations of modernist playwrights such as Samuel Beckett" (2010, pp. xvii–xviii). Drawing centrally on Beckett, Williams directed this comic disruption throughout the play until the final Act, with particular emphasis on Upton's adaptation of Masha's sensual words, sexual agency, and Vershinin's proneness to talk not action. As some reviewers noted, this was a very funny production, until the heavily symbolic emphasis (in Act 4) on the tree from *Waiting for Godot* (with Masha's sexy boots abandoned beside it).

And *yet,* as theatrical event, there was something crucial missing for me as a social audience member. Online reviewer Keith Gallasch captured some of the concerns I had as I watched. He challenges Upton's "excision of the sisters' final words; Olga's above all" because this "ignored the rigor of the play's emotional ebb and flow in which a pattern of crisis, acceptance and resilience play a key role in the overall arc of the work" As Gallasch argues, Vershinin is an optimist, even in this production: "whenever he despairs or the conversation slumps he swings into vigorous speechmaking, taking centre stage or standing on a table, speculating on the emergence of a benign society some 200–300 years hence (a position Olga takes at the end of the original play)" (2017).

By cutting those lines, Upton isolates *Three Sisters* in the time capsule of the 1970s, without reference to Chekhov *either* "now" *or* "then". What is curious here is that Williams teases his audience with reference to Trump in his programme notes, yet steps back from the global to a *personaliza-tion* of Chekhov's biography. "Chekhov...had tuberculosis, he was deeply unwell." So, "inside *Three Sisters* are existential questions around the pur-pose of living...the meaning of it, and the failure of it. Death and mortality hang over the play in a profound way" (Williams 2017, pp. 5–7). Likewise, for writer-adaptor, Andrew Upton, *Three Sisters* has "a deeply felt sense of anger at the corrosion of time, the hammering weight of loss" (2017, p. 15) "Chekhov...must have been coughing up a lot of blood because it's relentless about death and loss. He seems to be not only saying 'you can't take it with you', but also 'you don't even have it when you go'. You lose and lose and lose all the way through this play" (Ibid).

A clear intellectual and political difference lay between the Williams/Upton interpretation of Chekhov and Griffiths' or Greer's versions. For Williams/Upton, as with Icke's *Uncle Vanya*, *Three Sisters* is about death as part of the "human condition". There is rage on-stage (and, supposedly, off stage with its author). Hence "you lose throughout the play" (Upton Ibid). But significantly Upton cut out not only Olga's important finale speech, but the other sisters' speeches as well. Hence, in this adaptation, the three sisters in different ways all succumb to the failure of potential and collapse of their brother Andrei, who had dreamed of being a professor in the capital city, but ends up as a minor local bureaucrat who is subservient to the local council chairman, both at work and in his wife's bed.

Yet, sitting in the audience I—and others I spoke with there—felt that the *uncut* speeches of Vershinin as acted by Mark Leonard Winter sub-verted the "you lose all the way" directorial signature of this production. Some online reviewers puzzled about this, half articulated the problem, and in the end didn't like the production. Ben Neutze, commented that "Mark Leonard Winter's attempts to blow some life into his big speeches as the colonel Vershinin didn't quite gel with the pervasive realism of the other performers", adding that, for him, a key failure of the play was that this "realistic" performance of "angst simply oversteps its welcome" (2016). Cassie Tongue noted that despite the "highly stylized performa-tive despair *and hope* [my italics] between Masha and her new lover Vershinin....it's despair that succeeds the most in this production, other-wise so uncomfortable with itself that it resists connecting with its audi-ence" (2016).

So what *was* the missing "Chekhov then" which motivated those uncut lines?

CHEKHOV AND HOPE

In January 1902 Chekhov presented *Uncle Vanya* to the zemstvo medical association at the Eighth Pirogov Congress in Moscow. Afterwards he received a telegram. "The zemstvo doctors from remote corners of Russia who saw the work of the doctor-artist greet their comrade and will keep the memory of January 11 ever fresh". Chekhov wrote ebulliently to Dr. Chlenov: "The telegrams raised me to heights I had never dreamed of" (cited in Tulloch 1980, p. 70). What is missing from the "Chekhov then" narratives is the fusion of identities of Chekhov as writer and zemstvo doctor.

Russian scholar and historian Nancy Frieden tells the story of how zemstvo medicine, "a pioneering free rural health service" (1981, p. 77), emerged in Russia in the 1870/1880s. From its origins in the modernizing reforms and freeing of serfs by Tsar Alexander II, this new medical profession had two goals at its core: new science and practical community service. Its "sanitary science" emphasized preventing diseases in areas like cholera, diphtheria, tuberculosis and infant mortality; which is why, as causes for transmission of cholera and malaria were isolated, Chekhov could write that, offered all the ideals of the famous sixties in Russia "or the most wretched zemstvo hospital...I would choose the latter unhesitatingly", arguing that "I put my trust in Koch" (the discoverer of cholera aetiology). "To the contemporary medical student the period up to twenty years ago seems insignificant" (cited in Tulloch 1980, p. 17).

Public medical service was for the lower-class, rural peasants and workers in (often rurally based) factories via the local zemstvos. Chekhov wrote, "I don't conceal my respect for the zemstvo which I love" (cited Tulloch 1980, p. 55); and he held his profound faith in scientific zemstvo medicine throughout his life. Thus, he wrote to Dr. Chlenov in 1880, "To work for science and public ideals, that is personal happiness"; to his publisher Suvorin in 1894, "the natural sciences are achieving miracles now, and may rush upon the public and conquer it by sheer size and splendor"; to Dr. Orlov in 1899, "science is constantly pushing forward" (cited Tulloch 1980, p. 85)' and to Dyagilev in 1902 that modern culture based on science was the beginning of a quest for truth and a great future—a real god, whereas religion was a system of the past (cited Tulloch 1980, p. 86).

Chekhov had bitter cause to make that contrast because, as Frieden describes, members of the Orthodox Church had led superstitious peasants to attack and kill doctors aiding the poor in cholera epidemics.

One of the strengths of Frieden's account is her interweaving of Chekhov's stories (*Grasshopper, Wife, Ward Six, Enemies, Peasants*), plays *(Wood Demon, Uncle Vanya)* and medical dissertation *Sakhalin Island* with the struggle of zemstvo doctors for science, status and community service, arguing that "Chekhov's work ...helped to form the generalized world view of many of his colleagues" (1981, p. 16). Another impressive strength of Frieden's long-arc history is her scholarly detail embedded in contemporary sources, recounting the increasing politicization of zemstvo doctors (including Chekhov) after the assassination of Alexander III. She emphasizes Nicholas II's rejection of "senseless dreams" of social and political reform, and Minister of Finance Sergei Witte's secret memorandum to Tsar Nicholas' government that they could not continue to coexist with the zemstvos else "the autocracy would cede all its prerogatives" (cited Frieden 1981, p. 286).

Throughout the optimistic days of growing zemstvo medical professionalization Frieden discusses the key role of medical *communication* in forging professional consciousness. The weekly generalist medical journal, *Physician* (which Chekhov, like most of his colleagues, read) was founded in 1880, becoming "the voice, the conscience, and the backbone of the Russian medical profession" (Frieden 1981, p. 115) with its commitment to free public medicine. The medical association, the Pirogov Society, founded in 1883, led medical professionalization, initially in harmony with the state during the temporary arrangements of the 1892–3 cholera epidemics, but then into increasing hostility to its autocracy. The 1899 Congress marked a turning point, after the state stopped the Society's famine relief to thousands suffering from scurvy and typhus. At this Congress Chekhov's friend Dr. Zbankov pointedly asked what the use was of hospitals, clinics, medicine and sanitary science when so many were starving through state inaction: "you doctors must...devote your attention to easing the suffering of the unfortunate...These people cry out for bread" (cited Frieden 1981, p. 194). My own research discloses Chekhov's passionate support for medical journals, via subsidies from Suvorin, and his own practical help with censorship as the state reaction heightened.

When Chekhov received his telegrams from the Pirogov physicians who had just seen his *Uncle Vanya* he would have recognized the words used conveyed the core of their pride in professional identity: carrying medical care to the "remote corners" of Russia (Frieden 1981, p. 170). Many of Chekhov's friends and most admired colleagues were founding members of the Society; so he was fully aware of—and to the end of his life begged his doctor friends to keep him informed about—the politicization of the Pirogov Society. Six months before his death in 1904 Pirogovist leaders were calling for free voting (to replace the gentry-voting bias of zemst-vos), freedom of association (which the Society was increasingly being denied as the state increased its aggression), and freedom of the press.

Two books, Frieden's and my *Chekhov: A Structuralist Study*, were written about Chekhov and zemstvo medicine within one year without cognizance of each other, with completely different disciplinary and meth-odological profiles (with mine based on the translated and mostly un-translated Chekhov letters). Yet they agreed about the professional development, ethics, scientific identity, and reformist politics of zemstvo medicine (and Chekhov's profound identity within it). Frieden's book's major strength lies in the scholarly, source-based detail of the shifting struggles between modernizing state, zemstvo local government and bur-geoning medical profession over 50 years as political reaction waxed and waned. My *Chekhov* study lacks that historical dynamism, but its interdis-ciplinary profile offers a different strength. Based on PhD research, is puts under scrutiny what Judith Butler later described as "several different ways of considering ... what the object is" (Butler 2015, p. vi) as it brings together historically an *intra*-sociological dialogue about key markers of medical professionalization, concepts of modernizing autocracy from political science, Kuhnian paradigm theory from philosophy of science, and literary theory to isolate four indicators of professional identifica-tion—functional space, symbolic interaction, scientific paradigm and ideo-logical context—on *all* of which Chekhov scores highly (as already indicated with just a few of many examples cited in the book).

But as well as supporting Frieden's book evidentially, *Chekhov* extends it on one key indicator. Kuhn's "normal science" paradigm articulation (Tulloch 1980, pp. 73–76) spread in Russia via an ideology of Social Darwinism opposed to that of the United States. Challenging the "tooth and claw" US emphasis, Russian Social Darwinism emphasized the *sym-biosis within and between species* aspects of Darwin, especially via scientific leaders like the embryologist Mechnikov, the botanist Timiryazev, and the physiologist Sechenov, all of whom Chekhov admired. "I'm reading Darwin" Chekhov wrote in 1884, "I love him profoundly" (cited Tulloch 1980, p. 94). But this was the Darwin of his Moscow University medical professors Osipov, Erisman and Zakhar'in from whom he learned the importance of evidence-based, holistic and environmentally sensitive medicine. From Pirogov to Erisman Russian zemstvo doctors were taught to be educators of the underprivileged as well as scientific physicians; and, as Frieden says, "Erisman forged permanent links between the teaching and practice of public health, and trained a generation of zemstvo physicians" (1981, p. 103). Chekhov was one of those medical students, and worked as a zemstvo doctor until 1897 when doctors diagnosed his illness and ordered him to give up medicine, which, Chekhov wrote, was a great privation.

Speaking of Chekhov's *Uncle Vanya*, Frieden says that Dr. Astrov "may strike the Western reader as strangely preoccupied with the local ecology, but he personified the Moscow zemstvo physician whose tasks included the correlation of this with geographic factors" (1981, p. 93)—and Chekhov's close friend, zemstvo doctor P.I. Kurkin provided the topographical maps of progressive *de*forestation that Astrov shows to Yelena in the production of the play seen by the Pirogov Society in 1902. But Mechnikov spoke of how the scientific struggle against plague and cholera revealed that "to satisfy his aesthetic tastes, man revolts against the Laws of Nature which create races of sterile and fragile flowers, so he does not hesitate to defend the weak against the laws of natural selection" (cited in Tulloch 1980, p. 90). Planting trees was an important human agency in this defence, hence Chekhov's hope and pleasure expressed in a letter from Yalta at the time of writing *Three Sisters*: "Before I came here all this was waste land and ravines... covered with stones and thistles. Then I came here and turned this wilderness into a cultivated, beautiful place. Do you know that in three or four hundred years all the earth will become a flourishing garden" (cited Tulloch 1980, p. 140).

Chekhov's words about future progress via education and work underpin those of Colonel Vershinin, the new, scientific-style Russian army officer post-Crimean War in *Three Sisters* (Tulloch 1980, p. 173). The dead tree we see on stage in the final act of the Williams/Upton *Three Sisters* represents for Chekhov, in Tuzenbach's own words, the old-style aristocratic soldier's imminent death. But the *live trees* are upwardly mobile Vershinin's: "you have a genuinely healthy climate here, a true Russian climate. Woods, river...birch trees as well...It's a fine place to live" (*Three Sisters*, Tulloch 1980, p. 140).

Work, education and a healthy natural-social environment are key to Vershinin's *dialogue* with the sisters, as well as Olga's final words 'Just to know', Masha's insistence, "We must go on living", and Irina's hopes for the future "One day we will understand...the reason for all this suffering." All three sisters have adopted Vershinin's vision, not Andrei's failure. Clear historical data has long been available that Chekhov's "expressivity" in expanding the naturalist model was less a matter of theatrical history (developing towards Beckett's modernism) but of social knowledge, reforming ideology and epistemology. Chekhov's recognition of what Megson calls the "unpredictability" of causality was systemic. It was causality open to *social change*; and a new form of critical realism in theatre. Yet while there have been feminist and socialist theatrical challenges to Trump in theatres recently, there have been virtually none by way of the Chekhov who loved his planet.

CONCLUSION

I have argued that both reviewers' nostalgic memories and mono-disciplinary academic analysis can, unintentionally (yet systemically) restrict interpretation. My case study here was Chekhov, where I pointed to a systematic de-historicizing of Chekhov's very evident professional group affiliation as zemstvo doctor—a case of premediation wherein powerful institutions like the military, media (including theatre) and academia "provide schemata for future experience and its representation" (Erll 2008, p. 392, cited in Hoskins and Tulloch 2016, p. 26).

Underlying the analysis has been theatre scholar Wilmar Sauter's concept of "theatrical event" (which I have used loosely in this chapter and more systematically elsewhere; Tulloch 2005), and the notion of theatre as one of sociologist Scott Lash's *fluid sociations* which form, disassemble and re-form (Lash 2000) as we observed the temporal sequence of two productions of Chekhov by Greer and Griffiths. Also important has been Susan Bennett's take on theatre audiences which brings together Raymond Williams' cultural studies understanding of theatre as an "everyday" cultural commodity (Bennett 1997, p. 99) and anthropologist Victor Turner's focus on theatrical performance as structured experiences "which probe a community's weaknesses, call its leaders to account, desacralize its most cherished values and beliefs, [and] portray its characteristic conflicts" (Turner 1982, p. 11).

My point is dialogical: working within Judith Butler's argument that interdisciplinary research needs to go forward on the premise that intellectual problems can only be understood through several lenses. This is why I have profiled also the STC performance of *Three Sisters* and Icke's *Uncle Vanya*. Both contradicted Greer's and Griffiths' productions (and my own interpretation); and yet I and online reviewers experienced them as powerful theatrical events. So this is not a call to close off meanings, but to open them up to dialogue.

In the era of Trump tweets why does this *dialogical* interdisciplinary approach matter? First, it matters theoretically because in the face of Trump's media blitz about "fake news", confusing as he does unintended errors with manipulation, we must as academics avoid our own unintended distortions of "history then", especially when they become systemic by way of silo thinking. Denying that Chekhov sought hope after death is one such example. The Russian state's refusal to let physicians extend their care for the poor from medicine to food is a stark reminder of an autocratic closing-off of disciplinary meanings. Second, it matters methodologically when we as academics seek to challenge "fake news" via rational, reflexive claims on an evidential basis. It is in *material data* (as Chekhov kept arguing) that "truth", "realism" and "beauty" should be based. Third, it matters because the tree-planting, social evolutionary Chekhov offers perhaps a greater inflection of the present against Trump than any of the other recent productions that I have discussed—since, via global warming, the planet itself is in peril and Trump is a climate-change denier. Fourth, it matters because theatre is for the *public* as audiences. Chekhov from a century ago can offer important examples to populations struggling now with anxiety, disillusion, dismay, and cognitive despair. Zemstvo doctors adopted *before others* the ideal of providing health care at need to the public at large with the best medical science available—in contrast to Trump's dedication to repeal even the mildly liberal medical-access reforms of Obama. So zemstvo history and memory of "Chekhov then" must not be forgotten.

Of course "classic theatre" cannot be blueprinted to a single kind of interpretation, otherwise creativity would be dead. But the clear tension between hope *and* despair, life *and* death, endurance *and* collapse among Chekhov and his zemstvo colleagues is open to rich possibilities for alternative "ways of considering the object" (as my discussion of the Greer's and Griffiths' Chekhov indicates). Moreover, it is clear from reviews of the Icke *Uncle Vanya* that Astrov's "eco-friendly" words *remained intact*. Icke's production worked hard to remediate the positive future in Astrov's lines via a determining set-design and actors' performances. But where those words remain they do matter, and Chekhov's ecological vision still calls to account our contemporary political leaders, including Donald Trump.

REFERENCES

Alasuutari, Pertii, Ed (1999) Rethinking the Media Audience. London: Sage.

Barker, Martin (2011) "Watching Rape, Enjoying Rape…How Does a Study of Audience Cha(lle)nge Film Studies Approaches?", in The New Extremism in Cinema, Tanya Horeck and Tina Kendall (Eds.). Edinburgh: Edinburgh University Press.

Beckett, Lois (2017) "Trump as Julius Caesar: anger over play misses Shakespeare's point, says scholar", https://www.theguardian.com/culture/2017/jun/12/donald-trump-shakespeare-play-julius-caesar-new-york

Bennett, Susan (1997) Theatre Audiences: A Theory of Production and Reception. London: Routledge.

Bosanquet, Theo (2017) "The Cherry Orchard", https://www.timeout.com/london/theatre/the-cherry-orchard-9

Brown, Steven and Andrew Hoskins (2010) "Terrorism in the New Memory Ecology: Mediating and Remembering the 2007 London Bombings", Behavioural Sciences of Terrorism and Aggression 2(2),87–107.

Butler, Judith (2015) "Forward: Tracking the Mechanisms of the Psychosocial", in Psychosocial Imaginaries: Perspectives on Temporality, Subjectivities and Activism, S. Frosh (Ed.). Basingstoke, UK: Palgrave Macmillan.

Chinyanga, Munotida (2017) "The Cherry Orchard", https://playstosee.com/the-cherry-orchard-2/

Clapp, Susanna (2016) "Uncle Vanya–Chekhov rewired", https://www.theguardian.com/stage/2016/feb/21/uncle-vanya-review-almeida-robert-icke-observer-review

Cottle, Simon (2009) Global Crisis Reporting. Globalism in the Global Age. Maidenhead: Open University Press.

Cottle, Simon and Libby Lester (2011) Transnational Protests and the Media. New York: Peter Lang.

Eaves, Julian (2016) Review, The Hotel Cerise, http://britishtheatre.com/review-the-hotel-cerise-theatre-royal-stratford-east/

Elam, Keir (1989) "Text Appeal and the Analysis Paralysis: Towards a Processual Politics of Dramatic Production", in Altro Polo Performance: From Product to Process, T. Fitzpatrick (Ed.). Sydney: Sydney University Press.

Erll, Astrid (2008) "Literature, Film, and the Mediality of Cultural Memory", in Cultural Memory Studies: An Interdisciplinary Handbook, Astrid Erll and Ansgar Nünning (Eds.). Berlin: Walter de Gruyter, 389–398.

Fitz Files (2018) "Boom goes the fake news" Sydney Morning Herald, 6–7 January: p. 47.

Frieden, Nancy M. (1981) Russian Physicians in an Era of Reform and Revolution, 1856–1905. Princeton: Princeton University Press.

Gallasch, Keith (2016) "Three Sisters: seeing double", www.realtime.org.au/stcs-three-sisters-seeing-double/

Greer, Bonnie (2016) A note from Bonnie Greer. London: Theatre Royal program.

Griffiths, Trevor (1990) interviewed by Roger Stephens. Birmingham: Birmingham University.

Helmore, Edward (2017) "Broadway v Trump: 'feel bad' politics is new box-office draw", https://www.theguardian.com/stage/2017/jun/24/broadway-vs-trump-drama-of-feel-bad-politics-is-new-box-office-draw

Hoskins, Andrew and John Tulloch (2016) Risk and Hyperconnectivity: Media and Memories of Neoliberalism. New York, Oxford University Press.

Jarman Lab (2016) The Seasons in Quincy: Four Portraits of John Berger DVD. London: Curzon Film World.

Lash, Scott (2000) "Risk Culture", in The Risk Society and Beyond: Critical Issues for Social Theory, B. Adam, U. Beck and J. van Loon (Eds.). London: Sage, pp.47–62.

Lovell, Terry (1980) Pictures of Reality: Aesthetics, Politics, Pleasure. London: BFI Publishing.

Lunn, Matthew (2017) "The Cherry Orchard, Arcola Theatre", http://britishtheatre.com/review-the-cherry-orchard-arcola-theatre/

Mechnikov, Ilya (1910) The Prolongation of Life. London: Heinemann.

Megson, Chris (2010) Naturalist Plays. Abingdon: Methuen.

Naylor, Gary (2017) "The Cherry Orchard, Arcola Theatre", https://www.broadwayworld.com/westend/article/BWW-Review-THE-CHERRY-ORCHARD-Arcola-Theatre-20170223

Seymour, Claire (2017) "The Cherry Orchard", http://www.britishtheatreguide.info/reviews/the-cherry-orch-arcola-theatre-14052

Symons, Alex (2019) "Trump and Satire: America's Carnivalesque President and His War on Television Comedians in Catherine Happer", Trump's War on the Media, Andrew Hoskins and William Merrin (Eds.). Basingstoke, UK: Palgrave Macmillan, pp.181–195.

Tulloch, John (1980) Chekhov: A Structuralist Study. London: Macmillan.

Tulloch, John (1985) "Chekhov Abroad: Western Criticism", in A Chekhov Companion, Toby W. Clyman (Ed.). Westport: Greenwood, pp. 185–206.

Tulloch, John (2005) Shakespeare and Chekhov in Production and Reception: Theatrical Events and their Audiences, Iowa City, University of Iowa Press.

Tulloch, John (2006) Trevor Griffiths. Manchester: Manchester University Press.

Tulloch, John (2018) Class "Then" and Class "Now' in *Hotel Cerise*, in The Routledge Companion to Media Fandom, Melissa Click and Suzanne Scott (Eds.). New York: Routledge, 416–427.

Tulloch, John and Warwick Blood (2012) Icons of War and Terror: Media Images in an Age of International Risk. Abingdon: Routledge.

Trueman, Matt (2016) "Uncle Vanya at the Almeida Theatre", http://variety. com/2016/legit/reviews/uncle-vanya-review-almeida-theatre-1201707561/

Turner, Victor (1982) From Ritual to Theatre, New York, Performing Arts Journal.

Turney, Eleonor (2016) "Uncle Vanya at the Almeida", http://exeuntmagazine. com/reviews/review-uncle-vanya-at-the-almeida/

Upton, Andrew (2017) "In Conversation". Sydney: Sydney Theatre Company Program.

Wahlquist, Carla and Lois Beckett (2017) "'This is violence against Donald Trump': rightwingers interrupt Julius Caesar play", https://www.theguardian. com/us-news/2017/jun/17/trump-supporter-interrupts-controversial-julius-caesar-play-in-new-york

Williams, Holly (2016) "Uncle Vanya: as clear and fresh as a draught of water", http://www.independent.co.uk/arts-entertainment/theatre-dance/reviews/ uncle-vanya-the-almeida-theatre-review-as-clear-and-fresh-as-a-draught-of-water-a6875221.html

Williams, Kip (2017) "In Conversation", Sydney: Sydney Theatre Company Program.

CHAPTER 12

Trump and Satire: America's Carnivalesque President and His War on Television Comedians

Alex Symons

INTRODUCTION: TRUMP'S "CARNIVALESQUE" WAR

Studies have shown political comedy on television has developed an increasingly antagonistic relationship with American politicians since the 1970s (Matviko 2003; Day 2011). However, comedy as a combative means of criticism, catharsis, and exerting political power, has taken on an unprecedented significance during the political rise and administration of President Donald Trump. Whereas, back in 2011, Trump nodded in acceptance of grotesque putdowns during the *Comedy Central Roast of Donald Trump,* his attitude to satire changed dramatically in 2015. As I will explain, it was from the beginning of his political activities that Trump has provoked and retaliated to satire like no recent political figure—going from symbiotic coexistence to an effective state of war with America's television comedians.

This war may have started in February 2015 when Trump was audience to President Barack Obama at the White House Correspondents' Dinner. As Adam Gopnik reported in the *New Yorker,* it was at that ritzy

A. Symons (✉)
Department of Arts and Sciences, LIM College, New York, NY, USA

© The Author(s) 2019
C. Happer et al. (eds.), *Trump's Media War,*
https://doi.org/10.1007/978-3-319-94069-4_12

event that Obama, acting as a kind of "cool comedian," ridiculed Trump's career to date (Gopnik 2015). According to eye witnesses, the effect on Trump was profound. He "barely moved or altered his expression as wave after wave of laughter struck him" (Gopnik 2015). Since then, Emily Heil in the *Washington Post* has even documented the consensus among many journalists that it was this comic humiliation which spurred Trump to begin his first campaign. As Heil notes, Trump's entrance to the field could thus be blamed on "White House speechwriters and Hollywood comics" (2016).

It is ironic then, that beginning with his riotous campaign rallies in 2015, Trump countered his ridicule by Democrats and America's media institutions by taking on what reflects a traditional comic persona. Firstly, this is evident in his aesthetics, reflecting the kind of "theatrical" appearance and "performative" behavior popularized by America's iconic comedians of the 1930s, the Three Stooges, the Marx Brothers and W. C. Fields (Symons 2012, p. 91). Trump's modern variation is that of a disgruntled seventy-one year old man, tanned-to-orange, topped with unusual brushed-back hair, seemingly-tinted blonde. And as Kim Soffen documented during her investigation for the *Washington Post*, Trump does indeed have "unusually small hands—15th percentile small" (2016). Those hands point upwards, gesticulating wildly—and to inclined audiences; this even makes his sleeves appear oversized, reminiscent of the short ties worn by the Three Stooges, or Charlie Chaplin's oversized clothes as his character, the Little Tramp.

In the style of a vaudevillian monologue, Trump often breaks into biting comments and apparently off-the-cuff adlibs, diverging from normal logic—a variation on Groucho Marx's rambling and disruptive speech (Symons 2012, p. 86). For notable examples, his 2017 rally in Charleston, West Virginia, drifted into a diatribe on his use of hairspray; and his interview transcript with Peter Barker for *New York Times* moved between topics in a manner that borders on the surreal (Baker et al. 2017). His proclaimed opinions are often parodies themselves—spoof exaggerations of a conservative mindset reflective of America's satirical publication *The Onion*, not "serious" political discussion. Most notorious of these, so far, would be his suggestion that President Barack Obama founded terrorist organization Isis, his threat to have federal police surge Chicago, and his accusation that three million voters cast ballots illegally in the 2016 presidential election.

Trump's political persona even reflects contemporary American comedians through his notorious use of foul language (motherfucker, son of a bitch, shit, pussy)—all of which through its revelry elates his supporters. In fact, his political success with these traits is directly comparable to those same techniques employed by America's controversial "authentic out-sider" comedians, in particular, Doug Stanhope, Marc Maron, and Louis CK (Symons 2017). Just as those comedians appeal to new audiences by defying "family-orientated" conventions, as imposed in American's net-work television, Trump defies the norms of his political peers—he is too, unsuitable for "family" viewing. In this same vein, Trump's "vulgar" polit-ical persona draws on a long-running tradition of American satire. This persona came to prominence in the film *Duck Soup* (1933) with Groucho Marx as the cigar-chomping, anarchic president of *Freedonia*. Following in that same tradition, Mel Brooks performed the deranged, misogynistic and lecherous Governor LePetomane in his blockbuster *Blazing Saddles* (1974). In each case, these characters are "performed," and are not to be taken seriously.

Firmly in line with these "outrageous" comic characters, Trump fre-quently belittles his adversaries using comedy. Along with his numerous asides, Trump has even indulged in comic bits to mock his adversaries, notoriously including performing a declaimed impersonation of the dis-abled journalist Serge Kovaleski, in which he awkwardly manipulated his arms onstage (Borchers 2017). Similarly, Trump performed an imperson-ation of Republican senator Marco Rubio, mocking him for his awkward water-drinking during his response to the President's address. And as Tessa Berenson reported in *Time*, Trump "took out a water bottle and sprayed it around him while yelling, 'It's Rubio!'" (2016). In all these respects, Trump himself is a comical figure.

It is also according to Trump's inherently comic practices that he pres-ents a new challenge for television satirists. To understand this challenge, it is useful to consider the model of popular comedy proposed by theorist Mikhail Bakhtin, whose work has shaped studies of comedy to date. Bakhtin describes "carnivalesque revelry" in medieval folk culture, which he suggests appealed to the public through its liberation from all social propriety, whereby everyone can "play the fool and madman as he pleases" (p. 246). Notably, a similar purpose of comedy is proposed by Pierre Bourdieu in his landmark sociological study *Distinction* (1984), in which he suggests that popular comedy—including film and theater—satisfies the public in a similar fashion, by "overturning conventions and propri-eties" (1984, p. 26). Thus, like Bakhtin's study of "carnival," the pleasure of comedy is in the rejection of social convention and political structures.

As John Tulloch notes in his study of "'Classic Theatre' As Media Against Trump" (this volume) aesthetics can become political if conventions are disrupted, offering audiences anarchic revelry—just as can "carnivalesque" social behaviors. For example, Robert Icke turned George Orwell's dystopic ending of *1984* "upside down" in his stage adaptation by "including within the play Orwell's appendix on Newspeak." In the case of Trump, such formal disruptions are reflected in the "disrupted" narrative structure of his political speeches, the broken formalities of his television interviews and the rejection of conventional process in his political rallies. With all these models considered together, Trump is himself a profoundly comic figure, satisfying this public need for revelry and breaks with political social norms. It is in this context that political comedians on television are presented with a new challenge: in the case of Trump, there are no conventions left to mock or "overturn." Put simply, the difficult task for the political comedian confronted with Trump is to make into "carnival" what is already "carnivalesque."

Despite this difficulty, television satire necessarily plays an ongoing important role in American politics, and more so in recent years. The rising importance of American satire was recently examined by Amber Day in her book *Satire and Dissent: Interventions in Contemporary Political Debates* (2011). In that study, Day suggests American political comedians have become "legitimate players in serious political dialogue" (Day 2011, p. 1) and brought about the "blurring boundaries" (2011, p. 43) between political comedy and political journalism. Day attributes this shift to a concurrent decline in trust in "real" broadcast journalism which followed the broadly-acknowledged failure of network and cable news to voice opposition to the invasion of Iraq in 2003 (Day 2011, p. 4). In contrast, comedy has seen its impact rise. This impact has been enhanced by news shows themselves—including those on CNN, to MSNBC, and Fox News—by their practice of including clips of comedy skits and allowing political comedies to lead their discussions (Day 2011, p. 1).

Further to this same point, research has now added quantitative evidence for the impact of American political comedy. As James H. Fowler notes that Stephen Colbert's cult program, *The Colbert Report* was proved to have a serious impact on political finances. This is despite its format as a strict satire, presented by Stephen Colbert in the guise of a right wing commentator. While politicians who guested on the show had to "take the risk of humiliation," they also gained access to Colbert's educated audience, described as an "elite demographic" (2008, p. 534). Furthermore, when Democrats appeared, they received a "dramatic rise" in campaign contributions (Fowler 2008, p. 536). This considered, political comedy is both a contributor to "serious" political news coverage, and an influential platform in itself for political figures to communicate with the public.

Together, Tulloch's discussion of classic theater (this volume) with my own study here of television comedy suggests a wider phenomenon is occurring in the era of Trump: an increasing integration between entertainment and politics, as artists are drawn into political fracas. As Tulloch notes, this was strikingly clear with the 2017 Shakespeare-in-the-Park production of *Julius Caesar*, whereby the play was drawn into a discourse around resistance and democratic process. Similarly, the Broadway play *Hamilton*, while more dryly political by its nature, took on an explicitly combative stance in relation to Trump. Speaking more broadly, Tulloch makes a concise conclusion which parallels my own study: "theatre professionals are actively resisting the risk of Trump, and they deserve more analysis than they have received so far." In this same vein, America's television comedians, once a lower-tier of influence, are now more influential, and engaged in a "serious" political conflict with the president. Given this shift, they too require more thorough examination.

For just one unprecedented example, mild-mannered comedian Jimmy Kimmel employed his monologue on *Jimmy Kimmel Live* (ABC 2003–) to argue against Trump's Graham-Cassidy healthcare bill. This monologue received extensive press coverage, and was regarded to have contributed toward the bill's failure (Bruner 2017; Russonello 2017; McGee 2017). As I will explain, this instance is in fact typical of the new climate in which American television comedy has shifted from its traditionally gentle satire to outright political conflict and engagement. In addition, Trump's "carnivalesque" nature has required those comedians already predisposed to satire him to adopt new, more outlandish approaches. This is especially clear in his impersonations on *Comedy Central*, NBC's *Saturday Night Live* (1975–) and *The Late Show with Stephen Colbert* (2015–) as well as the satirical commentaries on HBO's *Real Time with Bill Maher* (2003–) and *Last Week Tonight with John Oliver* (2014–).

Trump As "Grotesque": Before He Was President

During Trump's campaign for Republican presidential candidate, resistance in television comedy came in the form of parodies focusing on his more menacing qualities, playing up his perceived despotism, lack of sympathy, and his vindictive characteristics. The purpose of this can be understood considering Bakhtin's study of comedy, in which he notes that during carnival activities, "All that was terrifying becomes grotesque" (p. 91). By this, Bakhtin suggests that by making fun of even authentically terrible concepts like "Hell"—a prominent fixture of medieval culture, popularized by establishment churches—it was possible to momentarily experience the "defeat of fear" (Ibid). As such, Bakhtin notes: "The people play with the terror and laugh at it; the awesome becomes a 'comic monster'" (Ibid). Thus, in the same tradition as American parodies including Charlie Chaplin's *Great Dictator* (1940), the pre-election parodies of Trump perceive the same kind of stark dictatorial threat, and exaggerate that threat into a "grotesque" meant to temporarily relive that public anxiety.

This kind of "grotesque" version of Trump was clearly evident in Comedy Central's special "The First Ever @midnight Presidential Debate" (2016). In that show, Anthony Atamanuik, appeared as Trump, wearing orange-colored make-up, and an overly high sweep-over wig. Atamanuik defined Trump as a tense and aggressive character, muttering menacingly, "Get him out of here! Waterboard them! Kill their families!" Yet while these phrases are shocking departures from political norms, they were each in fact recognizable from Trump himself—they couldn't be exaggerated. For example, Trump freely volunteered his "kill their families" mantra during an interview with breakfast show *Fox and Friends*:

> We're fighting a very politically correct war. And the other thing is with the terrorists, you have to take out their families. When you get these terrorists, you have to take out their *families*. They care about their lives – don't kid yourself. *You have to take out their families*. (Gass 2015)

Notably, Atamanuik manages in some key moments to exaggerate Trump's then-menacing persona, confronting anxieties about his much-discussed control of America's nuclear arsenal. It was during a discussion on ecology that Atamanuik announced: "Trees are terrible. And I promise you, if I become president, we will turn every tree into glass, I promise you – we gotta use these nukes, we haven't used them in years!" However, even this surreal reference to nuclear weapons reflects reports of Trump's own casual attitude. This was typified when Trump first attended a briefing on the United States arsenal, and expressed his eagerness, three times reportedly asking: "If we have them, why can't we use them?" (Neidig 2016). It this sense, Atamanuik's "grotesque" version of Trump offers audiences a momentary relief from their anxieties, delivering what Bakhtin would describe as a "victory over fear" (91). The effectiveness of this strategy is suggested by the special's impressive consumption, including 7.8 million views via Comedy Central's YouTube channel.

President Trump: "Childlike and Naïve"

After Trump was elected 45th president of the United States, an entirely different perception of him quickly emerged. It was following his initial post-election meeting with President Barack Obama that the press began to focus on Trump's lack of experience for the role of president. As reported by Michael Bender and Carol Lee in the *Wall Street Journal*, "Mr. Obama walked his successor through the duties of running the country, and Mr. Trump seemed surprised by the scope" (2016). This idea was further perpetuated by some telling footage of an unsure-looking President-elect Trump sitting with Obama—often framed by commentators as evidence of his lack of readiness. Typically, Steve Benen in an MSNBC editorial proposed the idea that Trump "applied for a job he knew very little about, never read the job description, and isn't quite sure what to do now that he has it" (2016).

Following this, new comic attacks on Trump were developed, reducing him to a childlike, naïve, and out-of-his-depth figure. This approach was popularized on *Saturday Night Live* (NBC 1975–) reflecting common-held anxieties that Trump would be exploited by other world leaders and his advisors. As reported in *The Hill*, Alec Baldwin's "childlike" Trump was defined in his first appearance in which he explained why he tweets carelessly: "I do it because my brain is bad" (Balluck 2016). Baldwin's Trump conveys Trump's naivety through a newly goofy pout, and hunched shoulders. His Trump is always dumbfounded, belittled, and led astray by his "superiors"—including a stripped-to-the-waist Vladimir Putin, and a traditional grim reaper representing his advisor Steve Bannon. These highly personal skits achieved maximum impact when Trump struck back, tweeting his distain: "Totally biased, not funny and the Baldwin imperson-ation just can't get any worse. Sad" (Balluck 2016).

Saturday Night Live (*SNL*) had similar success with Melissa McCarthy performing a "carnivalesque" impersonation of Trump's then-White House press secretary, Sean Spicer. As reported by Olivia Marks in *Vogue*, her appearance was regarded as a "resurgence" of *SNL*, having been viewed "more than 25 million times on Youtube" (2017). McCarthy exaggerated many of Spicer's distinctive faux pas, including chewing gum, erratic speech and his undisguised anger, even motoring around the stage on a mobile podium. It was notably after this relentless satire that Spicer eventually resigned, and Trump finally lashed back, remarking that Spicer had taken "tremendous abuse from the fake news media" (Thrush and Haberman 2017). The impact of the skits was further suggested in a report by Annie Karni in *Politico,* which noted the Spicer skit "did not go over well internally at a White House in which looks matter" (2017).

It is important to note that Trump's war on political comedians contrasts greatly to the appeasement and complicity of America's previous presidents and political figures. In 1992, following his defeat to President Bill Clinton, George Bush senior invited comedian Dana Carvey to the White House Christmas Party. Carvey's impersonation of Bush was relatively tame: spectacled and formal, an accurate imitation of Bush's croaky, yet thoughtful speech patterns. As Dan Fastenberg notes in *Time,* "Carvey helped create the image of Bush as the type of man who said things like, 'It wouldn't be prudent at this juncture'" (2010). Similarly, during the 2008 presidential election campaign, Tina Fey satirically performed Sarah Palin—introducing the diminishing catchphrase "I can see Russia from my house!" While that impersonation is still regarded as the "most savage" by Ryan McGee in *Rolling Stone* (2017), Palin nevertheless later appeared on the show along with Fey.

In fact, good-natured exchanges between politicians and comedians have been the hallmark of *SNL* since its very beginning. As John Matviko notes in his article "Television Satire and the Presidency: The Case of *Saturday Night Live,*" Chevy Chase's impersonation of a bumbling Gerald Ford often opened the show during its first two seasons (2003, p. 336). But rather than antagonize the show, the administration decided to "defuse the negative image" by having Ford's press secretary, Ron Nessen appear as co-host, with Ford himself speaking the show's opening line from the Oval Office (Cramer Brownell 2016). It is in the context of this history that the show's more personal attacks on Trump, and his own visceral, negative reactions, make evident a historically untypical move toward conflict.

PRESIDENT TRUMP: "CAMP" AND "RIDICULOUS"

The Late Show with Stephen Colbert (CBS 2015–) became an explicit opponent of Trump when Colbert replaced David Letterman as host, adopting a newly provocative "liberal" agenda. Certainly, the politicization of

Colbert's "mainstream" network show provides significant evidence for what Day describes as the "blurring boundaries" (2011, p. 43). Colbert's nightly monologues are personal, consistently satirizing Trump's every controversy with blunt criticism. When Colbert impersonates Trump, reading his onscreen tweets aloud, he imposes an elongated "camp" form of Trump's speech, making his words yet more flamboyant and "silly." Colbert's approach connotes many familiar "camp" qualities identified in Susan Sontag's seminal essay, in particular the "element of artifice" and the "spirit of extravagance" (2008, p. 47). However, once again, making a "camp" imitation of Trump is a difficult task as "campness" is already present in Trump's own appearances—often self-ware spectacles which as Sontag notes of camp culture, "cannot be taken altogether seriously" (Ibid).

Colbert's approach to "camping" Trump notably reflects that of British comedy actor Peter Serafinowicz, who was invited on *The Late Show* in August 2017 to discuss his "Sassy Trump" videos. As Colbert explained, these videos are distributed online via YouTube, are original recording of Trump, except with Serafinowicz speaking Trumps own words, unchanged—imposing an extremely "camp" emphasis and tone. As Serafinowicz remarked elsewhere, he perceives this "campness" as Trump's "true spirit coming through," since he is "*so* bitchy and *so* catty" (Herring 2017). To date, the most widely distributed of these, "Donald Gay Trump," posted February 3, 2016, has received over 1.9 million views on YouTube.

In another excessively "camp" technique, satirical comedian Jon Stewart has made some effort to portray Trump as a "ridiculous," clown-like figure. Despite having retired from the flagship program Comedy Central's *The Daily Show* (Comedy Central 1996–) back in 2005, Stewart returned in several appearances on *The Late Show*, as a guest of Colbert. In February 2017, Stewart appeared in the guise of Trump, managing to effectively exaggerate Trump's appearance and even his political ideas. As Zamira Rahim noted in *Time*, Stewart "emerged wearing an overly long tie and a 'dead animal' fixed to his head in a surreal imitation of the U.S. leader" (2017). Whereas in a previous era Stewart's "element of artifice" (Sontag 2008, p. 47) could have courted some significant redistribution on cable news, in the era of Trump, the lacking coverage of this appearance suggests it is now not artifice-enough.

"LEGITIMATE" POLITICAL COMEDY: SOPHISTICATED ATTACKS

The ultimate "blurring boundaries" (Day 2011, p. 43) between American comedy and politics is evident in the output of premium subscription service HBO (Home Box Office). As scholars of television have documented, HBO's branding offered audiences the promise of elevated "cultural status" that was "associated with high and legitimated arts" (Levin and Newman 2011, p. 33). By this same distinction, HBO's *Real Time with Bill Maher* (2003–) and *Last Week Tonight with John Oliver* (2014–) are America's more "sophisticated" comedy on television. Their joke structures are not primarily visual, with very few props, without skits, and with few impersonations of Trump. While being scattered with quips, puns, and ironies, both are strikingly informed, and set their own agendas, examining the bigger societal picture. As such, these shows are more intellectually demanding, and lack the explicitly "carnivalesque" appeal of America's "popular" comedies on network and cable.

Bill Maher, host of panel show *Real Time,* identifies himself as a "liberal" and is politically active. His involvement peaked in February of 2012, when Maher announced on *Real Time* that he had donated one million dollars to Obama's re-election campaign, in part, to encourage others (Kahn 2012). But for all his savage material on Trump in his own show, it was only when Maher appeared on "mainstream" network television in 2013 with Jay Leno on *The Tonight Show* (NBC 1954–) that he achieved a measurable impact. In that interview, Maher offered to pay Trump five million dollars if only he would produce documentation proving he was not born from an orangutan—imitating Trump's claim regarding Obama's birth certificate. This was acted on by Trump, who sued Maher for the declared amount. The case was rejected by the court, but even so, Maher's joke echoed through America's news media, including stories in E! News, *Variety,* the *Hollywood Reporter, Entertainment Weekly,* TMZ, CNN, ABC, Politico, *Vanity Fair,* the *New York Times,* and *USA Today.*

In contrast to Maher's approach, *Last Week Tonight with John Oliver* is focused around the direct-to-camera monologue of its host. In this respect, the show borrows its highly conventional structure from the numerous host-centered "popular" shows including Comedy Central's *The Daily Show* (1996), *The Jim Jefferies Show* (2017–) and *The Opposition with Jordan Klepper* (2017–), NBC's *Late Night with Seth Meyers* (2014–) and CBS's *Full Frontal with Samantha Bee* (2016–). However, *Last Week*

Tonight with John Oliver distinguishes itself from these shows by its significantly more detailed, contextualized reports of corruption and recent events—often leading the way on important new topics which are entirely neglected by cable news. For example, in 2017, Oliver has reported on the growing misuse of flawed forensic science in American courts, the unseen political operations of the NRA (National Rifle Association), and the practices of net neutrality lobbying.

Oliver has consistently been an aggressive critic of Trump, using comedy. Most notably, Oliver launched a campaign to rebrand Trump with his actual former family name "Drumpf." As Oliver explained on his show, this was an effort to undermine Trump's reputation as a "successful" figure in business. Oliver also explained his convoluted strategies in a guest appearance on *The Late Show with Stephen Colbert*—including imitating Trump's own merchandize by producing red caps emblazoned with the slogan "Make Donald Drumpf Again." Yet despite Oliver's efforts, his more "sophisticated" comedy has not had significant impact; Trump has not responded, and Oliver's segments are generally not replayed on America's cable or network news. In short, Oliver is too cognitive, meaning in the era of a "carnivalesque" presidency—more riotously comic than his own show—such satire is less able to effectively shape political dialogues.

Conclusion

Following Tulloch's compelling observations on the politicization of theater, television comedy emerges as another medium drawn deeply into political dialogues. As Tulloch notes in this volume, the reception of the 2017 stage shows *1984* and the *Cherry Orchard* provided evidence that audiences were consistently connecting them "to the emergence of Trump as part of a series of crises and catastrophes." Similarly, America's increasing politicization of television comedians provides further evidence of a changing climate in which entertainment is increasingly part of "serious" dialogues. In large part, this is, of course, a result of the president's own behavior. Whereas previous presidents appeased and participated in their television satires (Matviko 2003), Trump has provoked his. In return, Trump has elicited a new level of comic criticism, and from new platforms—thus ending the previously symbiotic on-off relationship with America's television comedians, and eliciting a continuous war.

Trump's war on television comedians stems from his "carnivalesque" persona, which breaks with American political norms through his theatrical overturning of social proprieties, his transgressions of etiquette, and his outrageous political ideas. In these respects, Trump himself reflects the satires of American politicians performed historically by Mel Brooks and Groucho Marx (Symons 2012). As such, Trump's persona and behavior has antagonized American television's comedians, and demands new strategies in comic critique. This means comedians must take on the difficult challenge of exaggerating opinions which are already extreme, playing up the "camp" artifice of what is already camp behavior, and pursuing increasingly harsh personal attacks.

Trump's war on media has taken many forms. In this study, the attacks on Trump range from his exaggerated portrayal as a "grotesque" threat to humanity on Comedy Central, to his dangerously "childlike" portrayal on *Saturday Night Live*, and his "camp" characterizations on *The Late Show with Stephen Colbert*. Each of these achieved a significant impact, measured individually by their press coverage, public consumption, and reactions from the president himself. Whereas HBO's more sophisticated comedians Bill Maher and John Oliver are equally critical of Trump, their more cognitive techniques mostly lack the extreme "carnivalesque" approach that now gains traction. This difference further underlines the reality of the newly combative climate, in which only excessive techniques—outdoing those of Trump—can now hope to significantly impact political debates.

References

Baker, Peter, Michael S. Schmit and Maggie Haberman. "Citing Recusal, Trump Says He Wouldn't Have Hired Sessions." *New York Times*. 19th July 2017. https://www.nytimes.com/2017/07/19/us/politics/trump-interview-sessions-russia.html?mcubz=2 (Accessed 12th October 2017).

Bakhtin, Mikhail. *Rabelais and His World*, trans by Helene Iswolsky. Bloomington: Indiana University Press, 1984.

Balluck, Kyle. "Trump slams 'Saturday Night Live' as 'unwatchable.'" *The Hill*. 4th December 2016. http://thehill.com/blogs/in-the-know/in-the-know/308658-trump-slams-saturday-night-live-as-unwatchable (Accessed 10th October 2017).

Bender, Michael and Carol Lee. "RNC Chair Reince Priebus Is Named Donald Trump's Chief of Staff." *Wall Street Journal*. 13th November 2016. https://www.wsj.com/articles/leading-contender-for-donald-trump-s-chief-of-staff-is-rnc-chairman-reince-priebus-1479069597 (Accessed 1st October 2017).

Benen, Steve. "Trump applied for a difficult job he knew very little about." MSNBC. 14th November 2016. http://www.msnbc.com/rachel-maddow-show/trump-applied-difficult-job-he-knew-very-little-about (Accessed 1st November 2017).

Berenson, Tessa. "Watch Donald Trump Mock Marco Rubio by Spilling Water on Stage." *Time.* 26th February 2016. http://time.com/4239357/donald-trump-marco-rubio-water-bottle-texas/ (Accessed 12th October 2017).

Borchers, Callum. "Meryl Streep was right. Donald Trump did mock a disabled reporter." *Washington Post.* 9th January 2017. https://www.washingtonpost.com/news/the-fix/wp/2017/01/09/meryl-streep-was-right-donald-trump-did-mock-a-disabled-reporter/?utm_term=.eb3e54f15b4a (Accessed 12th October 2017).

Bourdieu, Pierre. *Distinction: A Social Critique of the Judgement of Taste.* Cambridge: Harvard University Press, 1984.

Bruner, Raisa. "Read Jimmy Kimmel's Moving Healthcare Monologue That Everyone's Talking About." Time. 20th September 2017. http://time.com/4949522/jimmy-kimmel-healthcare-transcript/ (Accessed 1st January 2017).

Cramer Brownell, Kathryn. "The Saturday Night Live Episode That Changed American Politics." *Time.* 15th April 2016. http://time.com/4292027/gerald-ford-saturday-night-live/ (Accessed 10th October 2017).

Day, Amber. *Satire and Dissent: Interventions in Contemporary Political Debate.* Indiana: Indiana University Press, 2011.

Fastenberg, Dan. "Bush the Elder Invites Dana Carvey to the White House." *Time.* 29th July 2010. http://content.time.com/time/specials/packages/article/0,28804,2007228_2007230_2007252,00.html (Accessed 10th October 2017).

Fowler, James H. "The Colbert Bump in Campaign Donations: More Truthful than Truthy." *Political Science and Politics,* Vol. 41, No. 3 (Jul., 2008), pp. 533–539.

Gass, Nick. "Trump: We have to take out ISIL members' families." *Politico.* 2nd December 2015. http://www.politico.com/story/2015/12/trump-kill-isil-families-216343 (Accessed 15th October 2017).

Gopnik, Adam. "Trump and Obama: A Night to Remember." *New Yorker.* 12th September 2015. https://www.newyorker.com/news/daily-comment/trump-and-obama-a-night-to-remember (Accessed 1st October 2017).

Heil, Emily. "Is Obama's 2011 White House correspondents' dinner burn to blame for Trump's campaign?" *Washington Post.* 10th February 2016. https://www.washingtonpost.com/news/reliable-source/wp/2016/02/10/is-obamas-2011-white-house-correspondents-dinner-burn-to-blame-for-trumps-campaign/?utm_term=.efbc50170660 (Accessed 10th October 2017).

Herring, Richard. "Peter Serafinowicz – Richard Herring's Leicester Square Theatre Podcast #134." YouTube. 15th February 2017. https://www.youtube.com/watch?v=616Cm1lTaZA (Accessed 10th October 2017).

Kahn, Carrie. "Bill Maher's Obama SuperPAC Donation Causing Stir." *NPR*. 28th March 2012. http://www.npr.org/2012/03/28/149512215/bill-mahers-obama-superpac-donation-causes-stir (Accessed 1st October 2017).

Karni, Annie. "White House rattled by McCarthy's spoof of Spicer." *Politico*. 6th February 2017. http://www.politico.com/story/2017/02/melissa-mccarthy-sean-spicer-234715 (Accessed 10th October 2017).

Levine, Elana and Michael Z. Newman. *Legitimating Television: Media Convergence and Cultural Status*. New York: Routledge, 2011.

Marks, Olivia. "Is There Still A Place For Satire In The Age Of Trump?" *Vogue*. 1st August 2017. http://www.vogue.co.uk/article/current-affairs-satire (Accessed 9th October 2017).

Matviko, John. "Television Satire and the Presidency: The Case of Saturday Night Live." Eds, Peter C. Rollins, John E. O'Connor. *Hollywood's White House: The American Presidency in Film and History*. University Press of Kentucky, 2003.

McGee, Ryan. "20 Most Savage 'SNL' Political Impersonations." *Rolling Stone*. 8th February 2017. http://www.rollingstone.com/tv/lists/20-most-savage-snl-political-impersonations-w465555/sarah-palin-tina-fey-w465684 (Accessed 9th October 2017).

Neidig, Harper. "Scarborough: Trump asked adviser why US can't use nuclear weapons." *The Hill*. 3rd August 2016. http://thehill.com/blogs/ballot-box/presidential-races/290217-scarborough-trump-asked-about-adviser-about-using-nuclear (Accessed 10th October 2017)

Russonello, Giovanni. "Jimmy Kimmel Doubles Down on Criticism of Health Care Bill." *New York Times*. 21st September 2017. https://www.nytimes.com/2017/09/21/arts/television/kimmel-cassidy-health-care.html (Accessed 1st January 2017).

Soffen, Kim. "Yes, Donald Trump's hands are actually pretty small." *Washington Post*. 3rd August 2016. https://www.washingtonpost.com/news/morning-mix/wp/2016/08/05/yes-donald-trumps-hands-are-actually-pretty-small/?utm_term=.58f3a3bda7c0 (Accessed 1st October 2017).

Sontag, Susan. "Notes on Camp." Ernest Mathijs and Xavier Mendik, eds. *The Cult Film Reader*. Maidenhead: Open University Press, 2008, pp. 41–52.

Symons, Alex. *Mel Brooks in the Cultural Industries: Survival and Prolonged Adaptation*. Edinburgh: Edinburgh University Press, 2012.

Symons, Alex. "Podcast Comedy and 'Authentic Outsiders': How New Media is Challenging the Owners of Industry," *Celebrity Studies* (Volume 8, Issue 1, 2017).

Thrush, Glenn and Maggie Haberman. "Melissa McCarthy Plays an Angst-Ridden Sean Spicer on 'Saturday Night Live.'" *New York Times*. 14th May 2017. https://www.nytimes.com/2017/05/14/arts/television/snl-melissa-mccarthy-sean-spicer.html (Accessed 10th October 2017).

Tulloch, John. "Classic Theatre" As Media Against Trump: Imagining Chekhov, in Happer, Catherine, Andrew Hoskins and William Merrin (Eds.) (2019) *Trump's War on the Media*. Basingstoke: Palgrave Macmillan, pp.159–180.

PART V

Media Out of the Margins

CHAPTER 13

President Troll: Trump, 4Chan and Memetic Warfare

William Merrin

Trolling and Politics

The 'troll' has become one of the most important contemporary political and cultural figures. Or rather, I want to argue, *troll-culture* has now become central to our political processes, spreading through the mainstream to become one of the most important forms of political participation and activism today, employed by politicians, political commentators and the public alike. This is obviously a surprising claim to make, given that the 'troll' has also become one of the most famous contemporary hate-figures, regularly attacked by the press, politicians, the legal system and by academic critics. These attacks, however, are based upon a misplaced conception of trolling that prevents us from recognizing its broader take-up and its political impact and significance. It's only by understanding what trolling is and how it operates that we can understand how widely it has been politically appropriated and how it has become a key weapon in online debate and activism.

The troll I am discussing here, therefore, is not the same 'troll' that is the subject of press panic, of political complaint and of legal overreaction.

W. Merrin (✉)
Swansea University, Swansea, UK

© The Author(s) 2019
C. Happer et al. (eds.), *Trump's Media War*,
https://doi.org/10.1007/978-3-319-94069-4_13

That figure of fury and offence whose splenetic attacks fill social media and comments-sections and whose hate-speech, and rape and death threats, it is claimed, are ruining the internet for all decent people isn't actually a troll, for the simple reason that their abuse and hatred are serious (Merrin 2016a). And nor is this troll the same as that which is the subject of academic commentary, especially within academic psychology—a discipline that can only conceive of trolling as an individualized, psychopathological phenomena, seeing only a sufferer of 'anti-social personality disorder' (Bishop 2013) exploiting the 'toxic disinhibition' (Suler 2005: 184) of anonymous, online communication to express their anger. Hence psychology's continuing failure to understand trolling—their unconvincing attempts to define 'types' of troll-behaviour or troll-personalities (see Bartlett 2014: 28; Bishop 2012: 166; Hardaker 2013) and the ludicrous 2014 paper that claimed to scientifically identify the 'dark tetrad' of the troll-mind—their 'sadism, psychopathy and Machiavellianism' (Buckels et al. 2014: 97).

None of these approaches help us understand trolling. Instead we need to return to the history of the concept and what it names. The term originates in the mid-fifteenth century, probably in the French 'troller', meaning 'to wander here and there (in search of game')' and the Old German 'trollen', meaning to stroll (Oxford Dictionaries 2014). 'Trolling' later became a fishing term, referring to the dragging of baited line behind a boat to see what could be caught, and it was this meaning that survived through to the Vietnam War where US pilots described 'trolling for MiGs'—trying to draw out enemy aircraft, often as a decoy for other activity (Saar 1972: 28). It was these ideas, of sport and baiting and drawing out and playing with the target that inspired the early online use of the term. An influx of new Usenet users in 1992 caused irritation for established members and 'trolling for newbies'—trying to provoke a response that could be mocked—became a recognizable activity (Bartlett 2014: 28). Online trolling would develop in the following years but one of its defining elements would remain that of *sport*—of the pleasure of playing with and catching someone. But the Usenet example also highlights another defining aspect of trolling, as they mocked the newbies not because they were new, but because they *affected authority*. Trolling, therefore, is a baiting, a sport, a playing, that more than anything aims at those who get above themselves, or set themselves above others—at those asserting, or in, authority.

With this in mind, we can see, therefore, that trolling isn't new. It is not a contemporary, individual, pathological phenomenon that urgently requires a moral and legal campaign to eradicate it, but is rather part of a broader, cultural phenomenon with a much longer history. Online trolling, I would argue, is the contemporary expression of an older attitude: of a historical spirit of disruption, disorder, challenge, play and humour that takes as its target the entire profane realm of everyday life, the structures and values built on it and the authorities that defend it. Its roots are traceable back to the ancient cosmogonies and their discussion of the role of chaos as a force that not only precedes order but that also helps birth it. This is chaos as a fecund, productive, procreative force that remains intimately bound with its opposite, the world of order and reality and the political organization of life. Chaos must be overcome for the order of the real to exist and survive, but chaos is never finally destroyed, remaining in many cosmogonies as a force that threatens order and that undoes it in order for it to be remade and renewed (Merrin 2016b).

As every civilization has understood, therefore, the real 'spectre' haunting their systems (Marx 2004) is not 'revolution'—that historical arriviste that wishes only to substitute a different political order—but the much older challenge of chaos: of that festive spirit that threatens the overturning of *all order*, of all politics, hierarchies, laws, rules and the reality principle itself. The spirit of chaos, therefore, is an essentially *anti-political* force, in preceding and standing outside of order and the real and taking aim at the very possibility of the polis—of the ordered city and its affairs. Despite this, these chaotic principles have often held a strong appeal for political forces that have regularly coopted them for their own ends. The left has obviously flirted with this chaotic spirit, being drawn to its play, humour, disruption and dissent, but the right has traditionally abhorred such forces, condemning anything that opposes order and authority. There are notable exceptions to this, however, such as in the Futurist serate, or 'soirees'.

First held in January 1910, the serate were public events in theatres where the Futurists presented their art, their poetry and their music and declaimed their manifestos. These were day long events. The Futurists would announce their arrival in the streets and build-up excitement for the evening whilst fruit-sellers set up stall outside the theatre to sell missiles to the crowd. The performances were marked by their deliberate provocation and the audience's violent response—as captured in Gerardo Dottori's ink-sketch *Futurist Serata in Perugia* (1914) which records the view from the stage and the Futurists hiding from a hail of objects and abuse. The event carried on in the streets afterwards where crowds would attempt to fight the Futurists and the artists often ended up in prison (Merrin 2013).

For Marinetti the success of an evening was judged by the abuse and scandal created rather than the applause, for his intention was the mobilization of the masses. His aim was *chaos*—the unleashing in the moment of a kinetic energy of anger, violence and destructiveness for the political ends of overthrowing the established order and provoking in people the Futurist's own desire for war. But what was this established order that the Futurist's opposed? The answer is found in Marinetti's founding manifesto which (alongside an interesting attack on 'moralism' and 'feminism') railed against Italy itself, its accumulated and encrusted history and sclerotic art-museums, libraries and institutions (Marinetti 1909). Hence 'Futurism' was specifically conceived as a break with the past and its perceived domination of the present, but what is important here is that in order to unleash the radical forces that would bring this future the right-wing Futurists first had to construct *an image* of the present as dominated by an established order. It was this image that was then opposed, with their chosen weapons being the speed of kinetic provocation, destructive participation, the assault on anything already existing and *established* and the unleashing of chaos itself. This was a methodology that right-wing trolls and the 'alt-right' would rediscover just over a century later.

4Chan and 'The Great Meme War'

The modern online home of trolling and the spirit of chaos is 4Chan, the image-board set up by Christopher Poole ('Moot') on 1 October 2003. Consisting of un-archived, subject-based boards with anonymous posting, 4Chan soon became the must-see, cess-pit of the internet: as Obi-Wan Kenobi says (in a quotation often applied to the site): 'You will never find a more wretched hive of scum and villainy'. The most famous board is the /b/ 'Random' board, where almost anything goes. At any given moment the page overflows with gratuitous pornography, misogyny, racism, most forms of 'phobia', graphic insults, general grossness and maximum offensiveness. If this sounds like a site where every nihilistic teenager can post their most violent, angry, extreme and stupid thoughts, that's because that's what it is.

What makes 'random' tolerable, and perhaps even redeemable, however, is its troll-humour. Firstly, despite the horror of the site it has proven to be one of the most creative corners of the web, with its chaos birthing almost every major meme or aspect of internet culture over the last decade. Secondly, its defining attitude towards the world is 'zero fucks' and the biggest mistake any poster can make is to take their own or anyone else's post seriously. Its chaotic troll-spirit undercuts whatever is posted: as the /b/ masthead declares, 'The stories and information posted here are artistic works of fiction and falsehood. Only a fool would take anything posted here as fact' (4Chan 2017).

From 2008, however, 4Chan began to get political. Beginning with 'Project Chanology' its informational libertarianism overcame its Sadean libertinism and it began attacking the Church of Scientology for its attempts to censor information on the internet. This protest saw the birth of the hacktivist collective 'Anonymous' who, by 2010, were involved in a broader information war to defend WikiLeaks and by the year's end were active participants in the Arab Spring, aiding the Tunisian and Egyptian revolutions. Within a few years, therefore, the anons on 4Chan had moved from troll-raids on the children's virtual-world Habbo Hotel to participating in world-events. Their politics had become explicitly left-wing and over the following years Anonymous would pursue numerous progressive causes including supporting the Occupy movement (in 2011–12), attacking child pornography (2011–12), hacking the Koch industries website for their attacks on union members (2011), hacking the Ugandan Prime Minister's website in protest against Uganda's anti-homosexuality laws (2012), supporting Gaza against Israel's military 'Operation Pillar of Defense' (2012), supporting the victims of the Steubenville rape case as well as other rape victims (2012), supporting the 'Black Lives Matter' campaign (2014), and launching operations against ISIS and its supporters (2015–16).

Anonymous's politicization was controversial, with many anons criticizing the leftists as 'moralfags' for leaving behind the humour and chaos of 4Chan's trolling roots. When, as 'Agent Pubeit', Michael Vitale was filmed covered in Vaseline and pubic hair running into Scientology's New York offices and rolling around their soft-furnishings, his explanation was he wanted Anonymous to remain 'the assholes of the internet', up for 'any sort of motherfuckery' (Dibbell 2009). For a long time this trolling versus leftist 'moralfag' dichotomy seemed to define 4Chan/Anonymous but by 2016 the pendulum had swung a different way. Whilst Anonymous had continued its leftist-libertarianism, 4Chan and the associated troll-culture had returned to its Sadean libertinism and attracted and fused with the emerging online 'alt-right'.

Coined by Richard Spencer, the term 'alt-right' describes a range of extreme far-right movements and positions broadly unified by their

rejection of traditional, mainstream Christian conservativism and repub-
licanism in favour of white nationalism and supremacism. It's a nebulous
movement that incorporates Fascistic, racist, nationalistic, populist, anti-
feminist, anti-Semitic, homophobic, anti-immigration, anti-Islamic and
protectionist beliefs, but it also draws from and draws in a range of
related movements including online conspiracy-theorism, free speech
libertarians, palaeoconservativism, neoreactionism, the 'manosphere'
(encompassing the men's rights movement and 'pick-up artist' movement) and an increasingly right-wing internet culture, including Chan
culture and sites such as Reddit. Whether 4Chan's move to the right was
a result of a shift in its demographics and their politics or an active influx
of right-wing participants drawn in by its anything-goes libertinism is
uncertain, but the change was already noticeable by October 2011 when
4Chan set up the /pol/ politically incorrect board to replace the news
board and house the increasing number of extremist posts. /Pol/ would
become a centre of racist, misogynistic, trans-phobic, white-supremacist,
and neo-Nazi posting.

The first major, public expression of 4Chan's new alt-right sentiment
was 2014s 'Gamergate' hashtag movement. Gamergate's ostensible origins lay in the gamer-community's hyper-reaction to a perceived bias in
mainstream video-game journalism. By August 2014, 4Chan users were
falsely claiming that the female independent game-designer Zoe Quinn
had received favourable reviews for her browser-game *Depression Quest*
due to her relationship with the video-games journalist Nathan Grayson.
As part of the community's 'ethical campaign' against such mainstream
media bias, Quinn and her family (though not Grayson) were subjected to
a systematic, virulent, misogynistic hate-campaign organized from 4Chan,
other Chans and Reddit that included doxing, abuse, rape and death
threats. The abuse spread to other feminist commentators such as Anita
Sarkeesian (for the crime of analysing video-game sexism) and female
video-game developers such as Brianna Wu. Those coming to their defence
were dismissed as 'social justice warriors' ('SJW') and similarly attacked.
Hence a movement that claimed to be concerned with 'ethics' became an
organized, misogynistic hate-campaign designed to attack women and to
purify game-culture from the enemy of 'political correctness'. Though
4Chan banned discussions of Gamergate, Chan culture continued to feed
the campaign, with proponents moving to the even more permissive
8Chan. Along with Reddit and YouTube these sites formed a new alternative (and alt-right influenced) media for many younger people.

As Matt Lees argues: 'The similarities between Gamergate and the far-right online movement, the "alt-right", are huge, startling and in no way a coincidence' (Lees 2016). The Gamergaters used a range of rhetorical devices, he says, to present themselves as the underdogs and claim victim-hood: 'the targets were lying or exaggerating, they were too precious; a language of dismissal and belittlement was formed against them. Safe spaces, snowflakes, unicorns, cry bullies. Even when abuse was proven, the usual response was that people on their side were being abused too' (Lees 2016). Like the Futurists, therefore, they created an image of a dominant and dominating order (here comprised of mainstream media and Feminism) and attacked it with rapid, kinetic, violent verbal-missiles. This was a fast-moving, 'formless Fascism' remaining, Lees says, in 'an endless state of conflict' against a foe simultaneously caricatured as an 'impossibly strong' mainstream force and as 'laughably weak' PC-snowflakes (Lees 2016).

By 2016 it was clear the same strategies were being widely used by the alt-right who constructed a fictional establishment against which, as underdogs, they could rail. This order comprised three main elements: the mainstream political order including Washington's 'deep state' and 'swamp'; the mainstream liberal news media and their 'biases'; and the multicultural and 'PC culture' that, they believed, discriminated against whites and males and pandered to emasculating 'Feminazis', immigrants, the Black Lives Matter movement, homosexuals, transgenderism, Jews, Muslims and terrorists. Lacking access to the mainstream mass-media the alt-right, therefore, created 'a multi-layered alternative online media empire' (Nagle 2017: 45), ranging from explicitly Fascist websites such as The Daily Stormer, through to populist right-wing news sites such as Breitbart News Network. One of the most important elements of this alt-right media ecology was 4Chan, Chan culture and Reddit as they (1) delivered an important youth demographic, (2) played a central role in the attack on mainstream media, mainstream politics, the culture of 'political correctness' and Left-wing identity politics, and (3) coopted, diverted and weaponized troll-culture for neo-Fascist purposes, supporting and aiding the election of Donald Trump.

There's evidence that 4Chan's support for Trump was at first ironic, with the trolls enjoying the idea of trying to get a joke candidate elected president. As 'Marcus' reports on Trump's decision to run: 'For a lot of people, on the first day it was like, "This would be fucking hilarious," and then when he started coming up with policy stuff—the border wall, the

Muslim ban—people on the boards were like, "This can't be real. This is the greatest troll of all time"' (Schreckinger 2017). It remains difficult to determine motivations in the hall-of-mirrors of troll-politics but it seems that, for most, support for Trump and his policies wasn't a joke, as his politics closely chimed with the outsider-culture, anti-PC sentiment, racism and misogyny and the claims of post-truth 'shitposters' on 4Chan and Reddit. Hence these groups went to work for Trump, creating memes that promoted him such as the popular 'Trump Train' and 'You can't stump the Trump' images, the racist repurposing of Pepe the Frog, the 'Deplorables' memes and the refashioning of Pepe the Frog as Trump himself.

The result was what former participants refer to (only half-jokingly) as 'The Great Meme War': the flooding of the internet with pro-Trump and anti-Clinton memes. To take one example, consider the 'spirit cooking' meme. In March 2016 the personal email account of John Podesta, the chair of Clinton's campaign, was hacked, probably by 'Fancy Bear', a hacking group linked to Russian intelligence services, with 20,000 pages of emails being passed to and published by WikiLeaks in October–November. Employing what they ironically referred to as 'weaponized autism', 4Chan's /pol/ board combed the emails for anti-Clinton material, eventually discovering an email referring to a 'spirit cooking' session with the performance artist Marina Abromovic whose 1996 book *Spirit Cooking* included as ingredients breast-milk, semen and 'jealousy'. From this they created tweets, memes and internet stories claiming Clinton was a 'witch' and was involved, alongside her staff, in 'satanic rituals' (Lee 2016).

As Schreckinger says, Chan culture didn't win the election for Trump, but 'The meme battalions created a mass of pro-Trump iconography as powerful as the Obama "Hope" poster and far more adaptable', forcing the mainstream media to address outlandish topics such as conspiracy-theory accusations against Clinton that would never previously have been deemed worthy of coverage (Schreckinger 2017). They also produced a range of real-world reactions, including complaints by Pepe the Frog's creator and an armed assault on a Washington pizzeria.

This too had its origins in trolling. On November 2 2016 a /pol/ user jokingly suggested that mentions of 'pizza' in the Podesta emails were coded references to paedophilia (as 'child porn' was often abbreviated online to 'cp', which then became known as 'cheese pizza'). Another user responded, 'let's meme this into reality'. As Gregg Housh commented later, 'It was absolutely a joke and a guy just made it up on the spot'. /pol/ users, therefore, developed an elaborate conspiracy about Clinton being linked to a child sex-ring being run out of a DC pizzeria. They then pushed this message out through the #pizzagate hashtag on Twitter and onto The_Donald subreddit and onto the wider web (Schreckinger 2017). The story was so successful that on 4 December 2016 Edgar Madison Welch decided to investigate and free any children. He was arrested after entering the pizzeria with an assault rifle, firing three shots and holding staff hostage (Ortiz 2017). Two days later, one of Trump's campaign aides, Michael Flynn Jr., lost his job after fanning the 'pizzagate' conspiracy on Twitter (BBC 2016).

The Trump campaign had strong links to this mimetic culture. The right-wing, PC-baiting, troll-journalist Milo Yiannopoulos made his name reporting on and defending 4Chan and 'Gamergate' for Breitbart News, alerting Executive Chair of the site, Steve Bannon, to Chan culture and the potential of its support. After Bannon became chief executive of Trump's presidential campaign in August 2016 Trump Towers created a team of young staffers to monitor social media, including the 4Chan / pol/ board and the influential The_Donald subreddit which had become one of the most active communities on the web and a key forum for the alt-right. The Trump team didn't intervene in these forums but they did reap their activism, with staff, Trump aides, and Trump himself all retweeting alt-right videos and images created on these sites. As Schreckinger explains, 'one former campaign official said the goal was to relentlessly tilt the prevailing sentiment on social media in favor of Trump: "He clearly won that war against Hillary Clinton day after day after day"' (Schreckinger 2017).

The pro-Trump 4Chan and Reddit communities worked tirelessly to produce memes that would appeal to 'Normies' (the public), pushing them onto Twitter and spreading them with bots. The Trump campaign also picked up and boosted the most useful ones and those gaining most traction spread to other platforms such as Facebook to be widely shared by ordinary people. 4Chan and Reddit users also engaged in more hostile action, swarming and trolling a 'meme-generator' set up by the Clinton campaign, reminding black-voters of Clinton's comments on race, using 'sock puppets' to discredit support for Clinton, raiding other social-media platforms and harassing any expression of alternative, progressive or 'PC' views (Schreckinger 2017). Their efforts were noticed by Clinton who, to their delight, made them the focus of a speech on 25 August 2016 in which she accused Trump of 'taking a hate movement mainstream' (McCarthy 2016).

It's difficult to map the political use of memetic warfare, but we know it is intentional and well-organized. In 2005 Michael Prosser, a Marine Corps student at Marine Corps University in Virginia, wrote a Masters paper entitled 'Memetics – A Growth Industry in US Military Operations' suggesting memes would be an important part of future ideological informational warfare and recommending the establishment of a military 'Meme Warfare Centre' (Prosser 2006) and over the following years the idea of memetic war spread. One of those promoting it was Jeff Giesea, a right-wing Washington entrepreneur and consultant who, in Winter 2015, published an article entitled 'It's Time to Embrace Memetic Warfare' in the official journal of the NATO Strategic Communications Centre of Excellence (Giesea 2015). He argues here that 'warfare through trolling and memes is a necessary, inexpensive and easy way to help destroy the appeal and morale of our common enemies' (2015: 69). As he explains:

> Memetic warfare, as I define it, is competition over narrative, ideas, and social control in a social-media battlefield. One might think of it as a subset of 'information operations' tailored to social media. Information operations involve the collection and dissemination of information to establish a competitive advantage over an opponent. Memetic warfare could also be viewed as a 'digital native' version of psychological warfare, more commonly known as propaganda. If propaganda and public diplomacy are conventional forms of memetic warfare, then trolling and PSYOPS are guerrilla versions. (2015: 70)

Giesea's paper remains focused on the military application of memetic warfare, for example against Islamic State, but he gives examples of its domestic political use too:

> In the U.S. Republican Primary race, Jeb Bush recently attempted to paint Donald Trump as the "chaos candidate." But when his campaign tried spreading a #ChaosCandidate hashtag, trolls supporting Trump took it over and used it to denigrate Jeb Bush. Hashtags, one might say, are operational coordinates of memetic warfare. (2015: 72)

Influenced by the Russian government's use of 'troll farms', by Vladislav Surkov's disinformation campaigns around Crimea and East Ukraine and his appropriation and manipulation of language and invalidation of truth through 'alternative facts' (see Pomerantsev 2015), Giesea applied the same tactics to the US election.

Along with Mike Cernovich, Giesea created 'MAGA3X', a social media organization devoted to pro-Trump domestic memetic warfare, and recruited and coordinated an online troll-army to produce and share material. As Bernstein says, 'The MAGA3X accounts were a water cannon of memes, Breitbart stories, WikiLeaks theories, pro-Trump YouTube videos, and cartoons about #Pizzagate, and they swelled to the tens of thousands, eventually gaining public praise from Gen. Michael Flynn, the national security adviser to be' (Bernstein 2016). MAGA3x also built a meme-generator to promote the alt-right flashmobs they were creating. Overall, it's impossible to prove how influential or successful this memetic warfare was as people voted for Trump for many different personal, economic, social, cultural and political reasons, but one thing is certain: people voted for Trump. The 'troll' candidate won.

TRUMP AND TROLLING

The anons on 4Chan who'd reacted to Trump as a troll were, of course, wrong, for Trump was serious about his candidacy, but they were correct when they detected something *troll-like* about his politics. The sport of this cartoon-like, inexperienced reality-TV star running for president did feel like someone was trolling the political system, a feeling reinforced by Trump's random political opinions and almost absurdist statements and policies. Where Trump himself came closest to trolling, however, was in his use of Twitter.

Donald Trump joined Twitter in April 2009, taking the name @realDonaldTrump to distinguish himself from a parody account and posting his first tweet on 4 May advertising his forthcoming appearance on the David Letterman show. His account was initially run by a marketing team who posted bland, predictable, promotional material but something changed in 2011. His posts became far more frequent but they also became more personal and political. Whereas his first tweet of the year on 13 January 2011 was another reminder of a forthcoming TV appearance, by 3 August he was tweeting 'Wake up America – China is eating our lunch' (Oborne and Roberts 2017: 23, 32). Trump was famous for his lack of digital awareness and technological use, but something about Twitter gelled with him. Reportedly the only app on his smartphone, with Twitter Trump found his own unique political voice.

Twitter became Trump's primary vehicle of political communication. More importantly, it remained so *after* his election victory, with Trump becoming the first president to ignore and bypass the official channels of White House communication, as well as his own advisors and communications teams, to present his opinions and policies directly to the public and to the world. Interviews, speeches, press conferences and official policy-reveals all became secondary to the immediate declarations issuing from his Twitter account. His thoughts are unfiltered, often disconnected from each other and sometimes disconnected from sense or reality. Influenced by the motivational speaker Norman Vincent Peale and his 1952 self-help book *The Power of Positive Thinking*, for Trump untruths don't matter: you can simply will something into reality.

Just as Marinetti bypassed the art-establishment, taking to the stage to deliver his provocations straight to the people, so Trump uses Twitter's platform as a stage for his global declarations. And just like the avant-garde manifestos of the early twentieth century, what matters in Trump's communications isn't the logic, coherence, ideals or defensibility of his posts, but the mere fact of them being launched and of being *out there* for the public. For Marinetti—*the* theorist of speed—it was the immediate and instant connection with the public that counted: hurling the Futurist message to the crowds so fast that critical-thinking was short-circuited in favour of the chaos of the response. Similarly Trump employs the instantaneous, implosive power of digital technology to connect with the world, with the speed of thought and speed of Twitter coalescing into a mode of kinetic political violence that throws his audience, the political system, the official communicative channels, the mainstream media and the entire international order onto the back-foot and into chaos as they try to catch-up with what he's saying.

Trump, therefore, is followed by the world and is carefully watched by every political administration that wonders what he will do next. The South Korean government, for example, set up a Twitter watching position in the foreign ministry, explaining that they did it 'because we don't yet have an insight into his foreign policies' (Naughtie 2017). But Trump's Twitter use isn't just causing chaos internationally, it's having the same effect on his own administration as his press team has to continually respond to what he tweets and attempt to explain and rationalize what he might have meant.

The situation deteriorated to the point where branches of the US government are frightened what they might find out about via Twitter.

On 26 July 2017 Trump tweeted, 'After consultation with my Generals and military experts, please be advised that the United States Government will not accept or allow...'. There were nine minutes before the second part of the tweet announced transgender people would no longer be allowed to serve in the military which Pentagon officials reportedly spent on tenterhooks, worrying that 'Trump was going to declare war on North Korea' (Buncombe 2017). Trump's Twitter use, therefore, trolls his own administration and the US government system.

What's noticeable about Trump is his lack of traditional political vulnerability. Criticism from the mainstream media, seasoned political commentators, famous political figures and even international politicians and media are all brushed off by both trump and his supporters. As forces of the perceived establishment they only prove his outsider status and challenge to privileged authorities. Scandals, failed policies, gaffs and political attacks that should have damaged Trump appear not to have. So where then is he vulnerable? The answer is in humour and satire: the same troll-culture that supports Trump and which he incarnates has become one of the most important weapons against him.

This became obvious with *Saturday Night Live*. On 1 October 2016 Alec Baldwin first appeared as Trump in a spoof debate with Kate McKinnon's Hilary Clinton. His puckered lips, eyebrows, wig, calculated hand-gestures and pronunciation captured Trump's looks and mannerisms and the public's attention and he returned in the following weeks. By week three, Trump couldn't take any more, tweeting on 16 October: 'Watched Saturday Night Live hit job on me. Time to retire the boring and unfunny show. Alec Baldwin portrayal stinks. Media rigging election!' (Oborne and Roberts 2017: 223). The caricature was retired before the election but returned following Trump's victory, satirizing Trump and showing him being controlled by a shirtless Putin and Steve Bannon's Grim Reaper. Making fun of presidents wasn't new on *SNL*, but the disdain for Trump was particularly noticeable.

SNL continued to mock Trump. On 4 December 2016, they showed Trump in a security briefing only interested in his phone, saying 'I just retweeted the best tweet. I mean, wow, what a great, smart tweet', after sharing the thoughts of a 16 year-old high-school student called Seth. Kate McKinnon broke character as Kellyanne Conway to say 'He really did do this'. Hours later Trump responded on Twitter, 'Just tried watching *Saturday Night Live* – unwatchable! Totally biased, not funny and the Baldwin impersonation just can't get any worse. Sad' (Oborne and Roberts

2017: 237). Baldwin replied on Twitter 20 minutes later, 'Release your tax returns and I'll stop. Ha.' Trump, so implacable against mainstream media and political criticism, was clearly stung not just by the ridicule, but by the ridicule of those he wanted respect from—the entertainment community.

Perhaps *Saturday Night Live*'s best trolling of the Trump administration, however, was Melissa McCarthy's brutal impersonation of the White House press secretary Sean Spicer. First appearing on 4 February 2017, McCarthy skewered the look, mannerisms and modus operandi of his press conferences, screaming at the press, jabbing his finger and histrionically raging about the president and political reality: 'As you know, President Trump announced his Supreme Court pick on the national TV today. When he entered the room the crowd greeted him with a *standing ovation*! Which lasted a full *fifteen minutes*! You can check the tape on that. Everyone was smiling. Everyone was happy. The men all had erections and every single one of the women was ovulating left and right. And no- one, no-one was sad. Those are the facts forever...'. The sketch ends with Spicer attacking the questioning press with the podium and using a water-gun of soapy water on a reporter to 'wash that filthy, lying mouth!' (Saturday Night Live 2017).

By Monday evening it was being reported that Trump was furious about the sketch. The accuracy of the satire undoubtedly hurt, but the coup de grace was the fact that Spicer had been impersonated so well by a woman. To an administration infused with an alt-right anti-PC perspective and a president who boasted about grabbing women 'by the pussy', *this* was the real burn. The president 'doesn't like his people to look weak' an anonymous Trump donor explained (Karni et al. 2017). The Republican consultant and pollster Frank Luntz called the portrayal 'devastating', whilst former Obama White House press secretary Bill Burton noted of *Saturday Night Live*, 'It's effective in that it's getting under the skin in a way that it shouldn't be getting under their skin' (Smith 2017). Late night comedians have continued to roast Trump and women have remained at the forefront of this, with *Full Frontal With Samantha Bee* becoming one of the most important satirical critiques of the administration (Lewis 2017).

It wasn't just mainstream media trolling Trump. His own platform-of-choice, Twitter, became a political-satirical conflict-zone, with his every Tweet attracting satire and ridicule. The trolling wasn't new. In September 2014 Trump was fooled into retweeting a photo of serial-killers Fred and

Rose West as a fan's claimed parents (Monkey 2014); in September 2015 he tweeted a photo of Jeremy Corbyn sent to him as a supporter's 'dad' (Elgot 2015); and in February 2016 he retweeted a Mussolini quote from a Gawker bot-account that was presenting Mussolini quotes as Trump's (Haberman 2016). Soon after Trump's inauguration his administration got into a dispute about the relative size of his inauguration crowd compared to Obama's, after a comparison photo by Reuters was posted on the National Park Service Twitter account and then widely shared on Twitter and social media (Hunt 2017a). Others in the government also turned on him, with rogue NASA and EPA accounts being set up to challenge his administration's policies: as '@RogueNASA' said, 'come for the facts, stay for the snark' (BBC 2017a).

Trolling Trump and his supporters soon took off. Former Mexican president Vicente Fox had been abusing Trump and his border wall plans through 2016 and this continued after his inauguration. On 25 January 2017 he posted, 'Sean Spicer, I've said this to @realDonaldTrump and now I'll tell you: Mexico is not going to pay for that fucking wall. #FuckingWall', leading to #FuckingWall trending on Twitter (Cresci 2017). On 2 February it was reported hackers were breaking into the broadcast signals of radios around the United States to play YG's song 'Fuck Donald Trump', with one station, Sunny 107.9 WFBS-FM in Salem, South Carolina playing it on repeat for 15 minutes before it was halted (Strauss 2017). On 3 February Sweden's deputy PM Isabella Lovin posted a posed photo of herself signing a new law whilst surrounded by women, parodying a recent photo of Trump surrounded by a room of men whilst signing an executive order banning Federal money going to international groups which perform or provide information on abortions (BBC 2017b).

On 20 February 2017, Trump's comments in a rally in Florida about a non-existent terror attack—'You look at what's happening in Germany, you look at what's happening last night in Sweden…'—went viral. The hashtags #IStandWithSweden and #jesuisIKEA began trending on Twitter; UK broadcaster Gary Lineker tweeted 'Thoughts are with everyone in Sweden at this difficult time'; someone posted a photo of Abba under the headline 'four extremists responsible for the #Swedenincident still at large', and Chelsea Clinton (referencing another made-up terrorist attack) posted 'What happened in Sweden Friday night? Did they catch the Bowling Green Massacre perpetrators?'. One Twitter user posted flat-pack instructions for a 'Börder Wåll' to keep out immigrants, commenting

'After the terrible events #lastnightinSweden, IKEA have sold out of this' (Topping 2017; Malkin 2017). Irony, however, doesn't always win out: some Trump supporters, it was discovered, were posting that the attack *was* real and was being suppressed by the mainstream media.

At around the same time the 'Tiny Trump' meme started spreading across Twitter and social media. As 'Know Your Meme' reports, on 16 February 2017, Redditor theLAZYmd submitted a photoshopped picture of a shortened Trump walking down a tarmac with two secret service agents to /r/pics, where it received more than 181,000 votes (65% upvoted) and 2200 comments (Know Your Meme 2017a). The meme spread over Reddit and Twitter, as people joined in, photoshopping pictures to show Trump as a toddler-like figure signing orders in the White House, chatting to Obama, being petted by Putin, meeting political figures, being held like a baby and driving a toy car. As in Melissa McCarthy's impersonation, the meme stung because it struck not just at the political authority of Trump, but at his hyper-masculinist self-presentation.

Another meme emerged after the Saudi Arabian US embassy released a photo on Twitter on 21 May 2017 showing Trump at the opening ceremony of the Saudi 'Global Centre for Combatting Extremist Ideology' in Riyadh. The image showed Trump, Saudi Arabian King Salman and Egyptian president Abdel Fattah el-Sisi with their hands on a glowing orb—a decorative, illuminated world globe. This was a gift to online commentators. 'Hail Hydra!' (referencing Marvel comics' fictitious global terrorist organization) was one of many captions added to the photo. Other's referenced the Illuminati, or linked the photo to an image of Saruman with a 'palantir' seeing-stone from *The Lords of the Rings* films or to the eye of Sauron from the same trilogy, with both captioned 'one orb to rule them all'. A wide range of orbs were quickly unearthed from popular culture including an original-series *Star Trek* image of Captain Kirk being mind-controlled by an orb (Hunt 2017b). Again, international politicians took the opportunity to mock Trump: the Prime Ministers of Denmark, Finland, Iceland, Norway and Sweden, meeting in Bergen to discuss closer cooperation, reposted Trump's photo with another beneath, of themselves grasping a football together captioned 'Who rules the world? Riyadh vs Bergen' (Reuters 2017). It's unlikely that Trump—with his 'gossamer' thin skin, as *Vanity Fair* editor Graydon Carter described it (Carter 2015) and desperately needing to be taken seriously—would have wanted this to be the defining image of his first foreign trip.

The orb-meme was soon superseded as, within a week, Trump managed to invent a new word and melt the internet. At 5.06 am on 31 May 2017 Trump went to bed, leaving the world with his tweet: 'Despite the constant negative press covfefe'. Most agreed it was probably a typographical error for 'coverage' but Twitter-users enjoyed themselves anyway. US comedian Jimmy Kimmel admitted, 'What makes me saddest is I know I'll never write anything funnier than #covfefe'; another Twitter user posted a photo from the film *Arrival* showing a scientist trying to communicate with the aliens with a placard reading 'covfefe'; the Philadelphia Police tweeted 'Roads are still slick from last night's rain. Please use your wipers and drive with covfefe'; whilst a new account under the name 'Covfefe the Strong' was set up with its opening tweet being 'I have been summoned to this world. I know not why'. When Trump awoke he deleted the tweet and added, 'Who can figure out the true meaning of "covfefe"??? Enjoy!' (BBC 2017c).

Trump's own tweets participated in this troll-politics. On 2 July 2017 he tweeted a short video clip showing himself wrestling a person with a CNN logo for their head, under the headline '#FraudNewsCNN' (BBC 2017d). It was an altered video of his appearance at a WWE wrestling-event taken from a Reddit user, 'HanAssholeSolo', who had a history of posting anti-semitic, racist, Islamophobic and misogynist comments and images (Gabbatt 2017). Trump, therefore, was reposting an alt-right video created as part of the ongoing memetic political conflict and 'culture wars' (see Nagle 2017) and his take-up of the video was in turn mimetically reworked by his supporters and critics as another twist in the battle.

The best response came from CNN itself who posted a parody video of the CNN-face man explaining, 'My name is CNN and I was assaulted by the president of the United States'. The CNN man begins to tell the story of his online bullying illustrated by Trump's anti-CNN tweets, commenting 'Donald Trump started to call me fake news. Which was almost as painful as me having to call him President of the United States'. He next explains Trump's history of lying and the 'workplace' bullying of the channel before breaking down about having to explain his physical assault by the president to his kids, with giant blue, cartoon tears rolling off his logo (The Feed 2017).

CNN's decision not to expose the racist Reddit user's real identity unless they continued was a reasonable and ethical journalistic decision, but to the alt-right internet warriors it smelt of 'blackmail' and an attempt to shut down freedom of speech. This sparked a renewed alt-right versus

CNN meme war with Trump supporters superimposing the CNN logo and Trump's face onto anything and everything they could think of (RT 2017a). As the head moderator of /r/The_Donald subreddit, where the original video was posted, declared: 'This is an attack on the Internet and CNN has informally declared war upon it. In return we need to hit CNN where it hurts, and tell the advertise companies... that you do not approve of them by running ads at the network or endorsing CNN by running adds (*sic*)' (RT 2017b). On 15 August 2017 Trump himself reactivated the memetic battle, retweeting a meme of a train running over the CNN-face man, captioned 'Fake news can't stop the Trump Train' (BBC 2017e). Its imagery was especially insensitive, coming only three days after a white supremacist had run his car into a crowd of protestors in Charlottesville, Virginia, killing 1 and injuring 19.

The alt-right memetic war continues. One of the most popular recent alt-right memes was the 'based stick man' (Know Your Meme 2017b). It originated with Kyle Chapman, a 41 year-old Trump supporter who, on 4 March 2017, attended a pro-Trump rally in Berkeley, California dressed in home-made armour, including a baseball helmet, ski-goggles, face-mask and shin guards whilst wielding a large wooden stick and a DIY shield with the US flag painted on it. A video of him striking an 'antifa' (anti-fascist) protestor on the head went viral, leading to numerous remixes of the footage, dubbed with songs including by Rick Derringer, Styx, Imogen Heap and Hulk Hogan's theme-song. He was immediately celebrated on 4Chan's /pol/ board under the title 'based stickman' ('based' meaning having a strong foundation, knowing yourself and doing your own thing, which is generally considered online to be a cool pose) and the 'Alt-Knight' (referencing the right-wing vigilante Batman, 'the Dark Knight' and playing on the term 'alt-right'). 4Chan produced a series of memes photoshopping based stickman into a series of images including *Captain America: Civil War, 300, Game of Thrones* and the new Zelda game.

The left, however, already had their own counter-meme of the white-supremacist Richard Spencer being punched in the face during a TV inter-view in January 2017 (Burris 2017). Spencer knew what was coming, commenting afterwards 'I'm afraid this is going to become the meme to end all memes. That I'm going to hate watching this' and, sure enough, soon after a subreddit called 'r/RichardSpencerPunched' sprang up; a Tumblr user mashed a video of *Rick and Morty* characters beating-up a neo-Nazi with footage of Spencer; Tumblr and Twitter users juxtaposed the images with pictures of Captain America punching Hitler and Indiana Jones punching a Nazi; whilst on Twitter remixes of the video proliferated, such as one showing Spencer being punched to Celine Dion's song 'My Heart Will Go On' (Tiffany 2017). So too, clearly, would memetic political warfare.

'APPLY COLD WATER TO BURNED AREA'

The concept of 'memetic warfare' emerged out of military debates as an extension of informational war and psyops. To date it has been deployed by numerous governments as seen, for example, in China's '50 Cent Party', Russia's 'troll-farms', Israel's 'Hasbara' units, the Ukraine's 'iArmy' and the British military's 77th Brigade and GCHQ's Joint Threat Research Intelligence Group (JTRIG) (Benedictus 2016). What hasn't been fully recognized yet, however, is the extent to which this mode of ideational warfare has permeated domestic political debate and the life and activities of the broader public. By way of a conclusion I'd like to argue the following.

Firstly, memetic warfare is a real phenomenon, being used by governments, militaries, formal and informal organizations, groups and collectives and by engaged individuals as a mode of intervention in domestic political processes. It represents an emerging 'troll-politics' which is based upon the appropriation and weaponization of troll-culture and its tactics for political purposes. It takes trolling's use of humour and satire and chaotic intervention to attack or confuse an existing, established position, idea, argument, behaviour or order. But where it departs from real trolling is that it does so in order to advance an alternative order or position it believes in: unlike trolling, troll-politics *is serious*.

Hence what began on 4Chan as transgression became real sentiments to be promoted. In order to become serious it had to migrate from the jokey-chaos of the /b/random board to a dedicated /pol/ channel as real trolling gives zero fucks for white nationalism and supremacism. But the alt-right didn't entirely leave trolling behind, instead it coopted it as a tool, enjoying the continued reflected cool of memetic discourse, using memes to promote its political agenda and, when it suited, enjoying the protection of its irony. As Richard Spencer commented after footage emerged of him leading a Fascist salute shouting 'Hail Trump!' following the election victory, it was done 'in the spirit of irony and exuberance' (Wilson 2017a). That this is a ruse was admitted by Andrew Anglin in his article 'A Normie's Guide to the Al-Right' posted in August 2016 on *The Daily Stormer* website when he described the use of memes as 'non-ironic Nazism masquerading as ironic Nazism'.

Secondly, I'd argue that this troll-politics is now central to our political life, constituting, for many people, their most common mode of political expression, participation and activism. Time spent on traditional political activities such as engaging with political parties and local campaigning is eclipsed by the time spent on political posting and commenting. Our phones, apps, messaging, personal networks, favoured platforms, recommendations and peer-linked sources are at the heart today of our everyday political awareness, experience and activity and much of this activity is humorous, satirical, irreverent and sarcastic: lampooning, ridiculing and parodying the political opposition. If we broaden the concept of memetic warfare to include all forms of sharable content produced to make fun of and diminish another political position then we can see that a huge number of Facebook posts, tweets and other social media creations come under this rubric. Much of this includes linking to and reposting mainstream media news-stories and opinion pieces, but the actual link matters less than the humorous comment and critique we add to it: the journalism is secondary to the point and joke *we* want to make. Often the journalism isn't even read. Troll-politics, therefore, is everywhere, dissolving into our everyday life and use of digital media.

Thirdly, this memetic warfare is significant. It is common to claim today that we live in 'filter bubbles' (Pariser 2012), with social media functioning as an 'echo-chamber', connecting us to those who hold similar views and limiting our experience of and engagement with alternative perspectives. It's an important idea but it is too-uncritically accepted and often deployed simply to denigrate online activity. What it overlooks is how permeable our 'bubbles' are. Searchable, public hashtags on Twitter and trending topics and retweets all bring other views to us; on Facebook 'weak ties' link us to worlds, places, lives, opinions and activities different to our own (see Granovetter 1973), whilst others' 'likes' and comments elsewhere show up on our feed; on YouTube and other sites, recommendations for what to watch or listen to next gradually expand our experiences; across the web comments, postings and activities between people are visible; memes spread virally around the net, whilst newspapers and aggregation sites pick up on and spread internet culture. The result is a fractal ecology of experiences, posts and links that each of navigate—one that, inevitably, at some point, bursts our bubble.

Fourthly, this troll-politics isn't simply an online phenomenon. Older Gibsonian and Barlowian ideas of 'cyberspace' as a gnostic, separate, transcendental electronic world of 'mind' are now obsolete (Gibson 2016; Barlow 1996; Davis 2015). With mobile phones and public wi-fi and ubiquitous connections the online and real worlds exist as an imploded, electronically augmented space and with Web 2.0 real-lives are lived online and online-lives permeate and dissolve into the real-world. We can no longer separate the internet from everyday life, hence Chan culture and memetic warfare is a real-world phenomenon too. Jason Wilson reports on an alt-right rally at Boston Common in May 2017 where the right-wing protestors dressed themselves up with 4Chan's memes. There was Pepe the Frog cos-play, people dressed as Based Stickman and people carrying the flag of 'Kekistan', the imaginary country created by 4Chan members and the crowd chanted 'Normies out!' (Wilson 2017a). In the 'Unite the Right' rally in Charlottesville, Virginia, on 11–12 August 2017 the flag of 'Kekistan' could also be seen alongside the Confederate and Swastika flags. Indeed, internet politics suffused the meaning of the real-world rally too. The defence of the Confederate statues wasn't simply about historical events and persons for, as Wilson points out, 'white nationalists have been turning the statues into rallying points for resistance to multiculturalism, feminism and minority rights'—in other words, into resistance to that PC-world 4Chan and Reddit rail against online (Wilson 2017b).

Fifthly, I'd like to argue for the efficacy of memetic warfare. What at first appears as a minor and esoteric activity is, on reflection, a mode of political expression and engagement that includes the everyday online activities of a great number of people. Not everyone is as organized or as influential as 4Chan's /pol/ or The_Donald subreddit, but everyone can take part. Memetic warfare, therefore, is best understood as a mode of ongoing, continuous, real-time domestic, political psyops: an informational, hegemonic war carried out by each against all others. In this Gramscian battle we are all potential soldiers, firing our own individual memetic bullets into the fray. There are obviously attempts to organize and direct these soldiers by governments, groups and collectivities, but memetic culture remains essentially grassroots, bottom-up, popularly generated and spread. To have an effect it has to go viral and beyond control.

It's my belief that we've underestimated both the extent of this troll-politics and its impact. Memes have a powerful effect. They are weapons in a conflict but also, simultaneously, a means of solidarity, attracting support and binding those with similar views. They reduce and simplify political facts and arguments and represent another move away from the liberal ideal of rational, communicative debate, but they also cut through such discourse to deliver highly charged satirical critiques that damage opponents and their positions and that inflict a telling *ideological burn* upon them. They are part of a new politics of affectivity, identification, emotion and humour. They appear everywhere, are shared by huge numbers of people and will only increase in use and power. During the 2016 UK election, for example, stories about Jeremy Corbyn and anti-Theresa May comments, images and memes overflowed online. Whilst once the rightwing UK popular press seemed able to direct the public's mood and political beliefs, this time they proved impotent against a wave of online support. The people, it turned out, were too busy posting and trolling to listen to them. Ironically, for all the moral panic orchestrated by the press against trolls, today, perhaps, in a sense, *we're all trolls*.

REFERENCES

4Chan (2017) '/b/- Random', http://boards.4chan.org/b/

Barlow, J. P. (1996) 'A Declaration of the Independence of Cyberspace', 8th February, *Electronic Frontier Foundation*, https://www.eff.org/cyberspace-independence

Bartlett, J. (2014) *Dark Net*, London: William Heinemann.

BBC (2016) 'Trump aide Michael Flynn Jr. out after "pizzagate" tweets', *BBC News*, 7th December, http://www.bbc.co.uk/news/world-us-canada-38231532

BBC (2017a) 'Rogue NASA account fights Trump on climate change', *BBC News*, 26th January, http://www.bbc.co.uk/news/world-us-canada-38756447

BBC (2017b) 'Is Sweden's Deputy PM trolling Donald Trump in Facebook photo?', *BBC News*, 3rd February, http://www.bbc.co.uk/news/world-europe-38853399

BBC (2017c) '"Covfefe": Trump invents new word and melts internet', *BBC News*, 31st May, http://www.bbc.co.uk/news/world-us-canada-40104063

BBC (2017d) 'Donald Trump posts video clip of him "beating" CNN in wrestling', *BBC News*, 2nd July, http://www.bbc.co.uk/news/world-us-canada-40474118

BBC (2017e)

Benedictus, L. (2016) 'Invasion of the troll armies: from Russian Trump supporters to Turkish state stooges', *The Guardian*, 6th November, https://www.theguardian.com/media/2016/nov/06/troll-armies-social-media-trump-russian

Bernstein, J. (2016) 'This Man Helped Build The Trump Meme Army — Now He Wants To Reform It', *Buzzfeed News*, 30th December, https://www.buzzfeed.com/josephbernstein/this-man-helped-build-the-trump-meme-army-and-now-he-wants-t?utm_term=.nhRmZ6PJWy#.wneB9Wo5N2

Bishop, J. (2012) 'The Psychology of Trolling and Lurking: The Role of Defriending and Gamification for Increasing Participation in Online Communities Using Seductive Narratives', in Li, Honglei (ed.) *Virtual Community Participation and Motivation: Cross-Disciplinary Theories*. Hershey, PA: IGI Global, pp. 160-176.

Bishop, J (2013) 'The effect of de-individuation of the Internet Troller on Criminal Procedure implementation: An interview with a Hater', *International Journal of Cyber Criminology*, January-June, Vol 7 (1), pp. 28–48, http://www.cybercrimejournal.com/Bishop2013janijcc.pdf

Buckels, E. E., Trapnell, P. D., and Paulhus, D. L. (2014). 'Trolls Just Want to Have Fun'. *Personality and Individual Differences*. September. Vol. 16, pp. 97–102.

Buncombe, A. (2017) 'Pentagon "worried Trump was going to declare war on North Korea" during today's tweets about military', *The Independent*, 26th July, http://www.independent.co.uk/news/world/americas/us-politics/donald-trump-transgender-pentagon-fear-north-korea-declare-war-a7862091.html

Burris, S. (2017) 'White nationalist Richard Spencer punched in the face camera while doing interview', *Youtube*, 20th January, https://www.youtube.com/watch?v=9rh1dhur4aI

Carter, G. (2015) 'Steel Traps and Short Fingers', *Vanity Fair*, November, https://www.vanityfair.com/culture/2015/10/graydon-carter-donald-trump

Cresci, E. (2017) 'How former Mexican president Vicente Fox uses Twitter to troll Trump', *The Guardian*, 26th January, https://www.theguardian.com/us-news/2017/jan/26/no-pay-wall-how-former-mexican-president-vicente-fox-uses-twitter-to-troll-trump

Davis, E. (2015) *Techgnosis*, Berkeley, CA: North Atlantic Books.

Dibbell, J. (2009) 'The Assclown Offensive: How to Enrage the Church of Scientology', *Wired*, 21st September, https://www.wired.com/2009/09/mf-chanology/

Elgot, J. (2015) 'Donald Trump duped into retweeting picture of Jeremy Corbyn', *The Guardian*, 12th September, https://www.theguardian.com/us-news/2015/sep/12/donald-trump-duped-into-retweeting-picture-of-jeremy-corbyn

Gabbatt, A. (2017) 'Reddit user who took credit for Trump's CNN tweet has history of racist posts', *The Guardian*, 3rd July, https://www.theguardian.com/us-news/2017/jul/03/trump-tweet-reddit-user-history-hanassholesolo

Gibson, W. (2016) *Neuromancer*, London: Gollancz.

Giesea, J. (2015) 'It's Time to Embrace Memetic Warfare', *Defence Strategic Communications*, Vol. 1, No, 1, Winter, pp. 68-76 [PDF].

Granovetter, M. S. (1973) 'The Strength of Weak Ties', *American Journal of Sociology*, Vol. 78, No. 6, May, pp. 1360–1380, https://sociology.stanford. edu/sites/default/files/publications/the_strength_of_weak_ties_and_ exch_w-gans.pdf

Haberman, M. (2016) 'Donald Trump retweets post with quote from Mussolini', *The New York Times*, 28th February, https://www.nytimes.com/politics/first-draft/2016/02/28/donald-trump-retweets-post-likening-him-to-mussolini/

Hardaker, C. (2013) 'Internet trolls: a guide to the different flavours', in *The Guardian*. 1st July, http://www.theguardian.com/commentisfree/2013/jul/01/internet-trolls-guide-to-different-flavours

Hunt, E. (2017a) 'Trump's inauguration crowd: Sean Spicer's claims versus the evidence', *The Guardian*, 22nd January, https://www.theguardian.com/us-news/2017/jan/22/trump-inauguration-crowd-sean-spicers-claims-versus-the-evidence

Hunt, E. (2017b) '"One orb to rule them all": image of Donald Trump and glowing globe perplexes internet', *The Guardian*, 22nd May, https://www.theguardian. com/us-news/2017/may/22/one-orb-to-rule-them-all-image-of-trump-and-glowing-globe-perplexes-internet

Karni, A., Dawsey, J. and Palmeri, T. (2017) 'White House rattled by McCarthy's spoof of Spicer', *Politico*, 6th February, http://www.politico.com/story/2017/02/melissa-mccarthy-sean-spicer-234715

Know Your Meme (2017a) 'Tiny Trumps', *Know Your Meme*, http://knowyourmeme.com/memes/tiny-trumps

Know Your Meme (2017b) 'Based Stickman', *Know Your Meme*

Lee, B. (2016) 'Marina Abramović mention in Podesta emails sparks accusations of satanism', *The Guardian*, 4th November, https://www.theguardian.com/artanddesign/2016/nov/04/marina-abramovic-podesta-clinton-emails-satanism-accusations

Lees, M. (2016) 'What Gamergate should have taught us about the "alt-right"', *The Guardian*, 1st December, https://www.theguardian.com/technology/2016/dec/01/gamergate-alt-right-hate-trump

Lewis, T. (2017) 'Samantha Bee, the new heroine of American political satire', *The Guardian*, 13th August, https://www.theguardian.com/tv-and-radio/2017/aug/13/samantha-bee-full-frontal-donald-trump-interview

Malkin, B. (2017) '"JeSuisIkea": Trump's comments confuse Swedes as supporters cry cover-up', *The Guardian*, 20th February, https://www.theguardian. com/us-news/2017/feb/20/jesuisikea-trump-sweden-terrorist-attack-confuse-supporters-cover-up

Marinetti, F. T. (1909) 'The Founding and Manifesto of Futurism', http://www.unknown.nu/futurism/manifesto.html

Marx, K. (2004) *The Manifesto of the Communist Party*, https://www.marxists.org/archive/marx/works/1848/communist-manifesto/ch01.htm

McCarthy, T. (2016) '"Taking hate mainstream": trump and Clinton trade insults over racism accusations', *The Guardian*, 26th August, https://www.theguardian.com/us-news/2016/aug/25/hillary-clinton-trump-ad-white-supremacist-black-voters

Merrin, W. (2013) '12th January 1910: Futurism and Participation', in *Troll Theory*, 21st May, https://trolltheory.wordpress.com/2013/05/21/12th-january-1910-futurism-and-participation/

Merrin, W. (2016a) '12th September 2011 – Trolls and Tabloids', in *Troll Theory*, 8th May, https://trolltheory.wordpress.com/2016/05/08/12th-september-2011-trolls-and-tabloids/

Merrin, W. (2016b) 'From Chaos to Evil', in *Troll Theory*, 13th May, https://trolltheory.wordpress.com/2016/05/13/from-chaos-to-evil/

Oxford Dictionaries (2014) 'Troll', Oxford: Oxford University Press, http://www.oxforddictionaries.com/definition/english/troll

Monkey (2014) 'Donald Trump retweets serial killer photo in comedian's Twitter prank', *The Guardian*, 29th September, https://www.theguardian.com/media/2014/sep/29/donald-trump-retweets-serial-killer-photos-in-comedians-twitter-prank

Nagle, A. (2017) *Kill All Normies*, Winchester: Zero Books.

Naughtie, J. (2017) 'The Donald Trump tweets that say so much and reveal so little', BBC News, 7th January, http://www.bbc.co.uk/news/world-us-canada-38534308

Oborne, P. and Roberts, T. (2017) *How Trump Thinks*, London: head of Zeus Ltd.

Ortiz, E. (2017) '"Pizzagate" Gunman Edgar Maddison Welch Sentenced to Four Years in Prison', *NBC News*, 22nd June, http://www.nbcnews.com/news/us-news/pizzagate-gunman-edgar-maddison-welch-sentenced-four-years-prison-n775621

Pariser, E. (2012) *The Filter Bubble*, London: Penguin Books.

Pomerantsev, P. (2015) *Nothing is True and Everything is Possible*, London: Faber and Faber.

Prosser, M. B. (2006) *Memetics – A Growth Industry in US Military Operations*, Master of Operational Studies thesis, Marine Corps University, Virginia, http://www.dtic.mil/dtic/tr/fulltext/u2/a507172.pdf

Reuters (2017) 'Nordic prime ministers troll Trump's viral orb photograph', *The Guardian*, 31st May, https://www.theguardian.com/world/2017/may/31/nordic-prime-ministers-troll-trumps-viral-orb-photograph

RT (2017a) '#CNNBlackmail: Ted Cruz claims CNN may have broken law as meme war intensifies', *RT News*, 5th July, https://www.rt.com/viral/395412-ted-cruz-cnn-trump-meme-extortion/

RT (2017b) '"Entire Internet against CNN right now": Reddit moderator on #CNNBlackmail scandal', *RT News*, 6th July, https://www.rt.com/usa/395447-cnn-blackmail-internet-war/

Saar, J. (1972) 'Air Carrier War', *Life*. 4th February, pp. 26–31.

Saturday Night Live (2017) 'Sean Spicer press conference (Melissa McCarthy) – SNL', *Youtube*, 5th February, https://www.youtube.com/watch?v=UWuc18xISwI

Schreckinger, B. (2017) 'World War Meme', *Politico Magazine*, March/April, http://www.politico.com/magazine/story/2017/03/memes-4chan-trump-supporters-trolls-internet-214856

Strauss, M. (2017) 'Hackers Broadcast YG's "Fuck Donald Trump" on Radio Stations Across the Country', *Pitchfork*, 2nd February, http://pitchfork.com/news/69375-hackers-broadcast-ygs-fuck-donald-trump-on-radio-stations-across-the-country/

Suler, J. (2005) 'The Online Disinhibation Effect', *International Journal of Applied Psychoanalytical Studies*. Vol. 2 (2), pp. 184–88.

Smith, D. (2017) '"Vanguard of opposition": SNL adds Spicer to satire's resurgence under Trump', *The Guardian*, 11th February, https://www.theguardian.com/tv-and-radio/2017/feb/11/saturday-night-live-snl-sean-spicer-trump-melissa-mccarthy

The Feed (2017) 'CNN Responds to Trump's Tweet – The Feed', *Youtube*, 3rd July, https://www.youtube.com/watch?v=QotA7KHb7mo

Tiffany, K. (2017) 'Right-wing extremist Richard Spencer got punched, but it was memes that bruised his ego', *The Verge*, 23rd January, https://www.theverge.com/2017/1/23/14356306/richard-spencer-punch-internet-memes-alt-right

Topping, A. (2017) '"Sweden, who would believe this?": Trump cites non-existent terror attack', *The Guardian*, 19th February, https://www.theguardian.com/us-news/2017/feb/19/sweden-trump-cites-non-existent-terror-attack

Wilson, J. (2017a) 'Hiding in plain sight: how the 'alt-right' is weaponizing irony to spread fascism', *The Guardian*, 23rd May, https://www.theguardian.com/technology/2017/may/23/alt-right-online-humor-as-a-weapon-facism

Wilson, J. (2017b) 'Why is the US still fighting the Civil War?', *The Guardian*, 16th August, https://www.theguardian.com/world/2017/aug/16/why-is-the-us-still-fighting-the-civil-war

CHAPTER 14

Trump, the First Facebook President: Why Politicians Need Our Data Too

Jennifer Pybus

On March 12, 2017, Tim Berners-Lee, marked the 28th year since the inception of the Worldwide Web with three collective challenges: (1) The loss of control of our personal data, (2) the concentration of ownership and algorithmic practices which are facilitating the intensification and spread of misinformation and (3) the need for more accountability and regulation around political advertising. Each of these pressing concerns is interrelated. Moreover, as Trump's 2016 victory demonstrates, the social data that we generate is not just producing economic value but garnering political influence, raising important questions around the myriad ways in which political parties are now using algorithmic processes to reach potential voters. As such, what are the implications when a small number of platforms and companies, increasingly control terabytes of our socio-cultural data? More specifically, what does this mean when collectively, we have very little understanding about the ways in which this data is rendered actionable for economic and now for political gain? Data cannot simply be understood as a neutral asset, it is 'cooked' (Gitelman 2013), it produces value (Coté and Pybus 2011; boyd and Crawford 2012), it functions

J. Pybus (✉)
Digital Culture and Society, King's College London, London, UK

© The Author(s) 2019
C. Happer et al. (eds.), *Trump's Media War*,
https://doi.org/10.1007/978-3-319-94069-4_14

as a power knowledge-relation and therefore, most importantly, it is inherently political.

Contemporary politics, as Coté, Gerbaudo and Pybus (2016) argue, are being reshaped by data analysis in electoral campaign strategies. As a result, we have witnessed the rise of a new kind of political advertising, predicated on algorithms, analytics, tools and third party ecosystems. The techno-cultural assemblages (Coté and Pybus 2016) that facilitate the production of value and hence meaning from the quotidian data we generate on digital platforms are not new but have been directly borrowed from recent changes within the creative industries, most notably in advertising and marketing. New technologies and more data, coupled with powerful algorithms have enabled increasingly targeted ads. Additionally, such technological advances have allowed these industries to measure the results of campaigns in real time, across a host of different online channels, thereby optimising ads to account for unexpected market conditions (Hurst 2016). Such practices have been in development for some time. For example, in 2015, Lexus' *Beyond Utility 1000 to 1*, US Facebook campaign, won the 'Global Digital Marketing Award' (2015). The company made more than 1000 customised ads, based on the social media profiles of Facebook users. Each ad was tailored to follow the company's simple insight: "as advertisers, we know that when you are more relevant, you are more persuasive."[1] Lexus, therefore, used the likes, interests, geolocation, gender, demographics, career data and so on of Facebook users to generate 1000 similar but very different ads. The result, according to their campaign manager, was a 300 percent increase in their efficiency and a reckoning that the highly targeted video ads yielded very strong results. We might call this campaign an important, yet quaint, precursor for the kinds of political advertising witnessed during the Trump campaign.

The process of rendering our social data productive is often referred to as datafication (boyd and Crawford 2012; van Dijck 2014; Pybus et al. 2015). Specifically, this can be understood as: (i) the capture, transformation and valuation of collectively produced social data; (ii) a multivalent process, wherein the variability of any given data point has the inherent potential to be re-imagined and re-appropriated based on the algorithmic assemblage it finds itself within; and (iii) what Coté has referred to as 'motility' (2014) denoting the ways in which data moves intensively and extensively in a near autonomous fashion. Together, these elements have transformed the culture industries by facilitating hyper-personalisation which extends (but not limited) to our ads, our newsfeeds, our searches, our prices, our entertainment and even our news. Thus, processes of data-fication are recursive, drawing on our social data to propel the content that we will be predisposed to towards us, but increasingly, to generate those mediated objects that we will want to consume.

Personalisation from an advertising/marketing perspective refers to bringing users into contact with the content that they will want to like and/or share (creating more data) based on their unique data profile. However, the multivalence and motility of data equally means that these creative industries rely on our social data to actually produce those individuated pieces of *sticky*[2] content in the first place. And so, on the one hand, personalised data are used to make "assumptions about where citizens would want to focus their attention or where marketers need those citizen's attention" to be (Couldry and Turow 2014, p. 1712). On the other hand, personalisation is about a deeply affective, performative and recursive relationship that is intensifying the production of unique pieces of content, for unique consumers—not so unlike the memes that Merrin refers to. From this perspective, personalisation is not just about the transformation of mass-mediated to micro-mediated practices but equally about creating ads and content that draw potential users in a way that bypasses traditional content providers—those historically charged with entertaining and hence amassing audiences (Coté and Pybus 2007; Fuchs 2012). Coming back to Trump, at the peak of his Facebook election campaign run by Brad Parscale, he had 175,000 different ads, targeted at 175,000 unique user profiles, linked to 175,000 different pieces of unique content, thereby solidifying the value of personalised data mining practices within mainstream political campaigning (Lapowski 2016).[3]

Hyper-personalisation: Just Good Enough

A healthy democracy needs not only accountability in terms of the regulations of political advertising, but a much clearer understanding of the infrastructure that relies heavily on algorithmic processes to draw predictive insights from our collective personal data. Frank Pasquale argues that the proprietary infrastructure of digital platforms is entirely opaque—'blackboxed' to ensure that users are unaware of how their data are used for both political and/or economic gain. Facebook, according to Tech Crunch's Josh Constine (2017), is the largest social media platform with over two billion monthly active users and currently valued at over $500 billion (US)—surpassed only by Apple, Google and Microsoft (Egan 2017). One of the primary reasons driving Facebook's worth, revolves around their capacity to transform the data produced by their users into valuable assets which take on many forms, most notably as targeted advertising. However, this also includes building campaigns, audience insights, growing audiences, increasing the data profile of users by merging unique profiles with other databases, namely those generated by their growing number of 'marketing partners' and by producing various analytics. Furthermore, Facebook is also mobilising the social data of its users via one of its newest assets: Facebook Elections (2017), which promises to help anyone running a campaign to establish their online identity and to promote voter engagement.

Sue Halpern (2017), from the New York Review of Books followed Donald Trump's use of social media and provocatively called him "the first Facebook president." This proclamation was not simply made because he has a superior Facebook page but rather, as she argues, that:

> His team figured out how to use all the marketing tools of Facebook, as well as Google, the two biggest advertising platforms in the world, to successfully sell a candidate that the majority of Americans did not want. They understood that some numbers matter more than others — in this case the number of angry, largely rural, disenfranchised potential Trump voters — and that Facebook, especially, offered effective methods for pursuing and capturing them.

We must however, be careful. To entirely attribute Trump's victory to Facebook's capacity to deploy targeted political advertising would be an overestimation. We must resist an uncritical and easy conclusion that the likes of Cukier and Mayer-Schoenberger (2013), alongside others such as Chris Anderson (2008) or Sandy Pentland (2012), would have us believe. In short, the computational dream of an N = all verisimilitude—or rather the belief that a dataset can provide a one-to-one correspondence to any given phenomenon (Coté et al. 2016). This perspective is not only problematic; it is inherently flawed. More data does not mean more *truth*, nor does it mean instant persuasion.

So, how do we frame the empirical power of Big Data? And why is it so attractive to marketers, brands and now increasingly to politicians? Bernhard Rieder (2016) provides insight to this question as he puts forward an argument about how Big Data is deployed to produce "actionable forms of knowledge." In short, for him, the value of machine learning analytics lies not in the capacity to yield a descriptive truth but an advantageous outcome. Machine learning algorithms become powerful not because they can produce truth, in terms of knowing any given subject, but action, in terms of increasing conversion, or in Rieder's words: "better-than-coin-toss performances that increase with effects, measurable click-through rates and results." This insight serves as an important reminder—Big Data analytics, the rise of psychographic profiles and information silos cannot simply deliver an election, as evidenced by the failure of Ted Cruz[4] to be nominated for the Republicans, or even by Theresa May's recent failure to win a majority in the 2017 UK election. However, the datafied political campaign strategies that have been recently observed in the United States and the United Kingdom, were, nonetheless *just good enough* to have radically transformed political campaigning within our current historical moment. It would appear that their campaign managers learned from Lexus—you need to be relevant to be persuasive.

The relationality between our behaviour, our data, our ads and our political leaders cannot be understood as fixed but rather predicated on an affective and iterative logic of persuasion. Cathy O'Neil (2017) argues, that social media has facilitated an on-going series of experiments via thousands of data driven conversations to see what motivates action. To try and *nudge* a voter in a particular direction, thereby requires both the capacity to produce and situate content that can signify to potential voters. Thus, social data is not just a site of economic growth but an important modality of persuasion—nudge politics. Let us examine two companies: Cambridge Analytica and Facebook, both enlisted by the Republican campaign in 2016 and proved to be instrumental in the persuasion potential voters to either vote for Trump or not vote for Clinton (Halpern 2017).

BIG DATA POLITICS

There has been much attention given to the role of US based Cambridge Analytica, particularly as the software billionaire and Trump supporter, Robert Mercer is one of the largest investors in this advertising agency, which promises to "use data to change audience behaviour" (Cambridge Analytica 2017). Indeed, according to an article in the Guardian earlier this year by Carole Cadwalladr (2017a), Mercer now owns 90 percent of this company, which has boasted the gathering of 5000 data points on 220 million eligible voters in the United States. The data has apparently come from a host of different bodies, such as voter registration records, gun ownership records, credit card purchase histories, Internet account identities, mailing lists and so forth. The other ten percent of the company is owned by British SCL Group (2017), which specialises in "election management strategies" and "messaging and information operations." According to Cadwalladr (2017b), SCL Group has been refining its targeted approach for political campaigns over the past 25 years in a number of countries such as Afghanistan and Pakistan. In military circles, these kinds of interventions are known as 'psyops' or psychological operations. They are therefore hired to psychologically persuade individuals by playing directly on their emotions.

What we can learn from this historical relationship, is that seeking advantage via targeted political campaigning is a longstanding practice. What has changed, however, are new data driven approaches built on machine learning, algorithms and the big social data we collectively produce. Taking a step backwards, it is critical to appreciate why 'Big Data' is different from lots of data. As boyd and Crawford (2012) point out, it is not simply the amount or size of the data being extracted that matters; rather, what requires our attention is the inherent potential value produced from any given data point's relationship with other data points. Value and hence insights from our personal data are not derived from a singular link we upload or status that we write about ourselves. Instead, it comes from the associations which are determined by the digital traces we leave behind. In this sense, it is not simply procured from the petabytes of information, extracted and shared on social media platforms like Facebook, but rather comes out of an enhanced capacity to process large volumes of data from a multitude of different structured and unstructured points, at increasingly higher velocities (Kitchin 2014). These three Vs of Big Data, as they are crudely referred to, that is Volume, Velocity and Variability, hold the predictive promise of data analytics and ultimately explain why a platform like Facebook is highly valued. As they work together, they give rise to the predictive promise of Big Data, that is, to know you better then you know yourself.

The data that we collectively generate online has a depth and breadth of potential due to its varied form, routine generation and new modes of algorithmic processing. Cambridge Analytica was put forward by Steve Bannon, who was also on the agency's board, five months before the election. Their role was to use location data to determine where the undecided American voters resided in potential swing states that could influence the election. The big insight and value that Cambridge Analytica had to offer was (1) their capacity to determine which voters in US swing states were persuadable—as witnessed in the app they developed; and (2) their capacity to produce psychometrics, to influence those voters who were in fact open to a political message. Such metrics, also referred to as psychographics, measure an individual's traits and personalities. In the 1980s, according to Grassegger and Krogerus (2017), who initially broke this story in the Zurich based publication, das Magazin, noted that psychologists developed a model known as OCEAN, which was later picked up by advertising as a means of connecting with potential consumers.

Each letter in the OCEAN model seeks to represent a different personality trait, known as the 'big five': openness (how open you are to new experiences?); conscientiousness (how much of a perfectionist are you?); extroversion (how sociable are you?); agreeableness (how considerate and cooperative you are?); and neuroticism (are you easily upset?). According to Grassegger and Krogerus (2017), in 2008, two graduate students by the name of Kosinski and Stilwell developed and launched a small Facebook app called: MyPersonality at Cambridge University. The aim was to encourage users to fill out a questionnaire to learn about themselves; in so doing, they were also given the option of sharing their Facebook profile data with the researchers. By 2012, they had amassed the largest dataset ever collected, with millions of people's closest beliefs and convictions. With all of this raw material, Kosinski asserted with 10 likes, you could evaluate someone better than the average work colleague, with 70 likes you know enough to outdo what the person's friend knew, with 150 likes you know more than what their parents know and with 300 likes you know more than what their partner knows, and if you have more than 300 likes you could surpass what a person thinks they know about themselves! Once again, the promise of Big Data.

According to the investigative reporting of Grassegger and Krogerus (2017), Cambridge Analytica coopted this technology and used it to generate targeted advertising in addition to an application for the Republicans. The aim was to use the data that they had gathered to micro-target American voters by personality type. From July 2016, Trump canvassers were each given this application which was meant to easily identify the political views and personality types of the people they were targeting. Furthermore, canvassers were only advised to knock on the doors of the voters who were deemed in advance to be receptive. Finally, the canvassers were told to upload the reactions they received back into the app so that

Cambridge Analytica could continue learning and honing its predictive capacity by growing their database even further via machine learning techniques and practices.

However, despite the impressive capacity of Cambridge Analytica to determine psychographic profiles it is not the entire story behind Trump's digital success but rather one part of a very extensive decision to launch a highly sophisticated, well-funded data driven campaign. Instead, this company should be understood as an important node within a larger electoral strategy, which as Theresa Hong (one of Trump's key digital strategists) explained to BBC's Jamie Bartlett (2017), was called 'Project Alamo'. Briefly, this was the name given to the Republican's actively growing database about American voters. The data came from a number of bodies including Cambridge Analytica, Google and Facebook. According to Halpern (2017) and Winston (2016) there is a dispute among Trump's inner circle about which tool was the most effective. However, according to Hong, both played instrumental roles and worked together to maximise the party's capacity to gather data, create psychographic profiles and then most importantly to target the ads.

Facebook was introduced after a number of mass mailing attempts by the Republicans had failed in the earlier days of the campaign. Brad Parscale was then hired by Trump's son-in-law Jared Kuschner. Initially, he was given two million dollars to invest in a political advertising campaign. He made a decision to put this entirely into Facebook and went to the social media platform upon making a deal with the Republican National Committee to procure their existing database of Republican voters (Halpern 2017). Facebook then helped Parscale in a number of ways to maximise this list by introducing him to four key tools (Winston 2016): (1) Custom Audiences from Customer Lists—which was used to match the real people on the lists they had received from the RNC with their Facebook profile; (2) Audience Targeting Options—which allows ads to be targeted to people based on their Facebook activity, ethnic affinity, location and demographic data like age, gender interests and so on; (3) LookalikeAudiences—which is a tool used to automatically find 'common qualities' among the people you are targeting to find new profiles thereby growing your audience; and (4) Brand Lift—which is a survey capable of measuring the success of the ads you are placing. In addition, as the digital advertising spending increased to 70 million a month, the Trump campaign purchased data from certified Facebook marketing partners including Experian PLC, Datalogix,

Epsilon and Acxiom Corporation. It is worth noting that all these represent third party data brokers that specialise in generating audiences for advertisers and marketers and if Halpern is correct, helped to grow Project Alamo to more than 300 terabytes of data, which supposedly includes over 7.7 Billion micro-targeting data points, on nearly 200 million American voters (far surpassing the data procured by Cambridge Analytica).

During this time, Pascale worked with 100 people alongside Facebook's political advertising strategist for 'Right Wing politics' to generate anywhere between 40,000 and 175,000 targeted ads a day. More to the point, each of the ads that was created on Facebook was not only individualised but linked back to their own unique piece content which could be anything from an ad, to an article, to a website. The variance on this content could be fairly minor and was determined by the psychographic data profile that they had on their users. Some examples could be, a bigger button, a different colour, a different font or a different ad all together. Some in the advertising and marketing industry like KissMetrics (2017) might label what Facebook did for Trump as a very high-end kind of experimental A/B testing, wherein you test a number of different variables on a piece of content to determine what will maximise user engagement.

Nevertheless, experiment or not, Trump spent over $85 million on Facebook ads (Glasser 2017). The aim of these ads was not uniform. While many set out to persuade users to vote for Trump, when it became apparent that Hillary had the popular vote, many of the ads set out to dissuade Democrats from voting at all. These dark ads, which at times took the form of memes (see Merrin), where largely targeted with the help of Facebook's 'Look-a-like' Audience tool, allowing Republican's to easily locate Democrat voters on the platform (Martinez 2018). The aim of these ads was to supress voter turnout from three key demographics (Smith 2016):

1. One targeted idealistic white liberals—primarily Bernie Sanders's supporters
2. A second aimed at young women—hence the procession of women who claimed to have been sexually assaulted by Bill Clinton and harassed by the candidate herself, and
3. A third went after African-Americans in urban centres where Democrats traditionally have had high voter turnout

The small margins by which Trump won, indicate that indeed, this new form of political advertising might be just *good enough* in terms of influencing voter behaviour in this datafied landscape of nudge politics. In the same way that advertising no longer needs to seek out content which inherently attracts potential consumers, politicians no longer need to speak to a general public. Thus, Facebook and Cambridge Analytica demonstrate how processes of datafication can not only be used to target consumers but citizens via the social big data we produce. This sentiment is echoed in a recent piece published in Wired magazine by Antonio Martinez, a former member of Facebook's advertising team, who argued that Trump's use of Facebook needs to be understood outside of the zeitgeist of Russia's influence on the US Elections (2018). Rather, he points to the Republican's critical mastery of Facebook's advertising infrastructure to help win them the election.

In the aftermath, with Trump elected, and Facebook's quarterly revenue profits breaking $10 billion USD for the first time, Mark Zuckerberg promises more accountability and thereby "a higher standard of transparency than ads on TV or other media" (Cao 2017). In this new regime currently being tested in Canada, users will be able to view all of the ads run by particular candidates by simply visiting their page. On the surface, this appears to solve the 'filter bubble problem'. However, given that 98 percent of Facebook's 2017 profits totalling $33 Billion USD were generated via advertising, what we can be sure of, is, without regulation, political advertising, as seen in Trump's campaign, is destined to become increasingly sophisticated, customised and persuasive. Indeed, politicians need our data too and Facebook is only too happy to oblige! Following Martinez (2018): "If we're going to reorient our society around Internet echo chambers, with Facebook and Twitter serving as our new Athenian agora, then we as citizens should understand how that forum gets paid for." Understanding how our data is rendered actionable is an important first step.

NOTES

1. To see the campaign video following this link: https://www.youtube.com/watch?v=IyZawynWt2s&feature=youtu.be
2. Sticky here is a marketing term that refers to the amount of time a user spends with a piece of content. For more information refer to: Accumulating Affect: Social Networks and their Archives of Feelings (Pybus 2015).

3. While these practices were solidified during Trumps campaign this is not the first instance wherein they have been used. Most notably we have instances of data driven campaign practices with Brexit (Cadwalladr 2017a, b) and the 2017 UK election (Ellison 2017).
4. Ted Cruz made use of algorithmic campaign strategies and was among the first to deploy the services of Cambridge Analytica. For more information see Cadwalldr (2017a) or Halpern (2017).

REFERENCES

Anderson, Chris (2008). The End of Theory. *Wired*, 16 [online] (23 June) Available at: http://archive. wired.com/science/discoveries/magazine/16-07/pb_theory (Accessed: 14 October 2017).

Bartlett, J. (2017). The Digital Guru Who Helped Donald Trump to Presidency. *BBC News*, [online] (13 Aug). Available at: http://www.bbc.co.uk/news/av/magazine-40852227/the-digital-guru-who-helped-donald-trump-to-the-presidency. (Accessed: 14 October 2017).

Berners-Lee, T. (2017) Tim Berners-Lee: I invented the web. Here are three things we need to change to save it, *The Guardian*, [online] (11 March). Available at: https://www.theguardian.com/technology/2017/mar/11/tim-berners-lee-web-inventor-save-internet (Accessed: 14 October 2017).

boyd, d. and Crawford, K. (2012). Critical Questions for Big Data: Provocations for a Cultural, Technological and Scholarly Phenomenon. *Information, Communication & Society*, 15(5), pp. 662–679.

Cambridge Analytica. Available at: https://cambridgeanalytica.org/ (Accessed: 14 October 2017).

Cadwalladr, C. (2017a). Robert Mercer: The Big Data Billionaire Waging War on Mainstream Media. *The Guardian*, [online] (26 February). Available at: https://www.theguardian.com/politics/2017/feb/26/robert-mercer-breitbart-war-on-media-steve-bannon-donald-trump-nigel-farage (Accessed: 14 October 2017).

Cadwalladr, C. (2017b). The Great British Brexit Robbery: How Our Democracy was Hijacked. *The Guardian*, [online] (7 May)/ Available at: https://www.theguardian.com/technology/2017/may/07/the-great-british-brexit-robbery-hijacked-democracy (Accessed: 14 October 2017).

Cao, S. (2017) Mark Zuckerberg Promises Radical Ad Transparency as Facebook Profit Rockets. *The Observer*, [online] (2 November)/ Available at: http://observer.com/2017/11/facebook-q3-profit-hit-10-billion-mark-zuckerberg-tighten-ad-security/ (Accessed March 2018).

Constine, J. (2017). Facebook Now has 2 Billion Monthly Users...and Responsibility. *TechCrunch*, [online] (27 June). Available at: https://

techcrunch.com/2017/06/27/facebook-2-billion-users/ (Accessed: 14 October 2017).

Coté, M. (2014). Data Motility: The Materiality of Big Social Data. *Cultural Studies Review*, 20(1), p. 121.

Coté, M. and Pybus, J. (2007). Learning to Immaterial Labour 2.0: MySpace and Social Networks, *Ephemera*, 7(2005), pp. 88–106.

Coté, M. and Pybus, J. (2016). Simondon on Datafication. A Techno-Cultural Method. *Digital Culture & Society*, 2(2).

Coté, M., Gerbaudo, P. and Pybus, J. (2016). Introduction. Politics of Big Data. *Digital Culture & Society*, 2(2), pp. 5–16.

Coté, Mark and Pybus, Jennifer (2011). Learning to Immaterial Labour 2.0: Facebook and Social Networks. In: *Cognitive Capitalism, Education and Digital Labour*. Peter Lang Press, Frankfurt am Main, pp. 169–194.

Couldry, N. and Turow, J. (2014). Advertising, Big Data and the Clearance of the Public Realm: Marketers' New Approaches to the Content Subsidy. *International Journal of Communication*, 8, pp. 1710–1726.

Cukier, K. and Mayer-Schonberger, V. (2013): Big Data: A Revolution That Will Transform How We Live, Work and Think, London: John Murray.

Dijck, J. van (2014). Datafication, Dataism and Dataveillance: Big Data Between Scientific Paradigm and Ideology. *Surveillance & Society*, pp. 197–208.

Egan, M. (2017). Facebook and Amazon Hit $500 Billion Milestone. *CNN Money*, [online] (27 July). Available at: http://money.cnn.com/2017/07/27/investing/facebook-amazon-500-billion-bezos-zuckerberg/index.html (Accessed: 14 October 2017).

Ellison, M. (2017). Election 2017: Scottish Voters Targeted by 'Dark Ads' on Facebook. *BBC News*, [online] (7 June). Available at: http://www.bbc.co.uk/news/uk-scotland-scotland-politics-40170166 (Accessed: 14 October 2017).

Facebook Elections (2017). Available at: https://politics.fb.com/en-gb/ (Accessed: 14 October 2017).

Fuchs, C. (2012). Dallas Smythe Today: The Audience Commodity, the Digital Labour Debate, Marxist Poolitical Economy and Critical Theory. Prolegomena to a Digital Labour Theory of Value'. *TripleC*, 10(2), pp. 692–740.

Gitelman, L. (2013). *Raw Data is an Oxymoron*. Edited by L. Gitelman. Massachusetts: MIT.

Glasser, A. (2017). Politicians are Addicted to Data Like It's Campaign Cash. *Slate* [online] (17 October). Available at: http://www.slate.com/articles/technology/technology/2017/10/politicians_are_addicted_to_big_data_like_it_s_campaign_cash.html (Accessed: 17 October 2017).

Grassegger, H. and Krogerus, M. (2017). The Data that Turned the World Upside Down. *Vice Motherboard*, [online] (28 January). https://motherboard.vice.com/en_us/article/mg9vvn/how-our-likes-helped-trump-win (Accessed: 14 October 2017).

Halpern, S. (2017). How He Used Facebook to Win. *The New York Review of Books*, [online] (8 June). Available at: http://www.nybooks.com/articles/2017/06/08/how-trump-used-facebook-to-win/ (Accessed: 14 October 2017).

Hurst, M. (2016). 4 Reasons Why Your Promotions Need Real Time Data Right Now. *The Drum*, [online] (13 July). Available at http://www.thedrum.com/industryinsights/2016/07/13/4-reasons-why-your-digital-promotions-need-real-time-data-right-now (Accessed: 14 October 2017).

KissMetrics Blog (2017). A Beginner's Guide to A/B Testing: An Introduction. KissMetrics [online]. Available at: https://blog.kissmetrics.com/ab-testing-introduction/. (Accessed: 14 October 2017).

Kitchin R. (2014). Big data, New Epistemologies and Paradigm Shifts. Big Data and Society April–June: 1–12.

Lapowski, I. (2016) Here's how Facebook actually won the Trump presidency. *Wired*, [online] (Oct 15). Available at: https://www.wired.com/2016/11/facebook-won-trump-election-not-just-fake-news/ (Accessed: 14 October 2017).

Martinez, A.G. (2018) How Trump Conquered Facebook—Without Russian Ads: Why Russia's Facebook ads were less important to Trump's victory than his own Facebook ads. *Wired*, [online] (Feb 23). Available at: https://www.wired.com/story/how-trump-conquered-facebookwithout-russian-ads/ (Accessed: 1 March 2018).

O'Neil, C. (2017). *Weapons of Maths Destruction: How Big Data Increases Inequality and Threatens Democracy*. New York: Penguin.

Pasquale, F. (2015) *The Black Box Society: The Secret Algorithms That Control Money and Information*, Princeton, Harvard University Press.

Pentland, Sandy (2012). Reinventing Society in the Wake of Big Data. *Edge* [online] (20 October). Available at: https://www.edge.org/conversation/alex_sandy_pentland-reinventing-society-in-the-wake-of-big-data (Accessed: 14 October 2017).

Pybus, J. (2015). 'Social Networks and Their Archives of Feeling'. In K. Hillis, S. Paasonen, and M. Petit (Eds.) *Networked Affect*. Cambridge MA: MIT Press.

Pybus, J., Coté, M. and Blanke, T. (2015). Hacking the Social Life of Big Data. *Big Data & Society*. 2(2).

Rieder, B. (2016). Big Data and the Paradox of Diversity. *Digital Culture and Society*, 2(2).

Smith, A. (2016). Trump official says campaign has '3 major voter suppression operations underway' to discourage Clinton supporters. *Business Insider* [online] (27 October). Available at: http://uk.businessinsider.com/donald-trump-voter-suppression-2016-10. (Accessed: 14 October 2017)

The Best of Global Digital Marketing (2015, summer). Lexus' Facebook Campaign from USA Wins the Best of Global Digital Marketing Awards, Summer Edition. Available at: http://www.best-marketing.eu/summer-2015/ (Accessed: 14 October 2017).

Winston, J. (2016). How the Trump Campaign Build an Identity Database and Used Facebook Ads to Win the Election. *Medium* [online] (18 November). Available at: https://medium.com/startup-grind/how-the-trump-campaign-built-an-identity-database-and-used-facebook-ads-to-win-the-election-4ff7d24269ac. (Accessed: 14 October 2017).

CHAPTER 15

Trump's Foreign Policy in the Middle East: Conspiratorialism in the Arab Media Sphere

Abdullah K. Al-Saud and Dounia Mahlouly

INTRODUCTION

The success of Donald Trump's presidential campaign is commonly regarded as the sign of a trend toward populist identity politics, which partly resulted from today's controversial immigration debates and increasing perception of threat to global security. This phenomenon appears to have primarily manifested itself in recent European elections and referendums, as illustrated by *Brexit* and the success of the *Front National* candidate in the first round of the 2017 French presidential campaign. However, there is also reason to believe that Donald Trump's approach to national identity and political communication impacted on some of the politically driven ethnic and sectarian conflicts that occur in regions suffering high political instability, such as the Middle East. Therefore, in order to assess the significance of Trump's populist discourse on the global political culture, it is worth investigating the reactions to his foreign policy in the Middle East.

A. K. Al-Saud (✉)
International Centre for the Study of Radicalisation (ICSR),
King's College London, London, UK

D. Mahlouly
King Faisal Center for Research and Islamic Studies (KFCRIS),
Riyadh, Saudi Arabia

© The Author(s) 2019
C. Happer et al. (eds.), *Trump's Media War*,
https://doi.org/10.1007/978-3-319-94069-4_15

Some experts have already underlined the fact that Trump's controversial statements on Islam are likely to enhance anti-Western sentiment (Winter 2016; McKernan 2017) and that the inconsistency of his foreign policy raises further political uncertainty for the region (Burke 2017; Walt 2017). However, we still have to understand how his foreign policy is being framed to accommodate the distinctive media narratives that are competing in the Arab media sphere as well as how it is received in the regional public debate. Does Trump's foreign policy underpin diverging interpretations of the complex struggles for power that are currently at stake in Iraq and Syria and does this generate conspiratorialism (Hannah and Benaim 2016; Engel 2016)?

In order to reflect on these questions, this paper analyzes a sample of news reports from *Al Ahram*, *Al Arabiya*, and *Al Jazeera*, covering four specific major events during Trump's early presidency. By evaluating how the news was originally framed and commented on by the media outlets' readership, the article attempts to investigate how President Trump's foreign policy discourse and positions are received and reported in the Arab media, and to what extent, if any, do they exacerbate the current climate of uncertainty engulfing the region and beyond. In theory, as we shall see, conspiracy theories thrive in such environments. The aim is to investigate whether or not the reality validates that theory.

Conspiracy Theory and Political Uncertainty in the Information Age

What is a conspiracy theory and how does one operate in today's global media environment? From the aftermath of the Cold War to the rise of the 2000s' digital revolution, social scientists have opposed two divergent approaches to the study of conspiracy theories, which differ in whether conspiracy theorists embrace or reject the status quo. The first, as described by Serge Moscovici in his essay "Conspiracy Mentality" (1987), is that of an irrational feeling of resentment expressed by the majority toward a minority. In this case, so-called conspiracists are commonly blamed for the fact that they do not conform to the norm and are therefore regarded by the compliant majority as unfairly privileged. From this perspective, conspiratorialism is to be understood as "the psychology of resentment" (ibid. 162). It manifests itself as a prejudice toward the minority, which is induced by a rather "ethnocentric and dogmatic" (ibid. 154) form of social identity. As a result, resentment often manifests itself as a fear of the other and the foreigner, who potentially represent a threat to social cohesion. This perceived external threat endorses all sorts of phantasmagoric representations meant to emphasize the supposedly inexorable incompatibility between the in-group and the outsider (ibid. 163).

The alternative perspective can be found in the work of Parish and Parker (2001) and Dean (2000), who define conspiracy theory as a reaction to the uncertainty of the modern world (Parish and Parker 2001). In their view, conspiracy theory evidences one's ability to question the apparent truth and seek for a hidden meaning, however subjective or superstitious, of our social reality. Their conception of conspiracy theory is that of a cognitive process that potentially challenges the norm and allows one to think critically about the world.

This certainly demonstrates that what may be defined as a conspiracy theory remains intrinsically relative. In spite of this, researchers agree to define conspiratorialism by a common set of characteristics, such as paranoid skepticism, a tendency to displace responsibility for social problems (Showalter 1997), a feeling of insecurity, and a propensity to position oneself as a victim (Moscovici 1987: 163; Parker 2001: 198). The latter tradition however pays particular attention to how conspiratorialism relates to postmodernity and to the climate of anxiety generated by economic globalization and the emerging technoculture (Stewart 1999; Dean 2000). In this regard, Dean introduces a relevant reflection as to how today's increasing consumption of information might ironically intensify our feeling of uncertainty:

> [I]nformation does not necessarily correlate with clarity and transparency, not to mention goodness and accountability. (...) Information may obfuscate even more than it clarifies. This is an important insight today, the technocultural "post" to postmodernity. It reminds us that telling the truth has dangers all its own, that a politics of concealment and disclosure may well be inadequate in the information age. (Dean 2000)

This inevitably brings us to reflect on the relationship between conspiratorialism and the possible revival of information warfare. As argued by George Marcus (1999), it is a context similar to that of the cold war and characterized by information warfare and political uncertainty that precisely explains today's propensity to individual skepticism:

> [T]he cold–war itself was defined throughout by a massive project of paranoid social thought and action that reached into every dimension of mainstream culture, politics, and policy. Furthermore, client states and most

regions were shaped by the interventions, subversions, and intimidations pursued in the interest of global conspiratorial politics of the superpowers. The legacies and structural residues of that era make the persistence, and even increasing intensity, of its signature paranoid style now more than plausible, but indeed, an expectable response to certain social facts. (ibid. 2)

Assuming that today's conspiratorialism is, indeed, part of the legacies of the cold war, how does it fit within the recent interplay of proxy wars currently at stake in the Levant region? How does it react to superpower foreign policy in the information age, and how does it operate when different media narratives compete on the transnational scale? In order to explore some of these questions, this paper shows how Trump's position regarding foreign policy in the Middle East evolved since the 2016 presidential campaign. It examines how this may intensify the current climate of political instability in the Middle East and investigates how Trump's foreign policies in relation to the global security crisis have been reported by three distinctive Arab media outlets. Finally, by outlining the preliminary results of a thematic analysis conducted on a dataset of online readers' comments, this paper introduces a reflection as to how Trump's political communication impacts on the polarization of the political debate in the MENA region.

Trump's Foreign Policy Before and After the Election: Political Uncertainty Rising in the Middle East

Many of President Donald Trump's actions following his assumption of power in January 2017 stand at odds with his previous rhetoric on the earlier campaign-trail. The areas of foreign policy in which President Trump has reversed course are plenty, including his policy on NATO, the European Union, China, North Korea, and Russia. However, we will narrow our focus, for the purpose of this paper, to those pertaining to the Middle East region. With regard to the main Middle Eastern issue at the moment, the revolution turned civil war in conflict-ridden Syria, candidate Trump was very critical of any US involvement during the Obama years and wanted to stay out of it (Griffing 2017; Jacobs 2015). However, President Trump proved willing to enforce the red line drawn by his predecessor, President Obama, with his first major military airstrike hitting the Syrian airbase from which the Syrian president's planes launched the

Khan Sheikhun chemical attack, which killed more than 80 people in early April 2017 (*BBC News* 2017).

A couple of months later, on June 19, 2017 a Syrian army jet was shot down by a US warplane, which was framed by Russia as "an act of aggression" (Reuters and Haaretz 2017). This has put President Trump on a collision course with Russia, a country that has entered the war in Syria in support of the regime in Damascus. Russia was at the receiving end of Trump's soft approach and kind gestures during the campaign, thus fueling perceptions of a collusion between the two. However, during a press conference in April, President Trump said, "We are not getting along with Russia at all. We may be at an all-time low in terms of a relationship with Russia." While candidate Trump indicated that he would look into lifting the sanctions against Russia (Pager 2016), President Trump actually approved and signed a Russian sanctions bill in early August, 2017 prompting a Russian retaliation by ordering hundreds of US diplomats to leave the country (Tracy 2017), resulting in a tit-for-tat US response.

Regarding Iran, a blend of tough talk and targeted sanctions characterize both Trump's campaign rhetoric and the first 100 days of his administration. However, while he promised during the elections to tear up the nuclear Iran deal, he has yet to do that as of the time of writing this paper. Moreover, while candidate Trump, following the November 2015 Paris terrorist attacks, called for a temporary ban on all Muslims from entering the United States (Revesz and Griffin 2016), he, as president, issued a much narrower travel ban blocking migrants from only seven countries linked to concerns about terrorism, and then six after exempting Iraq, for a period of 90 days (Schear and Cooper 2017; Trush 2017).

With regard to the Arab Gulf states, apart from fleeting mentions about how he thought they should contribute more financially toward the stability and security of the region, candidate Trump did not elaborate on the nature of the relationship that he envisions or his opinion on his predecessor's "share the neighborhood" attitude to power politics—between Saudi Arabia and Iran, in particular. However, he chose Saudi Arabia to be the destination of his first foreign visit, from where he articulated his vision of "peace, security, and prosperity—in this region, and in the world" (The White House 2017). Despite President Trump briefly mentioning Qatar as "a crucial strategic partner" in his Riyadh Summit speech, he strongly supported the boycott imposed on it by the quartet of Arab states led by Saudi Arabia a week later. He tweeted that it is "so good to see the Saudi Arabia visit with the King and 50 countries already paying off. They said they would take a hard line on funding extremism and all reference was pointing to Qatar."

President Trump was propelled to victory on a wave of nationalist and populist sentiments sweeping across the West. While his campaign promises to put "America first" played a huge part in his appeal and success, it caused a great deal of anxiety in many US friends and allies around the world who started to fear that their relationship with the world's superpower could be jeopardized by divisive identity politics and protectionist ambitions. To those who were worried about his earlier rhetoric, it is positive that, as president, he reversed course on most of the controversial issues addressed earlier. To others who expected him to herald a break with traditional American foreign policy, this was certainly a disappointment.

In both cases, one could easily argue that Trump's unpredictable approach to foreign policy—and possible lack of long-term vision—implicitly calls for a remolding of political alliances in a region that has been suffering from political instability since 2011. Most importantly, beyond strictly geopolitical concerns, the inconsistencies of Trump's administration (both over time and among the members) is likely to have an impact on public opinion, by encouraging conspiratorialism in an environment where diverging media narratives are already competing on both the national and regional scale. Indeed, as the conspiracy literature mentioned above would suggest, conspiratorialism may be interpreted as the urge to explain the unexplainable, especially in a context of insecurity or the perception of threat. The process through which Trump has been shifting his position from the 2016 presidential campaign to the early stage of his presidency most certainly remains incoherent and can easily be considered as inexplicable by those, in the Middle East, who experience a strong feeling of insecurity today.

Four Media Events Covering Trump's Foreign Policy in the Middle East

In order to better understand the dialectic between Trump's foreign policy and the media narratives currently competing in the Middle East, the preliminary findings outlined in this chapter focus on four media events relayed in three Arab media outlets. The former have been selected to map the evolution of Trump's foreign policy in the region in the early stage of his presidency. Therefore, when analyzed together and chronologically, they reveal the inconsistency and lack of rationality pervading Trump's political stand *vis-à-vis* the Middle East, which, as per our hypothesis above, potentially offers more grounds for conspiratorialism.

The four media events we considered are:

1. November 2016 US presidential election concluding the controversial campaign, during which candidate Trump alluded to Islam as a vehicle for terrorism and welcomed the possibility of strengthening the United States' relationship with Russia.
2. The Executive order issued on March 6, 2017, following on from the January 27 travel ban, which prevented entry to citizens from Iraq, Iran, Libya, Somalia, Sudan, Syria, and Yemen. The new travel ban excluded Iraq from the list of seven Muslim-majority countries initially blocked.
3. US forces bombing the Syrian pro-Assad airbase, from which the Khan Sheikhun chemical attack against civilians was launched in April 2017.
4. President Trump's speech at the Arab Islamic American Summit in Riyadh, which took place as part of Trump's first foreign trip in May 2017.

In order to investigate the coverage of these events across the region, we explored how they have been reported in the three major Arabic media outlets representative of different political agendas in the Arab media sphere. A dataset of news reports relaying some of the events listed above has been published on the media's online portals along with a set of readers' comments. The three news sources were the state-owned Egyptian newspaper *Al-Ahram*, the Saudi news satellite channel *Al Arabiya*, and the Qatari channel *Al Jazeera*.

- *Al Ahram*—The Egyptian daily newspaper was originally founded in the late nineteenth century and is among the most influential and popular media outlets in the Arabic press. It has occasionally been criticized for being the subject of censorship and endorsing the views of the military elite. In addition to the daily printed version, the newspaper is now published online via its news platform *al Ahram Gate*.

- *Al Jazeera*—Since 1996, Qatar's state-owned satellite channel *Al Jazeera* has promoted itself as an independent and unbiased news source, claiming to deliver alternative information to that of Western and state-owned Arab media. However, *Al Jazeera*'s critical stance against local governments and Western powers and its support of political Islamists, especially the Muslim Brotherhood, along with its lack of any critical coverage of local Qatari issues, have discredited its claim to impartiality. In fact, many argued that the global news organization has contributed to the relative success of the Islamist opposition in countries that undertook a political transition following the 2011 uprisings. The media outlet was, in this regard, part of the reason why other Gulf States accused Qatar of underpinning terrorism, by supporting transnational political Islamist movements, such as the Muslim Brotherhood, and giving a platform to other more sinister groups and organizations, such as al-Qaeda.
- *Al Arabiya*—The pan-Arab news website and TV channel owned by the private Saudi media group MBC was launched in 2003. Experts commonly agree that the channel had been initially created to act as the direct competitor of the Qatari channel *Al Jazeera* and as a way to promote a more critical perspective on political Islamist opposition groups. *Al Arabiya* faced particular criticism from officials of two Shia-majority countries, namely Iraq and Iran. Along with its sister channel *Al Hadath*, the channel was criticized for raising criticism against the two governments—especially after the 2014 breakdown of Iraqi military forces in Mosul. In both countries, reporters were occasionally banned and the channel was threatened to have its local offices shut down.

The three news sources act as the voice of different kinds of leadership in the Gulf and North Africa, while reaching an equally large and diversified Arabic-speaking audience. As a result, one can expect that the process through which they frame US foreign policy—and Trump's administration in particular—may vary and potentially relate to different narratives. Their coverage of our chosen events is highlighted in Table 15.1 below and will be discussed specifically within the following context.

In Egypt, despite public opinion remaining highly polarized in the aftermath of the July 2013 coup, the pro-military government celebrated the election of Trump, whom they regarded as a stark alternative to the Obama administration and a more reliable shield against the Muslim

Table 15.1 News report dataset

	Media	Title	Date	Numb. of comments	Event	Type
			Dataset			
1	Al Ahram	ترامب يطيح بالقضي تطبيق قرارات حظر اللاجئين...	January 2, 2017	4	Immigration ban	News
2	Al Jazeera	ترامب يوقع أمرا جديدا بشأن الهجرة يستهدف دولة مسلمة	March 3, 2017	10	Immigration ban	News
3	Al Ahram	امريكا»وهران» حصد من تيرورات السلطات الاخيرة للانتخابات الامريكة	November 7, 2016	0	US presidential elections	Interview
4	Al Ahram	دونالد ترامب رئيسا للولايات المتحدة الامريكة	November 9, 2016	1	US presidential elections	News
5	Al Arabiya	دونالد ترامب رئيسا للولايات المتحدة الامريكية	November 9, 2016	25	US presidential elections	News
6	Al Jazeera	ترامب رئيسا للولايات المتحدة	November 9, 2016	41	US presidential elections	News
7	Al Arabiya	خطاب ترامب من الرياض...حديث عن وحدة في وجه الطوفان	May 20, 2017	1	Riyadh speech	News
8	Al Jazeera	خطاب ترامب في القمة العربية الاسلامية الامريكية	May 22, 2017	4	Riyadh speech	News
9	Al Jazeera	قصف امريكي بعشرات الصواريخ على مطار قرب حمص	April 7, 2017	51	Syrian military base airstrike	News
10	Al Arabiya	امريكا تخرج ب «59 صاروخا» النظام السوري	April 7, 2017	132	Syrian military base airstrike	News
11	Al Ahram	قصف قاعدة «الشعيرات» الجوية بـ 59 صاروخ توماهوك...ومقتل 9	April 8, 2017	4	Syrian military base airstrike	News
12	Al Arabiya	ترامب يوقع أمرا تنفيذيا حول الهجرة ويستثني العراق	March 6, 2017	5	Immigration ban	News
13	Al Ahram	تداعيات قرار ترامب «حظر السفر» على مصر تدعو امريكا وروسيا للتصرف لحماية إبادة الأرمنية السورية	February 8, 2017	0	Immigration ban	Editorial

Brotherhood. In an interview published in November 2016 by the pro-military Egyptian newspaper *Al Ahram*, the Lebanese-born American campaign advisor to Trump Walid Phares referred to the candidate as the representative of the silent majority—in both Egypt and the United States. Phares emphasized the fact that Trump had developed strong ties with President Sisi, calling him an "ally of moderate Arab and Islamic forces."

As mentioned above, the political tensions that were about to manifest themselves between Qatar and Saudi Arabia in June 2017 had apparently not been anticipated by the US president at the time of the 2017 Summit in Riyadh. This prompts the thought that Trump's relationship with Qatar may not have been as well-defined as his relations with the Egyptian military regime, and one could argue that Al Jazeera's coverage of the presidential campaign indicates that the country's leadership implicitly supported the Democrats (*Al Jazeera English* 2016). Alternatively, despite referring to candidate Trump as "a disgrace (…) to all America" in a tweet prior to the election, Saudi Prince Alwaleed bin Talal, was, with President Sisi, among the first leaders to congratulate Trump for his victory. On the eve of the US president's official trip to Riyadh, the two countries appeared to have "revitalised [their] friendship" and come to an agreement with regard to intensified military action in Yemen and the revival of a traditionally confrontational US foreign policy *vis-à-vis* Iran (Malsin 2017).

Media Framing and Readers' Comments

Trump's Election

While both *Al Arabiya* and *Al Ahram* remained largely factual and on point in their reporting on Trump's victory in the race to the White House, *Al Jazeera* tried to explain Trump's win by arguing that "despite polls showing that 60 per cent of Americans do not consider Trump fit to be president, the controversial republican candidate won the support of many voters who were disgruntled with Obama's policies." In the same news report, *Al Jazeera* highlighted the many controversial statements that Trump made regarding his foreign policy for the Arab world, such as "his call for the reoccupation of Iraq and the seizure of its oil to confront the Islamic State organization." In short, by including in its reporting statements that Trump is "classified as being very close to the far–right in the Republican party" and "he is known for his hostility to immigrants in

America, especially those who come from Mexican origins," *Al Jazeera* referred to the new US president in more negative terms.

Across the dataset, the news of Trump's election appears to have generated a commonly diversified set of comments. On the one hand, some posts stand out for suggesting—in a sarcastic tone—that Trump's administration will jeopardize US democratic values and accommodate the military authoritarianism that had been challenged by the 2011 Arab uprisings. Another category of readers' inputs, on the other hand, celebrates Trump's election and welcomes the end of Obama's administration. The most liked comments on *Al Jazeera*'s piece celebrate Trump's win because "he will herald the end of America and the end of the world". The majority of *Al Arabiya*'s comments, 15 out of a total of 25, were celebratory of Trump's win, congratulating him and hoping for a better future. Only three wished that Hillary had won. The single comment on *Al Ahram* expressed joy that "the supporter of Israel and the [Muslim] Brotherhood (...) and the so-called Arab Spring that caused wars and destruction in our region," meaning Clinton, did not win. The commenter continued to predict that Trump will certainly change after his election just like his predecessors before him.

Immigration Ban

In February, editorialist Dr. Ahmed Sayed Ahmed accused Trump's executive order of fueling a clash of civilizations in an *Al Ahram* piece that surprisingly contrasted with the interview of Trumps' campaign advisor published by the same newspaper prior to the US election. Both *Al Jazeera* and *Al Arabiya* remained relatively factual when reporting the ban. However, whereas *Al Jazeera*'s news report emphasized the popular demonstrations opposing the order, *Al Arabiya* focused on the security concerns related to the ban.

Between January and March 2017, Trump's immigration ban generated equally strong reactions among the readership of the three news sources. Across the dataset, this particular media event generated highly critical comments reflecting the controversial nature of the law. The United States was repeatedly called a racist state, and some readers suggested that similar restrictions should be applied in the case of US nationals trying to enter Arab states. Some comments called for boycotts of US products and for improved relationships with alternative powers such as Russia, which—in the latter case—could be considered as implicitly revealing pro-Assad views. The news of the new executive order issued in March 2017, which excluded Iraq from the original list of seven countries impacted by the ban, reactivated the debate on the US relationships with Shia-majority countries. A few posts, especially on *Al Jazeera*, suggested that US foreign policy catered to the interests of the latter, and that exempting Iraq—as suggested by more than one reader—will allow "Shi'a terrorists from Iran, Lebanon and Yemen" to enter the United States with an Iraqi passport, as "the US supported and continues to support the Iranian occupation of Iraq since 2003." Another reader commented on *Al Arabiya*'s reporting that the exemption of Iraq is evidence that the decision is illogical: "how can Iraq be included for clear reasons and then exempted days later?"

The Bombing of the Pro-Assad Military Airbase

Al Arabiya news report called US strikes on the pro-Assad military airbase a proportionate response to the chemical attacks on Khan Shaykhun. It underlined the measures taken to avoid civilian causalities by quoting statements from US Defense Department spokesman Jeff Davis and US Secretary of State Rex Tillerson. *Al Jazeera* addressed the event by focusing on its impact on US–Russian relations and the possible repercussions in terms of military action. It reported statements from the Russian Ambassador to the UN, Vladimir Savronkov, and relayed information from a local correspondent and the Syrian state television, so as to cover reaction to the events on the ground. *Al Ahram*, on the other hand, highlighted, in its headline, the Syrian press agency's allegation that the bombing killed nine civilians. It also stressed Egypt's official position calling for the United States and Russia to work together to put an end to the Syrian crisis.

Based on the three news reports from *Al Arabiya*, *Al Jazeera*, and *Al Ahram* considered in our sample, this particular media event proves to have generated the highest number of comments within the dataset. Reactions also appeared to be highly polarized, as they conveyed both skepticism of Trump's motivations and joy and enthusiasm at the thought of repressive measures against the Syrian regime. In this context, a significant proportion of comments suggested that the bombing was "a cheap ploy" designed as part of a strategy to alleviate internal pressure in the US, showcase the West's "humanitarianism," and divert attention from the possible interference of Russia in the US presidential election. This category of comments appears to have been particularly critical about the fact that Russian forces had been informed of US intentions to attack the airbase and the operation had been conducted so as to reduce the risks for Russian and Syrian airport staff. As a result of *Al Jazeera*'s news report framing the event in relation to the broader spectrum of political alliances involved in the conflict, its readers commented on the consequences of the bombings for the different military powers involved. More specifically, comments expressed resentment for Russia, Iran, and Hezbollah due to their support to the military regime, sometimes questioning the involvement of Israel and its security concerns relating to arms smuggling in the North of Lebanon. The most disliked comments on both *Al Arabiya* and *Al Jazeera* are those few comments defending the Syrian regime and its Iranian patronage, while the most liked, especially on *Al Arabiya*, are those showing support for the attack and expressing hope that this will herald the end of the Iranian "destructive" influence. The very few comments on *Al Ahram* were not supportive about the bombing. One reader asks, "[H]ow does killing more civilians contribute to solving problems? It is obvious that Trump is trying to divert attention from the scandals surrounding his administration."

The Riyadh Summit Speech

Al Jazeera published a transcription of Trump's speech at the Riyadh Summit after summarizing the main topics addressed at the event with an emphasis on global security issues, sectarianism, and the economic agreements between the United States and Saudi Arabia on the eve of the summit. Just before the start of the transcription, it also highlighted that the writer of the first draft of the speech, according to its correspondent, was Steven Miller who is "a known conservative right wing, and one of the most hostile to Muslims and immigrants, and a believer in the superiority of the white race." In doing so, it contributed to portraying Trump as unlikely to embrace the Arab Islamic perspective, bringing its readers to question his legitimacy in the particular context of the summit.

    Al Arabiya's report focused on Trump's call for unity to confront extremism and fight terrorism and on the part of his speech where he denied coming to the summit to give a lecture or teach people how to live or worship. Instead, as he himself said, "[W]e are here to offer partnership—based on shared interests and values—to pursue a better future for us all."

Al Ahram did not report directly on the Riyadh Summit's Trump speech, but focused instead on the speech given by President Sisi.

In contrast to Trump's speech, three out of the four posts commenting on *Al Jazeera*'s news report manifested sarcasm and resentment against Trump, calling him ignorant and unable to comment legitimately on issues relating to politics and religion in the Middle East. Readers also expressed discomfort at the thought that the US president could condemn sectarianism, despite being involved in the military and political reshaping of the region. In contrast, one single comment was added to *Al Arabiya* news report, welcoming President Trump in Saudi Arabia.

CONCLUSION

Admittedly, with the exception of editorials and opinion pieces, our dataset indicates that all three media outlets provide, in all appearances, a factual account of US foreign policy. Nothing, in terms of media framing, would suggest that any of the three media outlets is feeding a particular conspiracy theory. However, *Al Jazeera* undeniably distinguishes itself by referring to the United States in more critical terms. Alternatively, *Al Arabiya* delivers a perspective which is more in line with the US government's narrative, by relying specifically on US official sources. *Al Jazeera* appears to be more inclined to discuss US foreign policy in relation to the way that other international powers position themselves *vis-à-vis* the Syrian crisis. Its news reports may, for instance, refer to statements of Russian officials or local correspondents in Syria commenting on the position of the Syrian regime. The approach of the Egyptian newspaper *Al Ahram* to US foreign policy proves to be less consistent. This indicates that, despite Trump and Egyptian President Sisi equally prioritizing—and potentially capitalizing on—domestic and global security issues, Trump's administration remained, in its early stage, relatively controversial in the Egyptian public debate.

Within the scope of our dataset, the distinctive ideological inclinations of these media outlets, however perceptible, do not appear to have a direct impact on readers' comments. All three media outlets generate an equally diversified set of comments, from which conspiratorialism almost consistently evidences the intensively divisive Shia–Sunni conflict. In this context, conspiracy theory is therefore to be understood in the sense of resentment (Moscovici 1987). As it is debated by media audiences, the inconsistency of Trump's foreign policy proves to conveniently enable multiple and often selectively diverging interpretations of the geopolitical interests at stake in the region. However, instead of generating a constructive critique of the status quo (Dean 2000), this form of conspiratorialism contributes to the fragmentation and polarization of the debate.

Had we focused on other more universally controversial events, such as the attacks of September 11 or the 2003 US invasion of Iraq, we would have presumably encountered conspiratorialism on a larger scale. The Middle East is a region plagued with conflict, chaos, and instability. In such an environment, it is easy to understand why some people resort to the defensive psychological mechanism of "externalization," whereby they locate and project their problems onto an external other. External factors have played a role in many of the region's ills, but it has become increasingly difficult to demarcate, in the face of the current state of ambiguity and uncertainty, between fallacious conspiracy theories and legitimate criticism relying on rational arguments.

REFERENCES

Dean, J. 2000. "Theorizing Conspiracy Theory". Theory & Event. *Muse* 4(3) [online], https://muse.jhu.edu/article/32599 [accessed September 9, 2017]

Marcus, G., ed. 1999. *Paranoia within Reason: A Casebook on Conspiracy as Explanation.* Chicago: University of Chicago Press.

Moscovici, S. 1987. "The Conspiracy Mentality," in *Changing Conceptions of Conspiracy.* Edited by C. F. Graumann and S. Moscovici. New York: Springer, 151–169.

Parish, J. and M. Parker, ed. 2001. *The Age of Anxiety: Conspiracy Theory and the Human Sciences.* Malden: Wiley–Blackwell.

Stewart, K. 1999. "Conspiracy Theory's Worlds," in *Paranoia within Reason: A Casebook on Conspiracy as Explanation.* Edited by G. Marcus. Chicago: University of Chicago Press.

NEWS SOURCES

Al Jazeera News. 2016. "Craziest Moments from Donald Trump's Campaign." *Al Jazeera English,* November 9.

BBC News. 2017. "Syria Chemical 'Attack': What We Know." 26 April.

Engel, P. 2016. "Trump Is Playing into Popular Middle East Conspiracy Theories about ISIS." *Business Insider UK,* 11 August.

Griffing, A. 2017. "Donald Trump Threatening Syria Directly Contradicts His Campaign Promises." *Haaretz,* 2 July.

Hanna, M. W., and D. Benaim. 2016. "How Do Trump's Conspiracy Theories Go over in the Middle East? Dangerously." *The New York Times,* August 16.

Jacobs, B. 2015. "The Donald Trump Doctrine: 'Assad is Bad' but US Must Stop 'Nation–building'." *The Guardian,* 13 October.

Maslin, J. 2017. "President Trump Is Visiting Saudi Arabia to Cement a Friendship." *Time,* May 16.

McKernan, B. 2017. "Isis Hails Donald Trump's Muslim Immigration Restrictions as a 'Blessed Ban'." *Independent,* 30 January.

Parker, M., ed. 2001. "Human Science as Conspiracy Theory," in *The Age of Anxiety: Conspiracy Theory and the Human Sciences.* Edited by J. Parish and M. Parker. Oxford Blackwell Publishers, 191–207.

Pager, P. 2016. "Trump to Look at Recognizing Crimea as Russian Territory, Lifting Sanctions." *Politico,* 27 July.

Reuters and *Haaretz.* 2017. "Russia Threatens U.S.: Will Intercept 'Any Flying Object' in Syria Skies." 19 June.

Revsz, R., and A. Griffin. 2016. "Donald Trump Statement on Banning Muslims from US Disappears from His Website." *Independent,* November 9.

Shear, M, and H. Cooper. 2017. "Trump Bars Refugee and Citizens of 7 Muslim Countries." *The New York Times,* January 27.

Showalter, E. 1997. *Hystories: Hysterical Epidemics and Modern Media.* New York: Columbia University Press

The White House. 2017. "President Trump's Speech to the Arab Islamic Summit." Office of the Press Secretary, May 21.

Thrush, G. 2017. "Trump's New Travel Ban Blocks Migrants from Six Nations, Sparing Iraq." *The New York Times,* March 6.

Tracy, A. 2017. "Trump Silent as Russia Retaliates against U.S. Sanctions Bill." *Vanity Fair,* July 31.

Walt, S. M. 2017. "Making the Middle East Worse, Trump-Style." *Foreign Policy,* June 9.

Winter, C. 2016. "Trump Has Unwittingly Become an Asset for ISIS." CNN, November 3.

INDEX

© The Author(s) 2019
C. Happer et al. (eds.), *Trump's Media War*,
https://doi.org/10.1007/978-3-319-94069-4

Egeland, Tom, 6
Egypt, 248, 250, 252
Eisenhower, Dwight D., 56
Electorate, discontent of, 4
El-Sisi, Abdel Fattah, 216, 250
E! News, 192
Entertainment media, 138
Entertainment Weekly, 192
Epsilon (marketing agency), 235
Ergen, Mehmet, 167
Ernst, Jonathan, 72
Eustis, Oskar, 160
Experian plc, 234
ExxonMobil, 57, 58

F
Facebook, 4–6, 18, 27, 234
  censorship by, 6
  combating of fake news, 5, 41–43
  links to Russia, 18, 19, 38, 61–62
  MyPersonality (app), 233
  and Obama, 50
  and political advertising, 228–230,
    234, 236
  use of data in DT election campaign,
    230
  validation of accounts, 42
Factcheck.org, 5
Fairness Doctrine, 12
'Fake news,' 4, 5, 7–8, 15, 34, 37–40,
    69, 160
  and Brexit, 16
  identification of, 41–42
  implications for academics, 178
  and photography, 70–72
  political element, 16
  unintentional, 37
'Fancy Bear' (hacking group), 18, 208
Far right
  and internet, 13, 204, 205
  See also 'Alt right'

Fastenberg, Dan, 190
Federal Bureau of Investigation (FBI),
    63, 103
Federal Communications Commission,
    12
Fey, Tina, 190
Fields, W. C., 184
'Filter bubbles,' 12, 15, 70, 220, 236
Financial Times, 147, 151
First Amendment (US Constitution),
    38–40
*First Ever@Midnight Presidential
    Debate* (TV programme), 188
Fischer, Gregor, 71
Flynn, Michael, 209, 211
  links to Russia, 57, 58
Forbes, Michael, 115
Ford, Gerald, 120
For the Love of Money (song), 49
Fowler, James H., 186
Fox and Friends (TV programme), 188
Fox, Liam, 122
Fox News, 13, 14, 24, 107, 186
  and allegations about Obama's
    birthplace and citizenship, 104
  collusion with White House, 36
  reporting of election campaign, 104
  and Republican Party, 104
Fox, Vicente, and Mexico border wall,
    215
France, election (2017), 41, 239
Francis, Pope, 8, 77
  criticism of media, 8
Frankfurt School, 10
Frank, Thomas, 109
Free Beacon (website), 107
Frieden, Nancy, 173–174
Full Frontal with Samantha Bee (TV
    programme), 192, 214
Furlong, Christopher, 77
Futurists and Futurism, 203, 204,
    207, 212